PEASANT PASTS

PEASANT PASTS

HISTORY AND MEMORY IN WESTERN INDIA

Vinayak Chaturvedi

UNIVERSITY OF CALIFORNIA PRESS

BERKELEY   LOS ANGELES   LONDON

University of California Press, one of the most
distinguished university presses in the United States,
enriches lives around the world by advancing scholar-
ship in the humanities, social sciences, and natural
sciences. Its activities are supported by the UC Press
Foundation and by philanthropic contributions from
individuals and institutions. For more information, visit
www.ucpress.edu.

Parts of part 1 appeared earlier in Vinayak Chaturvedi,
"The Making of a Peasant King in Colonial Western
India: The Case of Ranchod Vira," *Past and Present*
192 (August 2006): 155–85. Parts of parts 2 and 3
appeared earlier in Vinayak Chaturvedi, "Of Peasants
and Publics in Colonial India: Daduram's Story," *Social
History* 30, 3 (2005): 296–320, www.tandf.co.uk.
Excerpt from "Theses on the Philosophy of History"
in ILLUMINATIONS by Walter Benjamin, copyright
© 1955 by Suhrkamp Verlag, Frankfurt a.M., English
translation by Harry Zohn copyright © 1968 and re-
newed 1996 by Harcourt, Inc., reprinted by permission
of Harcourt, Inc.

University of California Press
Berkeley and Los Angeles, California

University of California Press, Ltd.
London, England

Library of Congress Cataloging-in-Publication Data

Chaturvedi, Vinayak.
    Peasant pasts : history and memory in western India /
Vinayak Chaturvedi.
        p.   cm.
    Includes bibliographical references and index.
    ISBN: 978-0-520-25076-5 (cloth : alk. paper)
    ISBN: 978-0-520-25078-9 (pbk. : alk. paper)
    1. Dharalas—History—19th century—
Historiography.   2. Dharalas—History—20th
century—Historiography.   3. Dharalas—Political
activity.   4. Dharalas—Social conditions—19th
century.   5. Dharalas—Social conditions—20th
century.   6. Nationalism—India—Gujarat—
Historiography.   I. Title.

DS432.D45C43   2007
305.5'6309547—dc22   2006025558

Manufactured in the United States of America

15   14   13   12   11   10   09   08   07
10   9   8   7   6   5   4   3   2   1

This book is printed on New Leaf EcoBook 50, a 100%
recycled fiber of which 50% is de-inked post-consumer
waste, processed chlorine-free. EcoBook 50 is acid-free
and meets the minimum requirements of ANSI/ASTM
D5634-01 (*Permanence of Paper*).

For Bina

The past can be seized only as an image which flashes up at an
instant when it can be recognized and is never seen again.

Walter Benjamin, "Theses on the Philosophy of History"

CONTENTS

ILLUSTRATIONS

ACKNOWLEDGMENTS

The idea for this book would not have been conceived without the encouragement of Chris Bayly, who first suggested that I turn my attention to the study of agrarian social history in Gujarat. He served as an extraordinary thesis advisor while I completed my PhD at the University of Cambridge. I have kept his thoughtful comments in mind in the process of writing this book. I am grateful for his generosity and his belief in an ethos of intellectual pluralism.

At the University of California, Irvine, Robert Moeller and Ken Pomeranz have been wonderful colleagues and friends and supported my work in every way, reading multiple drafts and providing detailed comments and sharp critiques. I learned a good deal about the world of history through our engagements. In the process, my work and sense of humor were transformed for the better. I am thankful to Heidi Tinsman, whose comments helped me fine-tune the theoretical underpinnings of my work. David Arnold, Geoff Eley, and Ajay Skaria carefully read an early draft of this book and provided important comments that helped me to clarify my arguments. I hope they will see their respective imprints in the book.

A large number of friends and colleagues helped me in this venture. Daud Ali, Juan Buriel, Mike Davis, David Hardiman, Douglas Haynes, Rosalind O'Hanlon, Peter Robb, Sanjay Ruparelia, Krishna Tewari, David Washbrook, Jeff Wasserstrom, and Bin Wong kindly read and commented on parts of the manuscript and offered constructive advice. Discussions with Prathama Banerjee, Sandria Freitag, Vinay Gidwani, Dilip Menon, William Pinch, Mahesh Rangarajan, Vicki Ruiz, Samira Sheikh, and Sanjay Subrahmanyam helped clarify many of my ideas. I also thank Robert Brenner for first introducing me to the literature on agrarian studies and for encouraging me to think about antideterminist ideas in history.

In Gujarat, Gita Bajpai, Raj Kumar Hans, and Makhrand Mehta were very generous and helped me locate numerous sources that I would not have found on my own. Virendra M. Desai, Natvarsinh Solanki, and Amarsinh Waghela devoted a tremendous amount of time to helping me at every step, answering basic questions and introducing me to the local history of the region. Kanuprasad Shastri took time away from his own work to travel with me to numerous temples in Kheda district. I could always rely upon his language skills whenever I was unable to decipher aspects of the local dialect. Anupbhai Desai and his family provided a wonderful home in Nadiad so that I could complete the necessary research for this book in comfort. Most important, I thank the many individuals who shared their life stories with me while I was conducting my fieldwork. As requested, I have not mentioned the names of these figures here. However, I state unequivocally that, without their insights, knowledge, and analysis, much of this book could not have been written.

A large number of specialists helped me at the India Office Library (now the Oriental and India Office Collection of the British Library, London); Cambridge University Library; Centre for South Asian Studies (Cambridge); Maharashtra State Archives (Bombay); Office of the Deputy Inspector General of Police (Bombay); Gujarat State Archives (Vadodara); District Collectorate Records Room (Kheda); District Superintendent of Police Headquarters (Kheda); Roman Catholic Mission Archives (Anand); and UC Irvine's Langson Library. I especially thank Joan Ariel in Irvine, Alfred Christian in Kheda, Shri Pawar in Bombay, and Tim Thomas in London, who in their own respective ways made the task of doing research an enjoyable one.

I also thank the following funding bodies that provided generous financial assistance for research and travel for this venture: in Cambridge, the Holland Rose Fund, Cambridge Commonwealth Trust, Board of Graduate Studies, Smuts Memorial Fund, Charles Wallace Memorial Trust, and Dharam Hinduja Memorial Trust; in Irvine, the Humanities Center and Council on Research, Computing, and Library Resources.

Niels Hooper was a wonderful editor at the University of California Press. I thank him for his patience and for making the process of publishing this book a pleasurable one. Lynne Withey followed this project from an early stage; I thank her for all her comments and suggestions. I am thankful to Jacqueline Volin and Bonita Hurd for their editorial expertise, which has helped improve the quality of my work.

The contemporary abstract artist Akhilesh generously shared his work with me. I thank him for allowing me to use the serigraph on paper titled *Floating on Itself* for the cover art. Special thanks to Anuradha

Pathak and Ashish Anand of the Delhi Art Gallery for sharing the digital image of Akhilesh's artwork.

This book would not have been completed without the encouragement of friends and family. Michel Del Buono, Dorothy Fujita-Rony, Casiano Hacker-Cordón, Patrick Marmion, Rajit Mazumder, and Tom Mertes all provided necessary diversions along the way. My dear friend Sujata Tewari passed away suddenly when I was completing an earlier draft of this book. She had discussed parts of the manuscript with me and helped me to think through various problems of research. Her presence is greatly missed, not least because I ended up teaching at the same university where she taught for many years.

My grandfather Brindhavan Bihari Chaturvedi first introduced me to the texture of life in colonial India, regularly recounting tales of the good, the bad, and the ugly. He retired as Deputy Conservator of Forests in Madhya Pradesh, having spent his adult life in central India. For him, most individuals were decent but the institutional apparatus set up by the colonial state had systematically destroyed much of what was good. He would have read every sentence of this book carefully, taken copious notes, and then pursued a conversation with great kindness. He died in 1994, the first year of my graduate studies in Cambridge. While the origins of ideas are difficult to track, I like to think that his narratives had something to do with my conceptualization of this book.

In Bombay, the families of Rajesh Chaturvedi and Ramesh Chaturvedi exemplified all that is good about kin. Urmila, Naresh, Rajiv, and Sona Chaturvedi, my family from Northern Ireland, made my long stay in Britain a wonderful one. In Delhi, my grandfather Laxmi Chandra Chaturvedi has always demonstrated by example what can be accomplished with good humor and passion for life. Hemlata Parekh, Sachin Parekh, and Parul Parekh took time away from their busy schedules to ensure that I could complete my writing. Vinita Chaturvedi has been a source of great inspiration, in more ways than she knows to be true. My parents Yogeshwar and Kusum Chaturvedi helped me in every way, beyond what I could have ever expected. Arjun Chaturvedi has made writing this book a joy and provided a new perspective on my work.

Bina Parekh followed every idea in this book over the years. She has been a careful listener, a thoughtful critic, and a great support in everyday life. Without her it would not have been possible to complete this book.

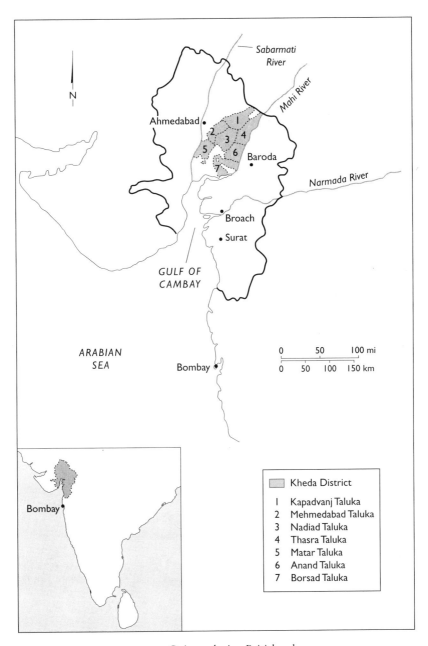

Map 1. Gujarat during British rule

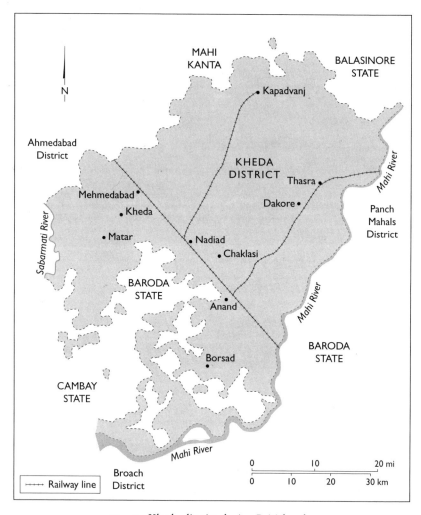

Map 2. Kheda district during British rule

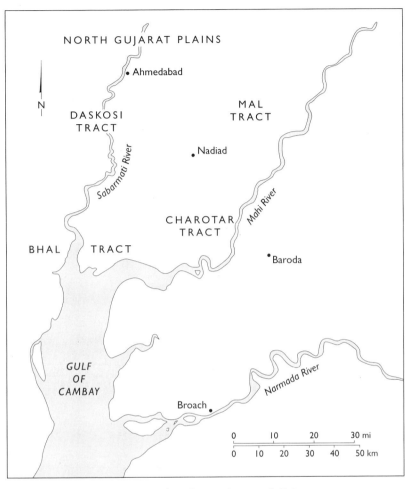

Map 3. Agricultural tracts in central Gujarat

INTRODUCTION

I

In the autumn of 1995, I began looking at early-twentieth-century police reports for western India in the Official Publications Room of the Cambridge University Library. I had decided to consider these reports quite by chance while searching for documents on the agrarian economy of Gujarat. I had expected to find the usual cases of local crime, such as robberies, disturbances, crop thefts, and murders, but much to my surprise I came across a comment by a district magistrate that immediately opened up a new direction of inquiry. He had reported that in 1918 village elites belonging to the Patidar community in Kheda district, in central Gujarat, were forcibly extracting labor from peasants known as Dharalas by abusing a colonial law known as the Criminal Tribes Act.[1] The application of the legislation in Kheda district was approved in 1911 and led to the immediate official classification of all Dharalas—approximately 250,000 individuals, or one-third of the agrarian population—as criminals in the eyes of the state.[2]

The fact that village elites were using extra-economic coercion to extract labor was not something new or unique to this area or time period. However, what stood out for me was that scholars writing on nationalism in India have recognized the same Patidars as harnessing one of the first movements for nationalism in that same year in alliance with Mohandas K. Gandhi—the Mahatma.[3] The implications of this seeming paradox were far reaching, especially since these Patidars historically have been celebrated as some of the most dynamic and creative peasant nationalists who led India's independence movement.[4]

Shortly thereafter I came across a similar reference in a speech given by Gandhi while he was campaigning for nationalist politics in 1925: "Patidars tyrannize over lower communities, beat them and extract forced labour from them."[5] He had asked the Dharalas to forgive the Patidars for the cause of the nation but had accepted the identification of

Dharalas as criminals and claimed that the community did not have an understanding of politics. The political exigency for Gandhi at the time centered on contesting colonial power and promoting the idea of an independent India in alliance with Patidars, rather than mediating a settlement of the conflicts within the structure of agrarian social relations, which would have certainly antagonized his primary support base in Gujarat. Patidar nationalists welcomed the coming of the nation-state, not simply as an end of colonialism, but as an opportunity to consolidate their own power in the countryside in an independent India. It came as little surprise when most Dharalas—primarily poor peasants, agricultural laborers, and servants—refused to participate in the Patidar-led nationalist movement in the locality from the 1910s to the 1940s. In fact, many actively opposed it.

It was evident that the narratives I had come across during my preliminary research had linked Dharalas to a history of criminality without considering alternative pasts. Dharala opposition to the nationalism led by Patidars (or even Gandhi) did not mean that these peasants lacked an understanding of politics or an ability to imagine a political community that was separate, if not independent, from the emergent form of the nation. I was convinced that the silences within the narratives had their own story to tell.[6] After all, nationalism was not the only articulation of politics in India or elsewhere in this period. My interest turned to further researching and explaining the nature of Dharalas' peasant politics in the shadow of British colonialism and against the background of an emergent nationalist movement. In many ways the idea for this book began here.

II

While considering the implications of such a conflict in the making of a nation within a colonial context, I began thinking about a theoretical question raised by Partha Chatterjee about nationalism: "Whose imagined community?"[7] It was clear that these nationalists were not saying that those subordinate to them were not going to become "Indians" in a postcolonial India, or that they would be excluded from the nation. Rather, it appeared they had conceptualized a nation in which they would continue to consolidate power and control of agrarian social relations. These nationalists understood what it meant to be dominant. Yet the project of nationalism required something more: those committed to nationalism had to convince and persuade the Dharalas to accept how *they* imagined the nation. In other words, the nationalists understood the idea of establishing hegemony within the nationalist project. Even Gandhi had argued that the problems within agrarian society would be resolved once India achieved its independence, at which time everyone would forge a national identity. His pronouncement anticipated an end to identifying oneself as a subject of the British raj, while offering hope for a future in which individuals could claim to be citizens of a postcolonial nation that was not mired in conflict. It remained unclear what independence from colonialism or freedom within a nation would mean for Dharalas, who were identified as criminals without politics by both the colonialists and the nationalists. In the meantime, Dharalas had asserted their own ideas, sentiments, and practices as a way to protect their everyday world while resisting the nationalist movement.

Chatterjee formulated his question in direct response to Benedict Anderson's explanation of the origin and spread of nationalism in the modern world. For Anderson, the idea of the nation as a political community had been imagined into existence in the age of the Enlightenment and Revolution in which other imaginings of community (namely, religious community) were already on the decline.[8] The nation acquired its shape through the emergence of what Anderson called "print-capitalism," which enhanced the rapid spread of newspapers and novels and allowed individuals to identify and conceptualize themselves as members of the same community. Anderson posited that the emergence of a "modular form" of this new political community first occurred in the Americas and western Europe; later nationalisms then adapted and replicated the modular form in their own respective projects of nation building.

For Chatterjee, the arguments on nationalism proposed by Anderson were situated within a "universal history of the modern world" which did not take into account that anticolonial nationalisms in Asia and Africa fundamentally differed from the modular form.[9] Chatterjee's objection was that anticolonialism was simply subsumed as part of a normative history of nationalism originating in the Americas and Europe, without considering the "creative results of the nationalist imagination" present in the struggles against colonial power.[10] If the nation was indeed an imagined community, then what was left to imagine for the formerly colonized who were reduced to choosing their nationalism from the modular form? Chatterjee argued for a "freedom of imagination" that exemplified the differences within the historical experiences of nationalism.[11]

I understand that Chatterjee's purpose of asking "Whose imagined community?" was to disrupt the interpretations of normalized processes of nationalism in the modern world. What was at stake, of course, was assessing whose imagination was being considered in the making of the nation. In addition, his claims for creativity and freedom within the nationalist imaginary served the function of illustrating that nationalism in India was not simply a derivative discourse, nor was it a derivative imagination.[12] Yet Chatterjee points out that, while nationalist elites in India provided multiple ways of thinking about political community that differed from the historical experiences of the Americas and western Europe, they nonetheless adopted the form of the nation-state. Why did this happen? For Chatterjee, it had less to do with a lack of imagination about how to conceptualize community and more with what he calls "surrender[ing] to the old forms of the modern state."[13] Inscribed within anticolonial nationalism was a demand that "Indians" be treated as equals within the domain of the state. The ideas of liberal democracy were taken as necessary by nationalists in conceptualizing the postcolonial state in which all Indians would be treated as citizens of the nation.

I do not fully accept Chatterjee's arguments. My objection has less to do with rethinking the modular form of the nation for the study of nationalisms in Asia and Africa than with his specific claim that nationalists ceded statecraft to the West in the "material domain." For Chatterjee, anticolonial nationalism divided social institutions and practices into two domains within colonial society—the material and the spiritual. The economy, statecraft, science, and technology were all part of the material domain—a domain, according to Chatterjee, where "the West had proved its superiority and the East had succumbed."[14] On the other hand, anticolonial nationalism maintained a domain of sovereignty within colonial India in the "spiritual domain"—a domain of cultural identity that remained out of reach of the colonial state. It is within the autonomous spiritual domain where nationalism was "brought into being," thereby making it a distinct part of a "non-Western national culture."[15]

In thinking about the implications of Chatterjee's claims, I questioned the idea that nationalists had actually accepted a freedom of imagination *within* anticolonial nationalism. In fact, what appeared to be creative results of the nationalist imaginary in relation to the modular form, as argued by Chatterjee, were simultaneously expressions of nationalist dominance and hegemony over other political imaginings within the making of the nation. I suggest that the nationalists accepted the coming of the modern state, not as a form of surrender, but as an opportunity to continue dominating agrarian social relations within the postcolonial nation. In other words, nationalists like the Patidars sought to establish control within the material domain. The distinctions between the material and spiritual domains were far more blurred than Chatterjee allows for within his argument. Moreover, it was evident that in order to maintain power in the transition from the colonial world to the postcolonial one, the nationalists had to ensure that alternative forms of political community remained marginalized, or were simply silenced in relation to the idea of the nation.

A central feature of this book is a consideration of the multiple ways Dharala peasants resisted both colonialism and nationalism, all the while continuing to conceptualize political futures. The outcome of the story is well known, in that India became a nation in 1947 and Dharalas its citizens. In order to achieve victory, Patidar nationalists, and other nationalists throughout the country, fought against the British and their "Indian" detractors and opponents.[16] They were victorious, not simply because the nationalists convinced the masses to accept the idea of becoming Indian in what Chatterjee calls the spiritual domain, but also because they had established controls within the material domain. Dharalas ensured that these processes were full of conflict for the nationalists, because the fight was not simply over who controlled the means of production but also whose imagined community would come into being.

III

My research took me to local and regional archives in western India, where district-level documents have been processed and filed since the early-nineteenth century.[17] For a historian, these are the obvious places to begin. I was aware that the type of information I was looking for was difficult to collect.[18] The documents that fill the vast imperial archive reflect a colonial administration established to maintain political stability and generate revenue from the countryside. Officials did not intend for historians to write political or social histories about peasants based on their administrative letters and reports. In fact, there is often no consistency or regularity within the sources—that is, if the files are not missing or destroyed. Peasants generally appeared within official documents under extraordinary circumstances, contesting the legitimacy and authority of colonial power or local elites in the form of revolt, rebellion, and robbery.[19] During these moments of violence and conflict, the anonymous tillers of the land were transformed into criminals within the official record, but they never figured as political actors or intellectuals. Many such peasants were prosecuted and convicted of crimes against the state, but subsequently were never mentioned again in official documents. At the same time, peasants also wanted to stay out of the imperial archive.[20] They were aware of the functioning of the colonial state and did their best to avoid the attention of officials. To have one's name and activities entered into the pages of an administrative report had potentially dire consequences.

Thus, from the outset of my research, it was evident that I would be confronted with materials that were largely fragmentary and episodic.[21] This situation is certainly not unique to scholars of colonial India; it is a difficulty facing nearly all historical research on peasants. In thinking about writing histories based on fragmentary sources or writing fragmented histories (I will say more about this distinction later), I found Carlo Ginzburg's writings on historical methodology particularly useful, especially his point that "the occurrence of a phenomenon cannot be taken as an index of its historical relevance."[22] The minor presence, or major absence, of any given set of ideas or practices in the official record, for example, did not necessarily mean that their impact in society was actually minor or absent. Ginzburg also points out that a discovery of "small numbers of texts" can be "more rewarding than a massive accumulation of repetitive evidence."[23] What was significant was the quality of the evidence, not the sheer quantity.[24] In my reading there was great potential even within the fragment.

Ginzburg warns, however, that sources are not "open windows" to the past, but function more like "distorting mirrors."[25] For a historian to acknowledge that distortions exist within historical records and are a characteristic of all sources does not make the records necessarily "useless."[26] In fact, Ginzburg claims that the scarcity of evidence still provides an opportunity to "reconstruct a fragment."[27] In other words, the discovery of a fragmentary source could lead to the making of a fragmentary narrative.[28] The point was not to expect a complete picture in the historical record—an impossibility in any case—but at the same time not to be deterred from researching and writing historical narratives about peasants.[29]

IV

The first part of this book is based on materials that I located shortly after my arrival at the Maharashtra State Archives in Bombay. Within a judicial department file, I read a description of a peasant named Ranchod Vira who declared the end of the British raj and proclaimed himself a king of a new polity in 1898.[30] He wrote letters that circulated throughout the region. He collected books and papers. He was a priest and a medicine man. He had a complex understanding of political identities in rural Gujarat. He was captured by the police following an armed battle with colonial authorities and subsequently tried and convicted for sedition and murder in a court case entitled *Imperatrix vs. Ranchod Vira and Others*. Needless to say, from my point of view a new direction for the study of peasant politics immediately suggested itself and opened up fresh questions about the ways in which Dharalas were thinking about their world within a colonial context.

Ranchod and his supporters spoke in court and offered insights into their thoughts sentiments about everyday life. Yet this extraordinary case is certainly not complete, despite the extensive testimonies and detailed reports provided by government officials. In addition, it is clear that some of the confessions and testimonies of the peasants who appeared in court were coerced by the police and magistrate involved in the case. However, the rich material presents important clues about how peasants conceptualized political identity and ethical government while refusing to cede statecraft to the British.[31] By carefully combing through the details of this particular case and the statements made by the peasants in court, I have reconstructed Ranchod's story, which constitutes the first part of this book. I provide a narrative that places Ranchod and Dharalas at the center of this history. My purpose is to illustrate how peasants participated in the production and circulation of political ideas. I argue that Ranchod sought to reinvent a form of governance considered by peasants to be legitimate. His discourses and practices of kingship provide a way to look at a peasant imagining of a political community.

I knew that it was impossible that Ranchod's ideas had existed autonomously within a larger peasant world. He was neither the first peasant to declare himself a king, nor the first to announce the end of the British raj.[32] The difficulty, of course, was finding evidence that would allow me to establish larger intellectual and political connections with Ranchod and his Dharala supporters. Although officials had alluded to the fact that Ranchod's ideas were spreading throughout Gujarat even after his death, there was no interest in pursuing any leads until an individual named Daduram attracted the attention of the district magistrate.[33] I came across documents that described Daduram as popular priest and a reformer who had regularly attracted thousands of Dharalas to his meetings. The sheer number of these peasants posed a threat to the stability of the countryside, but more important, officials were concerned that Daduram had been influenced by Ranchod. Consequently, the district magistrate set up an extensive surveillance network to monitor Daduram's activities for a period of three years, between 1906 and 1909.

The reports produced by the district magistrate were the most extensive I had read about one single peasant. In many ways Daduram was similar to Ranchod in establishing critiques of colonial power and the dominance of local elites, but his methods and strategies were fundamentally different. I illustrate the fact that, even within a small locality, peasants and their leaders offered multiple ways of thinking about politics. Daduram did not propose that his Dharala supporters establish a new polity. Rather, he demanded a political future in which they would break their patron-client bonds with Patidars. Daduram was a public figure who encouraged debate and dialogue at his meetings rather than armed conflict.[34] He denounced emergent forms of popular nationalism while participating in public discourses on conceptualizing a political identity for Dharalas. While Daduram did not claim to be a king, he had nonetheless adopted practices of kingship in relation to his followers.

In the second part of the book, I reconstruct a series of narratives around the theme of Dharala politics in the early decades of the twentieth century. I begin with Daduram's complex story. However, in my attempt to find further connections to Ranchod in 1898, I was confronted with a problem of relying upon official sources. Not surprisingly, local officials stopped their surveillance in 1909, believing that the peasant movement ended with Daduram's death that year. They shifted their attention to nationalist politics in the 1910s–1940s; the focus on Dharalas acquired secondary status in the colonial record. The reports on the nationalist movement increased dramatically in this period, but fewer commentaries about marginal groups and communities were produced, except to discuss the propensity of Dharalas to commit crimes. Ironically, if more Dharalas had actually participated in the nationalist movement, it is likely that they would have garnered more attention in the official record. However, once Dharalas were declared a criminal tribe, any moment of violence or even a minor violation of the law by an individual was interpreted as a crime committed by all Dharalas. One major consequence of such a legal precedent is the absence of specificity and details in official reports and correspondence. In addition, there was a more fundamental problem: the surveillance reports and judicial testimonies were simply not objective or neutral—nor could they ever claim to be. Despite these limitations, I illustrate in part 2 the fact that official sources are neither irrelevant nor meaningless in providing clues that otherwise would have been lost.[35]

In the process of my research, I was drawn back to the details of how Dharalas were classified as criminals by the colonial state. I was struck by the fact that, only two years after Daduram's death, the Criminal Tribes Act of 1911 was imposed in Kheda district restricting the movement of all Dharalas in the locality.[36] The impact of the legislation was immediate. Patidar landholders were responsible for monitoring the Dharalas in their respective villages and were required to inform police officials of all gatherings and meetings. In effect, surveillance and control over Dharalas increased despite the fact that colonial officials were not directly involved in the daily monitoring of peasants. Public meetings to discuss political issues, which had been made popular by Daduram, came to an end. Patidars reestablished their dominant patron-client bonds with Dharalas, strengthening their ability to use extra-economic coercion. Interestingly, the most severe application of the Criminal Tribes Act was in Chaklasi, the center of Ranchod Vira's movement, where more than two thousand Dharalas were forced to attend roll call twice a day.[37]

The first two parts of the book reconsider the nature of peasant politics in Gujarat. Ranchod, Daduram, and their supporters, in their own respective ways, were demanding a new political order in the years immediately before the emergence of Patidar participation in nationalist politics. In fact, the region became a center of anticolonial nationalism only *after* the rise of Dharala politics. Let me be clear: I am not saying that Dharalas were either the first or the only section of agrarian society to raise anticolonial concerns or promote ideas of alternative political futures. Nor am I suggesting that Dharalas directly influenced the emergence of Patidar politics or anticolonial nationalism. Rather debates and critiques about ethical governance, colonial power, and political community were already a central part of the political culture in the region before the rise of mass nationalism in Gujarat now famously associated only with the Patidars and Gandhi.[38] There were multiple dialogues existing within contemporary society. The role of Dharalas in the making of peasant politics provides alternatives to the study of the region. Of course, there are many more histories yet to be written.

My argument contrasts with David Hardiman's claim that the impetus for peasant politics was primarily derived from the Patidars. Hardiman's seminal writings have illustrated the ways in which Patidar peasants were able to mobilize as a community in the struggle for nationalism. Hardiman also argues that factors of class structure were central to understanding the rise of peasant nationalism among Patidars. He states, "Although the peasant nationalists were mostly rich and middle peasants, they were also Patidars[, and] besides being a nationalist struggle, this also became a movement by the Patidars for their self-assertion as a community."[39] Hardiman further points out that there was a "rough correlation between class and community" in popular participation in local politics: "The force behind such movements came from the demands of economic classes, the banner under which the peasants fought was, more often than not, communal in form."[40] Hardiman correctly locates the crystallization of a Patidar identity in the period between 1917 and 1934 as a dominant force in leading the nationalist movement in Kheda district.

There is a fundamental problem, however, in Hardiman's analysis: namely, his explanation of the mechanisms by which Patidars dominated as a class and a community during the colonial period.[41] Although he states that Patidar "dominance came through wealth," there is little to delineate the historical processes that established the dominance of Patidars in agrarian society.[42] By focusing on the intra-Patidar divisions, distinguishing landlords from rich peasants and middle peasants, as a way to establish the locus of political mobilization, he directs insufficient attention to the long-term processes and political dynamics in the locality that help to explain the rise of Patidars in the nineteenth century. Why is this point relevant? Although Hardiman emphasizes the class-based divisions of the Patidar peasantry—arguing that middle peasants influenced rich peasants, who then influenced landlords to participate against colonial rule—there is little on how internal patron-client relations (or the nature of a surplus extraction relationship) functioned in agrarian social relations that allowed Patidars to collectively dominate Dharalas and other subordinate groups during the period of colonial rule.[43]

Throughout the nineteenth century, colonial policies had generally privileged Patidars—both landholding elites and peasant cultivators—to acquire wealth and power in the locality, while *all* Dharalas were systematically marginalized from access to the means of production. By the end of the nineteenth century, Patidars had replaced traditional moneylenders in the credit market, providing loans for fellow community members at favorable rates not available to others. The colonial state, moreover, provided loans for investments in setting up Patidar villages, in colonizing new lands, in building wells, and in purchasing cattle. New legislation implemented in the twentieth century gave Patidars the ability to exploit other peasants. However, dual crises at the turn of the century—a plague epidemic and a famine—devastated the entire region, in which nearly 20 percent of the entire population perished. For many

Dharalas, the period of crisis confirmed that a transformation in their everyday lives was absolutely necessary.

This period witnessed the emergence of organized peasant politics challenging the authority of local elites and the legitimacy of the colonial state, and offered alternative conceptualizations of political community. Some peasants demanded changes regarding land and labor rights within agrarian society, while others opted to create their own polity. The colonial state was facing its own fiscal crisis at the start of the twentieth century because it could not generate revenue from the countryside in Kheda district at the rates it had grown accustomed to during the second half of the nineteenth century. Patidars were unable to simply extract a surplus from the Dharalas because of the nature of peasant politics in this period. All the while, colonial officials continued to demand complete payment of taxes from the entire agrarian society. Patidars began questioning the legitimacy of the colonial authorities' decision to forcibly extract revenue payments in the midst of a crisis. Further, Patidars claimed that the colonial state was not ethical in its treatment of its subjects—an argument that Dharala peasants had already voiced in the late nineteenth century.

Hardiman is correct in noting that political mobilization in response to nationalism was dominated by Patidars without the large-scale participation of other parts of agrarian society, especially the Dharalas.[44] Hardiman believes this reflects a general lack of political awareness or formal organization by poor peasants. Furthermore, because many Dharalas did not own land, unlike their Patidar counterparts, he claims they could afford to be militant and violent in expressing discontent and redressing injustice.[45] More crucially, Hardiman states, "it was the movement of [substantial peasant] castes and communities which provided the initial challenge to authority and which triggered off the more revolutionary movements of the poorer peasantry."[46]

I do not fully agree with Hardiman's claims, especially when considering the ideas and practices propagated by figures like Ranchod and Daduram. The colonial state had prevented Dharalas from participating in organized politics by making public meetings and gatherings illegal with the implementation of criminal tribes legislation. Hardiman notes that Patidars had the greatest success in their movements in the villages of the Charotar tract. Not surprisingly, the Criminal Tribes Act was applied most stringently in this area of Kheda, which helps to explain why many Dharalas decided to move their politics underground at this point. Dharalas were not willing to participate alongside Patidars amid such conditions; instead, the peasants took up alternative forms of protest. Some Dharalas engaged in conceptualizing a new political identity, some organized labor strikes against Patidar landholders, some simply migrated, and others challenged aspects of colonial legislation. The most prominent form of peasant politics taken up by Dharalas in the early twentieth century involved underground activities, such as raids on villages, as a way to obstruct nationalist politics.

I argue that these efforts were not inspired by Patidar protests against the colonial state, but were a reflection of the limited options that remained to Dharala peasants. Gone were the days when hundreds and thousands of Dharalas could gather for days at a time to discuss everyday concerns about colonialism and nationalism; instead, what remained were small raids and fragmented politics. Yet the concatenation of Dharala efforts forced the nationalists to reconsider their strategies. Still, any small Dharala victories were short-lived, as it was becoming evident that the British raj was inching closer to its end, and the nationalist project led by Patidars was going to be realized. Had Patidars accepted the ideas and critiques of Dharalas, it would have meant an end to their control of the social relations of production and a reconfiguring of their understanding of an imagined community. Instead, Patidars chose to use the colonial legislation as a way to control Dharalas while simultaneously contesting colonial power in collaboration with Gandhi.

V

In the process of researching and writing this book, I made the decision not to accept the judgments of colonial officials—the judge, the magistrate, the collector, and so forth. Perhaps this is an obvious point. Had I accepted the verdict that all Dharalas were criminals, there would be no reason to continue: one could read either the colonialist narratives or the nationalist ones. Yet in order to construct my narratives and provide my own interpretations, I had to learn how the officials reached their decisions—to learn how to judge the judges.[47] I return to Ginzburg on this point, who advocates that the historian must "learn to read evidence against the grain" and "against the intention of those who produced it."[48] For Ginzburg, the method of the historian, like that of the judge, is based on evidence or proof required to reconstruct a truthful account. He does not say that proof is a "simple mirroring" of reality, which he states would be naïve, but rather that proof provides a way to understand what is possible or probable between the representations in the sources and "the reality they depict or represent."[49]

Despite the convergence between the historian and the judge, Ginzburg notes that there are fundamental differences. To begin with, historians, unlike judges, do not produce evidence.[50] Judges use evidence to make decisions, and simultaneously they participate in the making of evidence for the state in the form of the judgment, which becomes the proof later used by historians to construct historical knowledge. Historians may use proof to write about human actions and contexts in which there does not need to be a final outcome and the matter at hand can remain an "open problem."[51] In most instances, such an approach would be unsatisfactory and unacceptable in a court. The historian can choose which position to take in the process of reconstructing the narrative without having to produce an outcome or decision to conclude a case. History by its very nature suggests that there can be no conclusion to the process: there is no end of history. Ginzburg accounts for the fact that both historians and judges make errors, but the judicial errors can have more immediate and serious consequences, especially for the innocent who are convicted of crimes based on contextual circumstances that cannot be confirmed, despite the use of evidence. For Ginzburg, what remains integral for the historian is using proof and making a choice not to write like the judge, all while understanding the relationship of power involved in the making of all evidence.[52] Only then can the historian successfully use the evidential paradigm for locating the fragments within the sources and, in the words of Walter Benjamin, "brush history against the grain."[53]

I have chosen to write narratives in this book in which Dharalas are interpreted as political actors, rather than adopting the colonial classification of "criminal tribe." Yet throughout the book, I use the category of *Dharala* with great caution, recognizing that it is a term of generality and at times imprecision. I refer to the vast majority of Dharalas, who were poor peasants, agricultural laborers, and servants, rather than the few who were educated elites or even large landholders. While colonial officials sometimes made distinctions based on class, status, and power within the Dharala population, it is worth noting that *all* Dharalas were classified as members of a criminal tribe. The problem of imprecision is also compounded by the fact that early-nineteenth-century officials sometimes referred to Dharalas as *Kolis* while adding the caveat that not all Kolis were Dharalas. For purposes of clarity, I have alerted the reader to these discrepancies in the text. By the early twentieth century, some peasants shed their Dharala identity by claiming to be "Baraiyas" or "Kshatriyas." In the end, there may not be a term that is altogether satisfactory or free from bias. I have mostly used *Dharala* throughout the book, following Ranchod's declaration in court, "I am a Dharala"[54] and Daduram's critique of both *Baraiya* and *Kshatriya*.[55]

There are two further aspects on the issue of judgment that require explanation. The first has to do with a question of form; the second with the idea of the political. My book is a narrative history, or more appropriately, a book of historical narratives. I have not shunned fragmentary sources when writing these narratives, with the result that some of the narratives themselves are fragmentary. It is important to keep in mind that this decision has permitted me to include evidence or proof that would otherwise remain outside the pages of history. In some archival sources, Dharalas are mentioned as part of a footnote or are simply mentioned in passing as an irrelevant administrative detail; but what the colonial official classified as marginal had relevance for me. I have made many such references central to my text. They are required to construct the series of narratives in the book; some may look complete, but in reality they can never be. Yet what was revealed in the process of finding the fragments within the sources was a complex world in which peasants were articulating ideologies, forming organizations, and promoting programs for a transformation in agrarian society. Of course, this was not the language used in the sources, but my own adoption. I have inserted the realm of the political in my own narratives about Dharalas, although in doing so I am not asserting that the world of the Dharalas of the nineteenth or twentieth century is the same as the world today. At the same time, their world is not incomprehensible to us.[56]

Claiming that peasants are political is not new. I build upon the ideas developed in writings on agrarian society within the tradition of political Marxism, especially Ranajit Guha's intervention.[57] Guha's study of peasant insurgency in colonial India focuses on the many forms of agrarian disturbances, from small-scale riots to warlike movements in the long nineteenth century. Guha argues that through insurgency peasants demonstrated they were not only the subjects of their own history but also the makers of their own rebellions. In Guha's words: "For there was nothing in the militant movements of [colonial India's] rural masses that was not political."[58] Central to Guha's argument is an understanding that the social relations of production within agrarian society were necessarily political, because they were not dependent on strictly economic forces. Specifically, the elite in agrarian society could at any given time extract a surplus from peasants by force or extra-economic coercion based on their position and status in local society and in the colonial state. The peasant insurgent, who is the central actor in Guha's story, appears at regular intervals to "destroy the authority of the elite."[59]

Guha notes, however, that there were limitations to peasant insurgencies. To begin with, nineteenth-century movements lacked the "maturity" and "sophistication" of more advanced movements of the twentieth century.[60] Peasant leaders did not conform to the ideals of a secular or national state, because the movements were constrained by "localism, sectarianism, and ethnicity."[61] Guha attributes a political consciousness to the insurgents as a way to affirm that peasants were aware of their own world and had a desire to transform it by challenging the dominance of elites. Yet at the same time, Guha identifies peasant consciousness as an "imperfect, almost embryonic, theoretical consciousness" that was "conservative" at the core because it adopted the existing culture of elites, in spite of demanding change.[62] As a result, Guha turns to a formal study of what he identifies as "elementary aspects" of peasant consciousness, which existed in a "pure" state in colonial India prior to the emergence of the politics of nationalism and socialism.

As I have pointed out, the start of my research began with a particular discovery of a moment in the political relationship between Patidars and Dharalas. I later learned that the use of extra-economic coercion by Patidars did not first emerge in the early decades of the twentieth century but, rather, had a long history. It is important to note that while Patidars were able to extract surpluses from Dharalas beginning in the seventeenth or eighteenth century (and perhaps earlier), the nature of their relationship fundamentally changed because of the establishment of colonial power. In fact, the ability of Patidars to use extra-economic coercion actually increased with the support of colonial institutions. Implicit in this circumstance is that the nature of politics also changed in this period. Yet this point is not evident in Guha's interpretation of politics; what remains a constant in his analysis is the ability of peasants to rebel and their inability to develop a "full-fledged struggle for national liberation."[63] Peasants are recognized as being political for participating in insurgencies, but still politically limited.

While I accept that peasants are political, I do not fully agree with Guha's arguments that peasant politics were primarily based on violence in the form of an insurgency, revolt, or rebellion. Other forms of politics were possible in agrarian society. Further, I disagree with the idea that all politics must necessarily lead toward the making of a nation or revolution.[64] Through a study of peasant practices and discourses, I argue that peasant politics were complex, dynamic, and contingent. By expanding the idea of peasant politics, I show that many peasants (like other sections of Indian society) had alternative imaginings for a political community *before* the creation of the nation-state. My purpose is neither to celebrate their politics nor to suggest that these politics were unique. On the other hand, I do not claim that the peasants necessarily *failed* because their politics did not coalesce into something larger in scale. By telling this story, I illuminate a world in which peasants made normative judgments by relying on practices and discourses already sanctioned by local custom.[65] I argue that peasants were keenly aware of the changing nature of society and articulated their concerns based on contemporary considerations.

VI

In order to understand the political realm, it is also necessary to consider the nature of peasant religion, not least because both Ranchod and Daduram gained their authority as leaders through their positions as *bhagats*, or village priests.[66] More important, the two men imagined a future in which they themselves did not distinguish between the political and the religious. This is no surprise. I say this not as a critique of how peasants understood their world, or to suggest that all politics in India are necessarily religious, but to indicate how most polities in the world functioned during most of the nineteenth century.[67] After all, the nearly six hundred princes and kings—the rajas and maharajas—of the existing princely states claimed that within the traditions of kingship they were the representatives of one deity or another. Similar arguments were made by thousands of smaller kings and minor rajas scattered throughout the countryside.

Religious thought, practices, and rituals were central to how Ranchod and Daduram contested the relations of power in colonial society, but also to how they conceptualized a world in which they were not exploited by local elites, nationalists, and colonial officials. What is unclear, however, is why peasants like Ranchod would turn toward the discourses of kingship, and why Daduram would function like a king in patronizing his subjects in the midst of a conjunctural crisis. Perhaps the answer has something to do with the fact that, in a world being transformed by colonial power, on one hand, and nationalism, on the other, the governance associated with kingship, though not perfect, was considered more ethical in relating to the everyday concerns of peasants.[68]

My point here is not that *bhagats* and their supporters simply adopted the traditions of kingship without an internal critique. In the first place, it is doubtful that the rajas and maharajas, or the high priests who performed rituals legitimating the authority of the rajas and maharajas, would have actually accepted *bhagats* as equals of kings or priests—something Ranchod and Daduram would have known. Instead, the *bhagats* built upon the ideas of kingship—political and religious—for their own purposes of creating new types of social order for Dharalas that reflected the changing nature of their world. For Ranchod, the creation of his polity did not mean that other polities, including the British raj, ceased to exist, but rather that the authority of the colonial state ended in his newly confiscated territory. In fact, he preferred to coexist with other polities, but at the same time he wanted to protect his supporters—poor Dharala peasants—from further exploitation and subordination. Daduram did not formally proclaim himself to be a king or chart out a territory as his polity. Rather, he served the functions of a king in relation to his supporters.

Despite taking different approaches, both leaders relied upon the *bhagat* ideology already accepted as legitimate among their supporters, while simultaneously interpreting and incorporating a range of elite ideas within their respective discourses. It is impossible to know when such moments of transformation took place. But what is known is that inscribed within the discourses are various critiques—of colonialism, of nationalism, of power, of domination—and indications of how the poor, the marginalized, the subordinated could coexist in a world where even a peasant could achieve leadership as a *bhagat* or assume the position of a king.

The difficulty of writing about *bhagat* ideologies is that they were transmitted as part of an oral culture. To rely upon colonial documentation in order to write about such ideas presents a problem. *Bhagats* tend to appear in colonial sources only when they posed a direct threat to the state, but of course this was not the primary function of these village priests.[69] The complexity of what *bhagats* articulated in both religious and political terms during the nineteenth century may be irretrievable. What remains in the official record are small fragments indicating that peasants, like their elite counterparts, were engaged in discourses and practices to rethink and reimagine their world.

I do not suggest here that these peasants maintained an autonomous domain of ideas, either political or religious, that could ever have been entirely separate from the domain of elite ideas. This is not to say that the ideas of peasants and elites were the same. I have adopted two separate but compatible concepts in addressing this issue. The first is the notion of circularity, as proposed by Ginzburg, which indicates that there was a "circular relationship composed of reciprocal influences, which traveled from low to high as well as from high to low."[70] In my understanding of this circularity, the production and distribution of ideas were processes that influenced one another over time, especially with the presence of new technologies that linked oral and written cultures. This does not, however, mean that there was equal acceptance or acknowledgement by elites and peasants that their respective ideas were literally in constant dialogue with one another. The second concept that I have adopted is Chatterjee's argument that the domains in colonial society were "mutually conditioned," especially at the height of the "hegemonic project of nationalism."[71] However, Chatterjee notes, even within these domains there existed "resistances to the normalizing project." I argue that, despite, or perhaps because of, an awareness of the range of ideas already present in society, Dharalas chose alternative futures because they were aware of the impact of colonial power and what nationalism offered them with the coming of the postcolonial state. Both the nationalists and colonialists, in their respective ways, ensured that such futures remained marginalized.

VII

Part 3 of this book begins with a discussion of my engagement with official archival sources in constructing the narratives found in this book. During my research, I was not convinced by those officials who declared the end of the peasant movements involving Ranchod, Daduram, and other Dharalas. Colonial power may have stopped one movement after another by force or other means, but I knew it was impossible for officials to prevent the production and circulation of political ideas even if criminal tribes legislation was strictly enforced.[72] I went to rural Gujarat in search of the legacies and memories of these early peasant politics. I traveled to villages and towns in Kheda district to locate individuals who could provide narratives of Dharala movements, especially those led by Daduram and Ranchod. But more specifically, I was looking for the intellectual descendants of the two peasant leaders and their supporters. The point was not to simply juxtapose the oral materials with the official written ones, or to search for an authentic interpretation of the past as told by today's Dharalas. My aim was to find oral sources that would suggest alternative ways of thinking and writing about Dharala pasts that were unimaginable or unknowable through the official record.[73]

In part 3, I offer an account of this historical fieldwork, which took place in the Gujarat countryside in 1996. Oral sources gave me new insights into writing historical narratives. I did not expect to find autonomous voices that would provide completely independent narratives, but in the process of conducting interviews I discovered new directions of inquiry. I discuss here only select encounters in a condensed form that provide new meanings for the earlier narratives in the book.[74] Some interviews took many days and many trips to complete, while others took less time. Many individuals whom I spoke to have been left out of the story, while the ideas of others have been discussed extensively. I include encounters that appear complete, as well as mention others that illustrate the problems I came across in the process of using oral materials.

I returned to rural Gujarat in 2004 to discuss my writings with those whom I had met in 1996. My aim was to get a critique of my own interpretations of colonialism and nationalism. My trip took place two years after central and northern Gujarat experienced some of the worst communal violence in India, in 2002, when an estimated two thousand Muslims were killed. I was aware that it would be impossible to expect that the descendants of the Dharalas were not affected by the violence. While many individuals noted that horrific things had taken place, most were unwilling to discuss specific events or how the violence may have affected the ways in which they remembered the past. Although I have discussed the nature of violence and conflict in the making of nationalism, the history of Hindu-Muslim relations and its impact on postcolonial nationalism remains outside the scope of this book.

My travels in Kheda district were extensive, but in conducting the interviews I confronted further obstacles. My reliance on colonial sources was met with a good deal of concern, because many individuals believed that the British must have lied in their records. When I was asked how I had come to know so much about figures like Daduram and Ranchod, I explained that I had read the information in documents kept in the government archives in Bombay. On a few occasions, I was accused of being a policeman. It did not matter that the records in my possession were from the colonial period; it was assumed I must hold an official position in the government that would allow me access to such sensitive information. In a state that maintained criminal tribes legislation for part of the postcolonial period and continues to prosecute peasants for distilling alcohol or cultivating marijuana and opium, anyone resembling an official is met with suspicion.

In spite of these concerns, most individuals agreed to speak with me about Daduram and Ranchod after I explained that I was writing a book in which Dharalas were at the center of the history, not at the margins. However, most individuals were unwilling to discuss the underground movements that involved large raids on rich agricultural villages, except in the most general terms, fearing that even cursory details that I might mention could potentially bring new criminal charges or punishment. As a result, I have not discussed these details in the book. Some individuals agreed to share their thoughts only on the condition that I not reveal their identities. I have maintained their anonymity in my book, but for the others I have included the names they gave me at the outset of the interviews. (I do not distinguish between actual and pseudonymous names in the text or footnotes.)

I also take account of the relationship between popular religion and politics that was of no interest to either the colonialists or the nationalists writing about Dharalas, but which is central to the concerns of today's followers of Daduram and Ranchod. The discourses of nationalism are now central to the way the earlier peasant leaders are remembered. The fact that a figure like Daduram was antagonistic to early nationalism is not mentioned; instead he is considered the father of the Indian nation and a deity in the Hindu pantheon. Peasants in Chaklasi still consider Ranchod a protector in the village and still criticize nationalists and colonialists. The descendants of Dharalas have adopted a new political identity, which lets them erase the old criminal label and assert their rights as citizens of India. The nature of politics has changed in the postcolonial period, but so too has peasant religion. The hegemony of the nationalist project continues, as it needs to ensure that new generations understand how their nation came into being. All the while, resistance to the project also continues. The descendants of the nationalists still dominate the means of production; the descendants of those who resisted the nationalist project remain marginalized. It would be impossible to expect that the memories of peasants would not be transformed by the discourses of nationalism.[75] Yet while peasants today elect their own representatives, they also remember a time in which they claim to have lived autonomously, free from all forms of domination. Perhaps such a memory provides hope for the future. In the meantime, peasants have to tend to their everyday lives within the nation.

VIII

I have chosen to write a history of what Benjamin calls "minor" acts, of "inconspicuous transformations" rendered irrelevant except for those who posit that "nothing should be lost for history."[76] My research began with an untold story from one of the most celebrated areas in India, where nationalism developed. If all nationalist politics in India, and perhaps beyond, includes such hidden histories, then only extensive historical details can illustrate how individuals, classes, groups, and communities were marginalized from the promises of the nation. These ideas may be familiar to some readers, but others may find something new in this book. Not all histories within a nation are the same. Neither are all peasants.

PART ONE

1 · RANCHOD

This story begins with a peasant named Ranchod Vira. He was born around 1848 in the village of Chaklasi, located on the plains of central Gujarat, in western India. He was married and lived with his son and grandson. He tilled seven or eight *bighas* of land belonging to the village headman Kashibhai Ranchodbhai.[1] He was a subtenant, a servant, or a sharecropper who cultivated simple foodstuff like millet, wheat, and yellow lentil. In fact, there was nothing extraordinary about him. He probably would have remained an anonymous figure, leaving no trace in the annals of history, had he had not declared the end of the British raj and proclaimed himself king of a new polity.[2]

On January 12, 1898, five or six hundred armed peasants gathered in Chaklasi in support of Ranchod. Within a few hours, news of the activities in the village had reached colonial officials in the neighboring town of Nadiad, and a group of eighteen constables led by Police Inspector Jagannath Sagun and the *mamlatdar*—a revenue officer—quickly set out to prevent any disturbance. Around 4:30 in the afternoon, Inspector Jagannath and his men arrived in Chaklasi with the intention of speaking to Ranchod; however, they were stopped by the armed peasants. Jagannath insisted on meeting their leader and asked the crowd to disperse. In reply, the peasants told Jagannath to worship and asked him if he was a Gujarati or a *topiwallah* (literally, "hat wearer," a term for someone who worked for the colonial state).[3] Ranchod sent a message to Jagannath demanding that the inspector communicate with him by writing a letter specifying his queries and concerns. Jagannath's refusal to comply with the request was viewed as a sign of hostility: Ranchod emerged to the resonating sounds of a trumpet and booming drums and signaled his supporters to attack all representatives of the colonial government.

The battle lasted a few short hours, quickly being stopped by the police.[4] Constables shot into the large crowd, killing five peasants. Ranchod and some of his supporters ran away, while other peasants began chasing constables through the village. One constable was killed, and three others were attacked and stripped of their uniforms and weapons. On the following day, January 13, two hundred infantrymen of the British Indian Army's Fourth Bombay Rifles were dispatched from Ahmedabad to quell any further conflict.[5] Ranchod and ten other peasants were captured as they were attempting to flee the village. The police confiscated Ranchod's possessions for evidence, finding a wide range of items, including weapons, police uniforms, two letters, moneylenders' account ledgers, a loose bundle of account registers, a small book collection, twenty-two pieces of blank paper, and a list of twenty-one villages.[6]

For an individual who could neither read nor write, Ranchod appears to have been well aware of the power of the written word.[7] Although peasants in colonial India had often destroyed writings as symbols of elite dominance, especially documents recording peasants' debts, Ranchod chose to confiscate, collect, preserve, produce, and distribute writings as a way of establishing his own authority and leadership.[8] His desire to receive a written message from colonial officials like Inspector Jagannath suggests that he was behaving in consonance with the norms of courtly tradition that required formal communication from representatives of other states. Alternatively, it indicates that Ranchod had appropriated the written form at a time when the bureaucratization of the colonial state had advanced to the point where peasants were keenly aware of the significance and impact of rent notes, legal documents, and account ledgers in their everyday lives.[9] The use and incorporation of writing may be interpreted as a practice that symbolically affirmed Ranchod's ascendancy. But, then, Ranchod appears to have turned to other courtly practices and traditions found throughout western India, dating back several centuries, to establish his legitimacy as a king and to uphold a new social order.[10]

Colonial power had stopped a small peasant movement from coalescing into something larger. The introduction of the military and police ensured that the peasants of Chaklasi could no longer gather for political or other reasons. Local representatives such as the village headman and village accountant were dismissed from service and quickly replaced with individuals viewed as loyal to the government. Surveillance practices were enforced in the village, and peasants were required to attend daily roll call as a way of monitoring their everyday activities. Yet despite the swift conclusion to Ranchod's reign as a king, colonial power was not able to suppress the circulation of his ideas.[11] Officials reported that a letter dictated by the peasant leader declaring the end of the British raj was spreading throughout the region: "The letter is finding its way in the province . . . [and] people are enjoining to keep copies and forwarding [them] to the next village."[12]

2 · THE *BHAGAT* AND THE MIRACLE

Ranchod was not an ordinary peasant in the small world of Chaklasi: that much is clear. He was a *bhagat*—a village priest—who claimed to have supernatural powers. He was also a popular medicine man who had knowledge of herbs and spells. Ranchod may have learned these skills as a disciple of a figure named Bama Kuberdar from the village of Sarsa. But little is known about Kuberdar's relationship with Ranchod, especially during the period of Ranchod's ascendancy. At some point in the years preceding 1898, Ranchod had acquired a prominent position in Chaklasi and neighboring villages. This may have been connected to his role as a healer or to his popularity as a messianic leader who espoused ideas of a new beginning. There is, of course, very little information about the origins or background of the early years of Ranchod's leadership.

Ranchod's rise to power is not easy to understand from the testimonies presented by his followers and other villagers in Chaklasi. When Surta Ragha, another disciple of Bama Kuberdar, was asked in court, "What do you know about Ranchod?" he replied, "[Ranchod] used to recite Bhajans [devotional songs] formerly. . . . He built the mandwa [canopy], and gave out that he had met Shri-Ranchodji. He assembled the Bhagats around him and recited Bhajans. His *arti* [set of rituals] was performed . . . [and] worship was made to him as to a god."[1] Surta was stating what he had remembered about the activities of early December 1897. Others also reported that Ranchod had constructed a part of a temple called a *mandwa* for the purpose of organizing peasants from Chaklasi and the surrounding villages. In fact, this site became the center for all of Ranchod's subsequent activities, including the battle with the police. However, Surta's revelation of Ranchod's encounter with Shri Ranchodji was not mentioned elsewhere. This bit of information was ignored by the public prosecutor who questioned Surta; even Ranchod had not discussed this encounter when he spoke in court. But what was its significance for Ranchod's disciples?

Ranchod's meeting with Shri Ranchodji, a manifestation of the deity Krishna, can be understood as a spiritual encounter that had legitimacy for the peasants in Chaklasi.[2] On the whole, Ranchod's claim would not have been viewed as unusual, especially as *bhagat*s frequently commented on their supernatural abilities to contact and communicate with various Hindu deities. The fact that Ranchod had, in essence, the same name as Shri Ranchodji must have elevated his status and possibly enhanced his authority and legitimacy. Ranchod could not only assert that he was the principle devotee of Ranchodji, but he could also posit that he was a manifestation of the deity. In fact, he did make such a claim. By establishing a direct connection to Ranchodji, Ranchod constructed the popular idea of traditional divine kingship in which worshipping the king or the deity was viewed as ritually homologous.[3]

During the first week of December 1897, Ranchod prophesied a miracle in the village of Chaklasi. He stated that during the full moon on December 9, Ranchodji, his temple in Dakore, and a lake would magically arrive in Chaklasi. Ranchod began organizing daily public meetings at the *mandwa*, propagating messages about the miracle and attracting large numbers of peasants from Chaklasi and neighboring villages. In court, Surta testified that, on the full moon, "thousands of people assembled to do the Dars[h]an [to view a deity or person] as the *Bhagat* had given out that Ranchodji would come there."[4] Kashibhai, the village headman, reported, "About 2,000 people collected there from surrounding villages; they put a garland of flowers on a wooden frame and lit a *ghee* lamp. They also said that a village [water] tank was to spring up."[5] When Ranchod was later asked about the gathering by the magistrate, he had little to say except that "there were collected about 1,000 or 1,500 people, but I do not know them. They were Dharalas, Patidars and others."[6]

3 · DHARALA/KOLI/SWORDSMAN

During Ranchod's first appearance in court, he told First Class Magistrate J. Becharlal, "I am by caste Dharala, my occupation is agriculture."[1] Later, when the magistrate asked Ranchod what "class of people" were his supporters, he responded, "They were all Dharalas." Ranchod's identification placed him squarely within the largest agricultural community in Kheda, constituting nearly one-third of the district's total population. (In Chaklasi alone there were nearly twelve hundred Dharala families, most of whom were small peasant cultivators.) Dharalas had achieved some notoriety in the area for their martial skills in sword fighting; in fact, the name *Dharala* was believed to have been a derivation of *dhar,* literally "the edge of a sword."[2] British officials had noted that these swordsmen were formerly members of the "military classes" in Gujarat; they were "generally strong and well-made" and were "respected" by fellow members of their clan—the Kolis.[3] However, the term *Koli* posed difficulties for the government: some officials defined it to mean "clansman, clubman, or boatman"; others applied it to a number of "tribes that differ widely from each other"; at times it was defined as an "aboriginal of the plains," and at others it meant "bastard or half-caste."[4]

In Kheda, four separate communities—Dharalas, Patanwadias, Khants, and Chunvaliyas—were all classified as Kolis, with Dharalas constituting more than 80 percent of all Kolis.[5] Officials acknowledged that Dharalas "do not like to be called Koli. . . . They consider themselves to be superior"; in fact, the Dharalas asserted their status by choosing not to dine or intermarry with other Kolis.[6] Yet the early-nineteenth-century official correspondence and reports use only the term *Koli* to describe Dharalas. While these distinctions were not at the center of the court case, the magistrate referred to Ranchod and his supporters as Dharalas throughout the duration of the trial, except once, when he asked Surta, "What had the *Kolis* with them in their hands?"[7] The magistrate's question was significant since the right to possess weapons was at the center of much official debate about all the Kolis living in British territory.

By the end of the nineteenth century, only a few Dharalas had maintained their martial skills and worked as guards, village watchmen, and
trackers. Most others had taken up settled agriculture or worked as
sharecroppers, laborers, or servants. This was no accident. The British
had an interest in disarming and settling all Kolis in the years following
the East India Company's (EIC) annexation of Kheda and its neighboring
lands, in 1803.[8] At the beginning of the nineteenth century, Kolis posed a
serious "law and order" problem for the new government, leading officials to declare that they were one of the most "turbulent, predatory
tribes" in India.[9] Many Kolis resided in villages outside the EIC's territo-
rial jurisdiction but viewed the imposition of new legislation and colonization in the territory as a direct challenge to established local customs.

Koli chieftains and their peasant supporters were probably aware that
the expansion of the EIC's land acquisitions would impinge on their own
privileges and legitimacy, and they were threatened by the British settling
the agricultural plains and establishing new modes of governance in the
area. In protest, some chieftains filed petitions in the Court of Law
(Adalat) in Kheda, stating that, according to local custom, the government had no authority over Kolis. Other chieftains simply ignored the
authority of the EIC and organized peasant raids into towns and villages
in British territory, claiming a customary right to plunder villages as a
form of their own tax collection, or a levy called *giras*. The idea of collecting *giras* was not new in this period; in fact, it was a practice that
dated back to the twelfth century.[10] The district magistrate responded by
stating such actions were "evil" and perpetuated by Koli chieftains from
"an ancient period."

By 1808, Koli chieftains had begun organizing raids into towns and villages in the territory controlled by the EIC, to steal crops and other possessions.[11] The town of Dholka and its neighboring villages became
favorite targets. Dholka was in the northern borderlands of British territory, adjacent to land controlled by the chieftains. Groups of armed men,
numbering between fifty and a hundred Kolis, easily entered Dholka and
returned to their respective villages without difficulty. British officials
lacked the manpower and local knowledge of the terrain to capture these
men. However, there were instances when a chieftain was arrested and
jailed for leading attacks on Dholka, as in the case of Bachur Khokani.[12]
On February 20, 1808, within a few days of Khokani's capture, a group of
fifty Kolis stormed the jail and released their leader.[13] Two policemen were
killed and six were wounded in the battle, and apparently, on the very
same night, Khokani and his men organized another raid on the town.

In an attempt to prevent further raids on Dholka, Kheda's magistrate, R. Holford, coordinated a plan that required local elites within the EIC's control to capture the raiders.[14] Holford recognized the limitations of the EIC's power to arrest individuals residing outside its control, but he believed that officials could force the elites who had villages within their legal jurisdiction to cooperate. Holford wrote to an individual named M. F. M. Purmar for this specific purpose:

> In consequence of the number of robbers who infest . . . Dholka . . . for the purpose of plundering, you will cause your sepoys and horsemen to prevent their so doing. Hence forward, should any person be plundered, you will be called upon to answer for it. This is written to you, in consequence of your holding villages belonging to the Sircars. . . . You cannot have a right to those villages, should the Government dispossess you of them. If you require a continuance of the Government's favour, you must continue to perform its service.[15]

The outcome of the official strategy had some success: in 1810, large numbers of Kolis had been arrested and convicted of crimes against the EIC. Judge H. W. Diggle recommended that the prisoners be transported out of the locality to the British colony the Prince of Wales Island (formerly called Penang), or to a distant jail, for a minimum of seven years.[16] It was argued that such an extreme measure would "overawe" and "check the daring and ferocious nature" of Kolis while simultaneously serving as a deterrent for others. However, as in the case of Bachur Khokani, a group of four hundred to five hundred armed men descended upon the jail at Kheda and released the imprisoned Kolis. Most of the prisoners dispersed into areas outside of British jurisdiction and were saved just days before being transported to the Prince of Wales Island.

The raids continued in Dholka, and colonial officials urged the EIC to increase and strengthen the size of the police force in Kheda. In addition, officials requested the support of soldiers from neighboring Baroda State, who were supposed to have local intelligence networks in the borderlands that could be used for recapturing the convicted Kolis and their accomplices. But the outcome of using greater force had a minimal impact on what had developed into a serious law and order problem for the EIC. Colonial officials were not able to prevent Koli raids. Earlier attempts to press chieftains to cooperate in preventing attacks on government towns and villages had had limited results.

In 1824, A. Crawford, the district collector of neighboring Ahmedabad, suggested that a new strategy be adopted, including forcibly taking the possessions of Koli chieftains suspected of either participating in the attacks or simply having any information about them.[17] In addition, Crawford introduced the idea of using the military to destroy villages where Koli chieftains were hiding. This strategy marked an important departure from the policy of not entering areas that lay outside the jurisdiction of the EIC with the intention of using military force to capture chieftains or other raiders. However, the idea of completely destroying villages as a way to create "future peaceable conduct" did not prevent Kolis from challenging the authority and legitimacy of the EIC, and certainly it did not eliminate the armed excursions into British-controlled territory. In fact, it further intensified the demands of those Kolis who had been claiming that their customs and privileges were being violated by colonial officials.

The raids continued through the 1830s with some regularity, leading Crawford to state, "Some special regulations should be made about the Kolis. No measures of ordinary severity have any effect. We never hear of a reformed Koli, or of one whose mode of life places him beyond suspicion. All seem alike, rich and poor, those whose necessities afford them an excuse for crime, and those whose condition places them out of the reach of distress, are alike ready on the first opportunity to plunder."[18] But by the 1840s, the application of colonial policies and the use of military force led to the subsidence of Koli attacks in British-controlled territory. Officials argued that the character of all Kolis—chieftains and peasants—had improved, as many had taken up settled agriculture and become hardworking and peaceable.[19]

Despite this acknowledgment of the transformation among the Kolis, the early-nineteenth-century encounters continued to influence the implementation of official policies in the district. To begin with, in 1857 and 1858, the government imposed regulations restricting Kolis from carrying weapons in Kheda district.[20] Officials began disarming various groups in this period who were viewed as a threat to the stability of India's countryside based on the administrative concern that the peasant rebellions in northern, central, and eastern India would spread to Gujarat and further exacerbate the legitimation crisis of the colonial state. Officials confiscated swords and other weapons from Kolis as a preventive measure and outlawed their possession, except by those individuals who were so authorized by the government. For many Dharalas, this measure was a fundamental violation of their customary rights: after all, how was a swordsman to fulfill his service without a sword?

4 · THE PATIDARS AND THE KANBIS

The government's use of force and coercion had an impact on settling Kolis, but the process was facilitated by strengthening the dominance of another section of agrarian society—the Patidars. According to Ranchod, Patidars were also present on the night of December 9. Perhaps Ranchod and his Dharala supporters wanted other villagers to participate in the gathering, or Patidars simply arrived to view the spectacle. Chaklasi was a Patidar-dominated village located in the flourishing agricultural tract in Kheda known as the Charotar—in common parlance "the goodly land"—and was important to the colonial government for being one of the villages in the Bombay Presidency with the highest assessment on land rates.[1] The Charotar tract was largely controlled by members of the Lewa Kanbi caste, who shared payments of revenue within a coparcenary system of land tenure known as *narwadari*.[2] Lewa Kanbis had used this land tenure system probably as far back as the seventeenth century as a communal form of protection and resistance against exploitative modes of governance. However, in the nineteenth century, Lewa Kanbis used their networks within the *narwadari* system as a way to establish controls over other direct producers in the area, namely Dharalas and Kolis.[3]

Lewa Kanbis had developed a surplus-extraction relationship with other peasants by applying levies and demanding "gratuitous services," "labour rents" *(veth),* house rents, and the free use of carts, bullocks, and plows.[4] As early as the eighteenth century, Lewa Kanbis established a distinction within the caste: the direct cultivators were called Kanbis, and the caste elites who had abandoned the tilling of land and collected revenue were identified as Patidars.[5] The two sections of the Lewa Kanbis typically resided in the same village, but they often maintained separate dining and marital rites.[6] Yet by the latter part of the nineteenth century, colonial officials began classifying both as Kanbis, often dropping the "Lewa" label when referring to caste elites. In other instances, officials referred to both as Patidars, failing to distinguish between caste members. Ranchod's comment about "Patidars" has similar problems, as it is unclear if he was referring to caste elites or using the term as a reference to both sections of Lewa Kanbis in Chaklasi.

By all official accounts, the Charotar tract was a uniformly well-managed area with a beautiful landscape: the manicured fields, carefully planted rows of "high hedges," and "clusters of large shapely trees" were symbols of order and efficiency with no parallel throughout the region.[7] The flat plains, consisting of a light, shallow loam called *goradu*, were skillfully tilled to produce a "belt of rich vegetation."[8] It was an area that had been celebrated since the fifteenth century for its productivity levels and the high revenue-generating potential of its cash crops: cotton, tobacco, and food grains.[9] The agricultural tract was acclaimed as "perhaps the finest in India," and for some officials, like James Forbes in 1775, the visual aesthetic of the area was comparable to the home country, evoking memories of the English countryside.[10] As early as 1830, Major General John Malcolm had written that "the Coonbees of Guzerat . . . deserve all the encouragement which the protection and consideration of Government can extend them."[11]

Officials claimed that Lewa Kanbis were the most "industrious" and "thrifty" cultivators in the area, and that through the *narwadari* system they had used their communal networks to control the political economy of the locality. Officials had encouraged the maintenance of the *narwadari* system in nearly 90 villages (out of 570-odd villages controlled by the British in Kheda district), in which peasants in a given village were "jointly responsible" for making land revenue payments to the government. If one shareholder was unable to make a timely payment, the village community would make the payment or secure a loan for the peasant. Some *narwadar*s opted to make direct payments for their individual landholdings and shared payments for common land.[12] These options were not available for most peasants.

The government wanted to increase its land revenue by encouraging the Lewa Kanbis to take over land in the northern and eastern parts of Kheda district, known as the Mal tract, which lay beyond the *narwadari* villages of the Charotar. The majority of the "arable area" of the Charotar was already under cultivation, which left little room for further agricultural expansion.[13] In contrast, the Mal largely consisted of uncultivated grassland officially classified as a wasteland, but officials believed it could be colonized and improved to resemble the Charotar. But the Mal presented administrative problems for the government. This area bordered the lands traditionally under the control of Koli chieftains; in fact, most of the peasants residing in the Mal were Dharalas.

By the 1840s, the government established its administrative control of the area by pacifying Koli chieftains and reducing raids and excursions into British territory. Next, Dharalas (and Kolis, more generally) were either coerced or encouraged to abandon the practice of temporary occupancy of land and any peripatetic lifestyle and take up settled agriculture.[14] In fact, officials claimed that their actions had directly increased the number of Koli cultivators by nearly 60 percent between 1846 and 1872, a rise from 175,829 to 281,252.[15] Yet despite this transformation, officials raised concerns about the "unproductive" and "indolent" nature of Dharalas, who were perceived as impeding the growth of the agrarian economy. In the 1850s, the government was still apprehensive about the potential for Dharalas to take up arms and rebel, leading officials to confiscate all weapons. Because of their concerns, officials had regularly advocated that "productive" Lewa Kanbis from the Charotar tract be given proper incentives to permanently occupy and cultivate any available land in the Mal.

In the early 1860s, the government conducted the first Revenue Survey and Assessment of Gujarat and replaced the older systems of revenue collection with the *ryotwari* system, which required peasants to make individual land revenue payments to government officials.[16] By reorganizing the administrative apparatus to establish direct contact with peasants and eliminate the revenue-collecting middlemen, colonial officials expected to cut costs and increase total land revenue in the district. The rent rates on *ryotwari* lands were typically fixed for a thirty-year period (e.g., 1860s–1890s; 1890s–1920s) and revised in accordance with the government's fiscal interests within a particular village or agricultural tract. In some villages, including Chaklasi, two land tenure systems existed side by side: Lewa Kanbis were allowed to function within a *narwadari* system, while other peasants had to adapt to the new *ryotwari* system.[17] In addition, the government required that peasants permanently occupy any land suitable for cultivation, marking a departure for peasants who paid rents on the temporary occupancy of land or practiced shifting cultivation. The policy also promoted the permanent occupancy of common lands, grazing lands, and "waste lands" that traditionally had been held by peasants on a rent-free basis: a customary right that had been granted to select peasants in exchange for services to the government prior to the British annexation of western India in the early nineteenth century.

Colonial expansion into areas like the Mal tract was common throughout India in this period and typically led to the creation of new settlements with financial support from the government. Often such penetration into the inner regions of the countryside disrupted local patterns of everyday life and introduced new systems of governance that were alien to local inhabitants. In Kheda district, Captain C. J. Prescott, the head of the Revenue Survey and Assessment, proposed giving *tukavee* (loans) to cultivators, especially to "agricultural capitalists" who agreed to pay a moderate rent on the "poorest and most thinly populated 'mal' villages."[18]

In most cases, the government created financial incentives to assist Lewa Kanbis. The district collector even posited that "the Patidars [would] gradually take possession" of the land and the "thriftless Kolis . . . will be the labourers of the Patidars."[19] However, the Irish Presbyterian Mission was also granted 1,023 acres in the villages of Samalpura and Chetarsumba to create a Christian colony. The *desais* of Nadiad, Patidar elites who were once the chief revenue-farmers under the administrations of the territory prior to the arrival of the British, received incentives to take up land on speculation during the 1860s.[20] By the 1880s several deserted villages had been taken up. In 1880, the government gave Amratlal Maneklal Desai "a large grant of special terms" to establish a village for Lewa Kanbis.[21] Within five years, officials claimed that the village was "flourishing" and had achieved "considerable pecuniary success." Bechardas Veharidas Desai initially had applied for 500 acres in the Mal, but the government provided him with "special conditions" under which to take over 1,200 acres for tobacco cultivation and agricultural experiments.[22] In the 1890s, Maganlal Laxmilal Desai received a loan of four thousand rupees from the government for settling Kanbi families and providing them with financial resources to construct wells, purchase cattle and fertilizers, and hire agricultural laborers.[23]

By the mid-1890s, nearly one-half of Kheda district's wasteland was occupied under the terms established in the 1860s. Many Dharalas throughout the district had been forced to abandon their possessions and work as agricultural laborers if they were unable to take up the permanent occupancy of land for a thirty-year period based on the new rates. The resettlement surveys of the 1890s reinforced the government's land policies in the area that privileged Patidars and Kanbis while marginalizing other cultivators. In many villages, including Chaklasi, the government had doubled rent rates for specific plots of land as a way to force Dharalas to give up their possessions, thereby, creating further advantages for Patidars.[24] Additionally, Dharalas in the village were no longer able to rely upon rent-free common lands for grazing animals and cutting grass and trees as a means of supplementing their income. Sometime in early 1897, the twelve hundred Dharala families residing in Chaklasi gathered their belongings and left the village to protest these land policies.[25] Ranchod's role in this *hijrat*—protest migration—is not clear, but it may be assumed that he and his family also participated in the event.

News of the mass migration quickly reached the commissioner of Bombay Presidency's Northern Division, who immediately repealed the order to levy a full assessment on the village based on the new rent rates. He suggested that the old rates be restored and that the government reconsider its endorsement of all policies in the locality.[26] The Dharala families returned to the village, having secured assurances that rent rates would not be increased.[27] But if the government was interested in displacing Dharalas through the implementation of its policies, why would it opt to negotiate in this instance? Although officials wanted Kanbis to settle and permanently occupy Dharala land in Chaklasi as a way to guarantee a fixed rent rate, there was also an assumption that the "displaced" Dharalas would remain in the village and take on new roles as servants and agricultural laborers for the *narwadars*.

5 · BECOMING A COLONIAL EMISSARY

When Kashibhai was asked to identify himself at Ranchod's trial, he never mentioned that he was a *narwadar*. Perhaps this was an obvious point that everyone in court would have known. According to the court record, he said, "I state on solemn affirmation that my name is Kashibhai, my age is 52, my caste is Patidar, my profession is Mukhi and that I reside at Chaklasi." Kashibhai then testified that "accused number one tills . . . a field belonging to me."[1] This was a direct reference to Ranchod. The public prosecutor did not raise any further questions about Kashibhai's relationship with Ranchod. And it appears that Kashibhai did not offer any additional information about how long Ranchod had worked for him or in what capacity. Was Ranchod one of the many Dharalas "displaced" by the implementation of the new land policies? Was he forced to abandon his own possessions to work on a Patidar's land? Was he an agricultural laborer, a servant, or something else altogether? Unfortunately, there are no complete answers to these questions.

Individuals like Kashibhai played an important role for the colonial government in the everyday functioning of villages.[2] Prior to the British annexation of Kheda district, the *mukhi* had assisted individuals called revenue-farmers with the collection of land payments in villages, a process that dated back to the sixteenth century.[3] Revenue-farmers were individuals who collected land payments for the early governors of the territory. They provided a specific guarantee of payment to the governors; in return they were allowed to keep any surplus that they were able to collect from villages.[4] As an institution, revenue-farming had been condemned by peasants throughout western India for employing extra-economic coercion to extract a surplus beyond the required payments. However, by the early nineteenth century, the government dismantled revenue-farming, arguing that it promoted corrupt practices that prevented the expansion of agrarian productivity and large-scale profits. In its place, the government established a new land administration system in which revenue payments were collected directly from peasants by government agents.[5] In most instances, *mukhis* were assigned this position, and they quickly assumed the role of the government emissary in a village. Rent rates were set for a three- or five-year period, marking a shift from the local custom of negotiating rents on an annual basis. These initial administrative changes in land policy at the beginning of the nineteenth century later formed the basis for the development of the *ryotwari* system.

These resolutions, however, raised additional concerns. Officials noted that some *mukhis* frequently neglected their formal responsibilities to the government, while others actively participated in criminal activities. Some were declared unqualified to occupy the post due to their age or inability to read or write; others were described simply as "inefficient," "corrupt," and "useless."[6] In 1814, the government implemented new legislation (Regulation II of 1814) that required all villages to maintain an accountant *(talati)* as an official agent of the government to better administer the countryside.[7] The *talati* was responsible for preserving village land records, monitoring everyday activities, and gathering information on individuals, including *mukhis* and village elites.

In 1815, Ajoobhai Prabhudas, Ragubhai Vallabhbhai, and Ajoobhai Kishandas—three prominent leaders of the Lewa Kanbi community—organized a meeting in Chaklasi for a large number of *mukhis* to discuss the imposition of the new legislation.[8] The headmen had opposed the idea of having an official agent of the government residing in their respective villages and considered it a violation of local custom. The headmen were certain that the presence of a *talati* in each village was meant to limit their authority while providing the British with more power. The leaders of the group required all individuals present at the meeting to take an oath and sign a pledge of solidarity against the new policy.[9] In addition, they decided to pay land revenue only at the annual rates determined by local custom, rather than abiding by any long-term policies set by the government. It was also agreed that any village headman who violated the group's decisions and cooperated with the British would have to "forfeit his caste" as a Kanbi. Colonial officials labeled these actions as a "conspiracy" and "a crime against the state."[10]

The three leaders were arrested for the crime of sedition; officials argued that the men not only wanted to "overawe the Government" but also had hoped "gradually to annihilate it altogether."[11] The EIC had decided to charge the leadership of the movement with crimes rather than pursuing all the village headmen. Officials simply did not know the names of the individuals present at the meeting and were unable to locate the pledge signed by the headmen. More important, officials wanted to set an example by punishing the leaders, hoping to destroy the solidarity of the headmen. In November 1815, the leaders were convicted and sentenced to five years in prison, fined ten thousand rupees per person, and denied the right to ever hold an official position with the EIC.[12]

In 1818, after having spent nearly three years in prison in Kheda town, Ajoobhai Prabhudas and Ajoobhai Kishandas petitioned the Court of Superior Tribunal for an official pardon:

> We have patiently submitted to the sentence passed on us and remained in imprisonment in this jail to this day. We look up to you to mediate in our behalf and beg therefore most humbly to represent that we are subjected to the greatest privations, and that we have from a due sense of our conduct felt the full force of our punishment and do therefore humbly petition through you for our deliverance[,] for which we will ever lay under the greatest obligations and continually pray for the prosperity of the State. We have long anxiously entertained the hope of being relieved from our troubles[,] and now from your presence here our expectation is raised that through you our petition may be favourably heard.[13]

Officials acknowledged that their strategy of punishing the Kanbi leaders had led to a transformation in governing villages and securing land revenue. The village headmen were now cooperating and willing to apply new legislation without protest. The same men who had been described as committing the most "heinous offence" in 1815 were considered to be "as quiet and obedient as any subjects" in British territory.[14] In fact, pardoning the leaders was considered a "beneficial" strategy that would demonstrate the benevolence and fairness of the government in dealing with criminals who had finally agreed to serve as proper subjects of a new government. But more important, as the British were still in the process of expanding their territory in western India, it was hoped that such precedents would prevent other community leaders and village headmen from protesting the application of legislation. Ajoobhai Prabhudas and Ajoobhai Kishandas were pardoned and released from prison in 1818.[15]

Ragubhai Vallabhbhai, the third leader involved in the case, had escaped from prison in 1817 and had eluded capture.[16] However, upon learning that his kinsmen had been pardoned by the courts, Ragubhai also petitioned the government for a reprieve from his sentence. He claimed that while in prison he had had an illness that prevented him from thinking clearly, resulting in his decision to break out of the prison. He stated that he was feeling much better and was willing to turn himself in to the authorities. Officials no longer considered Ragubhai a threat to law and order in the countryside and agreed to pardon him as well.

In 1826, Ajoobhai Prabhudas petitioned the government to allow him to resume the office of *desai*.[17] The EIC had recognized the authority of the *desai* in the locality, but dismantled the post after Ajoobhai Prabhudas and the others were arrested and prosecuted for the crime of sedition. In considering the petition, officials noted that "the Desais had long possessed a leading influence and valuable interest in the Pergunnah [subdistrict]," and that restoring Ajoobhai to his post would help further establish the legitimacy and authority of the government.[18] It was suggested that officially acknowledging Ajoobhai's important position in local society as a member of the "first Kanbi family of Gujarat" would be "hailed by the community with great satisfaction."[19]

In the process of acquiring additional territory in 1818, the EIC became interested in establishing its authority without dismantling the legitimacy of local figures, especially those viewed as assets. Ajoobhai Prabhudas was reestablished as an administrator working for the EIC, as well as an official leader of the Kanbi community in the locality. However, the terms of his employment were significantly modified: rather than receiving an annual allowance of sixty-five hundred rupees, Ajoobhai was accorded three thousand rupees.[20] His power to set rules and regulations within Kanbi villages was significantly reduced, and any changes in administration had to be authorized by colonial officials. Although Ajoobhai had organized a large movement against new legislation in 1815, officials felt that the circumstances had significantly changed, especially since Ajoobhai and the protesting village headmen had accepted "subordination and good Government."[21]

In spite of these early protests by Lewa Kanbis, the institution of the *narwadari* system was maintained: the British had negotiated a settlement that allowed the Kanbi leadership to maintain its authority and legitimacy in the countryside. In fact, these early negotiations with the Kanbi leadership provided a basis for future cooperation with Kanbi peasants and incentives for colonizing land in the district—a stark contrast to the strategy used against Koli chieftains and peasants. Most *mukhis* acquired their posts through hereditary privilege, but the appointments had to be approved by the district collector or the assistant collector. In *narwadari* villages, the position typically was held by a large landholder, or it rotated among men from a dominant family. In some instances, officials intervened by rejecting candidates deemed inappropriate to serve as emissaries of the government. It was believed that such regulations would eliminate the earlier problems of *mukhis* in government villages.

By the 1860s, the *mukhis'* formal responsibilities to the colonial government were actually expanded through the Village Police Act (VIII of 1867). Officials argued that it was necessary to require *mukhis* to police their respective villages to ensure that emergent law and order problems did not interfere with the fiscal interests of the government. In some villages the responsibilities were divided between two individuals, but in most instances one *mukhi* was "entrusted with both revenue and police duties."[22] *Mukhis* were responsible for all aspects of policing the village and were allowed to administer punishment to peasants. The government also required *mukhis* to provide surveillance information to district-level officials about any suspicious activities.

6 · THE *MUKHI* AND THE *FOUZDAR*

In court, Kashibhai did not say very much about his own position as a *mukhi*. However, a fellow Patidar from Chaklasi named Baji Bapu mentioned in court that "the Mukhi is sometimes called . . . the Fouzdar."[1] He continued: "I said before the Magistrate that it was the Fouzdar who told me to go . . . to the field, I meant the Mukhi by the Fouzdar." The reference to Kashibhai's status as a *fouzdar* (or *faujdar*) was not pursued by the prosecutor. In fact, as the trial proceeded, the prosecutor also began referring to Kashibhai as *fouzdar* instead of *mukhi*.

Under the Mughal empire, a *faujdar* served as a military commander of a district and was responsible for "protecting forts, escorting treasures, and assisting in revenue and police duties."[2] *Faujdars* often led troops to quash disturbances and control ambitious revenue-farmers or landlords who posed a threat to the stability of the countryside. In addition, the *faujdar* functioned as a magistrate or criminal judge with the power to administer punishment on behalf of the Mughal administration. As early as 1780, the British had transformed the role of the *faujdar* by removing the military requirements and limiting his jurisdiction to matters of criminal justice.[3] One contemporary observer noted that the responsibilities of the *faujdar* had been reduced to the point that the office resembled that of a *kotwal,* an official who policed Mughal towns for the purpose of gathering intelligence and preventing crimes.

By 1790, the government also had modified the *faujdar's adalats* (courts) and replaced them with Circuit Courts administered by British judges and "native" assistants.[4] Following the British acquisition of territories in Gujarat in 1803, a judge and magistrate were appointed to handle the judicial administration in Kheda. Frequent changes were made within the administration throughout the early decades of the nineteenth century, with the district collector handling some cases and one or two district judges responsible for others. By the 1870s, criminal justice was handled by eighteen officers and fourteen "native subordinate-magistrates," with the district magistrate supervising the entire district.[5]

The *mukhi* was assigned a central role in the criminal justice system, as legislated by the Village Police Act of 1867, and Chaklasi even had a *kotwal*, or police chief, with limited responsibilities in 1898, but there does not appear to have been an official role for the *faujdar*.[6]

The British had transformed the institution of the *faujdar* throughout India and in many places eliminated it altogether. However, at the end of the nineteenth century the term continued to be in use throughout Gujarat, albeit with a different meaning. The military was still called the *fauj* in this period, but in local parlance *faujdar* was an authoritarian or powerful individual, possibly echoing the characteristics of the military commander of the Mughal administration. Does this tell us something about Kashibhai? Possibly. Baji Bapu stated that Kashibhai was "sometimes called *fouzdar*"—not always. The emphasis on "sometimes" suggests that this was not a formal position held by Kashibhai, but a term used by fellow Patidars to describe Kashibhai's position of power or effectiveness as a village elite. It is not known why Baji Bapu used *faujdar* and not another term, but Kashibhai was clear when he stated in court, "my profession is Mukhi."[7]

7 · MONITORING PEASANTS

At some point in early December 1897, Ranchod had had a falling out with Kashibhai. He publicly denounced the *mukhi* and confiscated his land, on which he then constructed the *mandwa*. Later, in court, Ranchod even made a statement indicating that the land was his and not Kashibhai's: "The mandwa was constructed in *my field* . . . for praying [to] the god."[1] Kashibhai had fulfilled his obligation as the village headman by reporting the peasant activity to higher level officials in the area: "About December 6th I sent a report to the Jamadar [chief or leader]: he came on the 6th and the Chief Constable came there on the 7th or 8th. I went with the Chief Constable to the mandwa: there were about 200 or 400 men assembled there."[2]

Kanji Samal, the head constable, verified this information: "On December 6th I went on my rounds to Chaklasi and I heard that accused number one was in the field of the Mukhi. I went with the Mukhi to the mandwa: there I saw accused number one was sitting on a bench and other[s] were sitting round. I asked [him] what he was sitting there for, and he said he was praying. We went to the Chora [village center] and gave a report to the Rawania [watchman], telling him to take it to the Chief Constable."[3] On December 7th, the Chief Constable Surajram Mahipatram arrived from Nadiad, a town six miles from Chaklasi, to investigate the information provided by Kanji Samal. Surajram testified in court: "I know accused number one. I first went to his mandwa . . . owing to the report from the Jamadar. There were 500 or 600 at the mandwa. . . . I told them to disperse and come back on the Punem [full moon] when Ranchodji would come there. On the Punem I sent Kanji to the field, and I wrote to all the Chief Constables of the district not to allow the people to come on the Punem, and I sent a report to the District Superintendent of Police on the 7th."[4]

By the end of the nineteenth century, officials were well versed in documenting information about any activity that posed a threat to the stability of the countryside. This was, in part, an administrative response to the 1857–58 rebellions that had created a legitimation crisis of the colonial state. By making the village officials (the headman and the *talati*) responsible for monitoring the daily lives of peasants, the government was confident it had the power to immediately check the emergence of law and order problems, given the development of new modes of communication—the electric telegraph and expanded railway lines. District-level officials could be quickly informed, and the military or police immediately dispatched, if necessary. The Dharalas in Chaklasi had already achieved notoriety for the protest migration in 1897, and officials were concerned that the gathering of several hundred peasants might lead to further conflict.

8 · PROPHESY UNFULFILLED

Ranchod's prophesy on the fateful night of December 9 was not fulfilled. He had little to say about it in court, but others were quite willing to discuss the event. Kashibhai testified: "As the idol and the tank did not appear, the people began to abuse accused number one, and so he went away into another field, and the people went away."[1] Head Constable Kanji Samal corroborated: "On the Punem when I was there 4,000 or 5,000 were assembled, but no idol turned up. We sent the *Bhagat* to his own house and the people dispersed."[2] Similar comments also were made by Surta Ragha: "Thousands of people assembled to do the Darsan as the *Bhagat* had given out that the Ranchodji would come there from Dakor[e] and a temple would appear, and the gomtiji [a tank of sacred water] would be formed. The people said he was false, and he ran away into his house."[3]

By all accounts, Ranchod's prophecy had failed; even his own Dharala supporters seem to have been disappointed, if not angry. Ranchod's story could have ended here, but he made sure that it did not. After six or seven days, Ranchod returned to the *mandwa,* apparently claiming that "Ranchodji would come in the future."[4] He offered no other explanation and resumed his daily *bhajans* and prayers on Kashibhai's land. Other fellow Dharalas from Chaklasi and neighboring villages joined him within a few days, but the Patidars stayed away. According to one supporter, Meru Mitha, many Dharalas went back to the *mandwa* around December 24: "These people remained night and day in the *[mandwa]* and took their meals also there. They sang bhajans . . . [and] sat continually in the *[mandwa]*."[5]

Gema Mitha, one of the participants in these daily activities, stated, "Things began to go on as before," and he added that "all the *Bhagats* [were] assembled."[6] According to Gema, Ranchod was also actively seeking the support of local Dharalas, possibly those individuals who had rejected him after December 9: "Then the *Bhagat* began to pay visits to the people in the village. He visited Banna Khoda, Ramtu Sura,

Rama Nara, Teja Bawa, Gator Jesa and Wala Lala. He also visited my house. Fourteen persons, including myself, used to accompany the *Bhagat* during his visits."[7] It is not easy to understand how Ranchod was able to reestablish his authority in such a short period of time, but this may have had something to do with his declaration of the end of the British raj during a new crisis facing peasants—the bubonic plague.

9 · DEFEATING THE PLAGUE, CONTROLLING DHARALAS

Government intervention in the everyday lives of the general populace, especially poor peasants and workers, reached an unprecedented level at the height of a plague epidemic in the 1890s.[1] Never before had the colonial state responded with such rapidity and panic to an epidemic in the nineteenth century. Why did the official declaration of the arrival of the bubonic plague in the city of Bombay on September 23, 1896, elicit authoritarian measures to control the epidemic throughout western India?[2] It was reported that the specter of the fourteenth century's "Black Death" haunted policy makers, who were only too aware of the potential impact of a demographic crisis on the agrarian economy.[3] Sanitation and public health officials believed that resorting to repressive measures was the necessary solution to an epidemic capable of decimating a population. In addition, officials argued that entrepôt points on India's western coastline—Bombay, Surat, Bharuch, and Cambay—needed to be protected from the spread of the plague to ensure that global markets would continue to accept commodities leaving British colonies. An international embargo could worsen the colonial state's fiscal crisis, and in order to ensure a balance in trade with global partners, the entire Bombay Presidency was put on maximum alert to wage a war against the bubonic plague.

Outside the main urban centers in the Bombay Presidency, colonial plague measures were implemented throughout the countryside, especially in the heart of the prized Charotar agricultural tract.[4] By the end of 1896, the first case of the plague was documented in Kheda, and in January 1897 "protective measures" were set in place. Sixty miles of the Mahi River on the eastern part of Kheda district was cordoned off to prevent individuals from traveling between Baroda State and British territory. Dakore's temple and market were forced to shut down after four or five cases of the plague were reported to have spread from Dakore to Ratlam, in central India. Pilgrims were prevented from entering the town, and the full moon festivals were suspended indefinitely. However, the plague measures were inconsistent: prominent Patidar families were allowed to travel without restrictions, but Dharala agricultural laborers were denied permission to move around the district for work. The general population in Kheda was confronted with many hardships emerging from the government's plague policies, especially the traveling restrictions, village evacuations, and detainment at a disinfection and observation camp. These policies were officially acknowledged at the time as creating difficulties for merchants and peasants that resulted in a widespread "depression in trade."

The government began an aggressive campaign to control the spread of the plague in Anand, a town that had developed into an important market center with the coming of the Bombay-Baroda and Central India Railway.[5] The Anand Observation Camp, established on November 24, 1897, was located only five miles from Chaklasi on approximately sixty acres of land, and was capable of holding between three thousand and five thousand individuals.[6] All railway passengers traveling through the locality were required to disembark at Anand for plague screening. Europeans and first-class passengers were exempt from all medical examinations, along with individuals who had acquired special medical certificates prior to arriving in Anand.[7] Most second- and third-class passengers were viewed as "suspicious plague carriers" and were forced to take a bath and have all their clothes washed before further travel.[8] Interestingly, the bathwater was recirculated among many passengers; plague officials were later forced to admit that "reusing water may actually have spread the disease."[9]

Passengers suspected of being carriers of the plague were confined in quarantine camps for a minimum of ten days, but this policy was inconsistent, as many were kept for two or three months. Despite the monitoring of railway passengers at Anand, colonial officials believed that Dharalas principally were responsible for importing and spreading the plague in rural Gujarat.[10] Plague officials were not interested in individuals who carried the disease. They preferred to tackle the problem by forcibly evacuating entire communities within villages and relocating them to Anand. Hence, plague measures were popularly viewed as a mask for control and a direct attack on society that disrupted both the movement of commodities and people and affected local custom.[11]

10 · THE DAKORE PILGRIMAGE

Perhaps it was within the context of the epidemic and the colonial plague measures that thousands of peasants from Chaklasi and neighboring villages had gathered around Ranchod's *mandwa*.[1] It appears that either colonial officials were unable to prevent the movement of people on that night, or they chose not to interfere with this auspicious celebration, despite the plague epidemic. Ranchod had claimed that, if the peasants could not go to Dakore during the full moon, the pilgrimage site in effect would come to Chaklasi in the forms of Ranchodji, the temple, and the lake. But what was significant about these symbols for Dharalas and others in the locality, including Patidars?

The Ranchodji temple in Dakore was constructed in 1772, and it quickly transformed the town into an important commercial and religious center in central Gujarat.[2] However, the idol of Ranchodji was reported to have been brought to Dakore in the mid-twelfth century from a temple in Dwarka, in the princely state of Kathiawar. The monthly full moon festivals attracted between five and ten thousand pilgrims to the town, and during the autumn month of Kartik, as many as a hundred thousand individuals would arrive in Dakore.[3] By the mid-nineteenth century, these festivals also served as bazaars for commerce in the opening out of the regional economy, especially with colonial investments in communication and transportation networks that linked the town with the main trade centers in western and central India.[4] The introduction of railway lines in 1874 and metaled roads in 1880 marked a further expansion of Dakore as a center for trade and commerce, but also as one of the most important pilgrimage sites in Gujarat.[5]

These transformations made it easier to get to Dakore, but they did not prevent the emergence of other problems for pilgrims. In 1883, temple priests instituted an entrance fee of four *annas* per pilgrim during specific full moons of the year, leading the district collector to comment that the new charges created "dissatisfaction." The government imposed a one-anna levy of its own in 1888, known as the Municipal District

Pilgrim Tax. Unlike the fees imposed by the temple priests, this tax was a permanent charge imposed on all individuals entering Dakore during the full moon festivals throughout the year. The first year of the new pilgrim tax yielded revenue amounting to Rs. 11,553, and the tax soon became the primary source of income for the Dakore municipality. Immediately, the number of pilgrims visiting Dakore decreased during the full moon, and many individuals visited the temple only when the charges were not applied.

In 1888, an anonymous author published a pamphlet, *Pilgrim Taxthi Dakoreni Dhoordhshano Haval*, requesting that the government cancel the tax.[6] The pamphlet begins with an appeal to G. F. Sheppard, the Northern Division revenue commissioner, to recognize that the tax had led to Dakore's decline not only as a pilgrimage site but also as a center for trade and commerce, and it continues with poems regarding the impact of the tax on agrarian society. A poem titled "The Terror of the Tax" illustrates these sentiments:

Oh, God, Lord of the Universe,
We don't know what will happen to us now!
We are facing the terror of the tax.
Oh, God, what is our crime?
What is our mistake?
The entire temple complex has been robbed.
The people are suffering.
All hopes for the future are gone.
If this tax continues, what will people eat?
We are sure death approaches.
We are suffering from a lack of money.
We do not understand how the tax is going to benefit us.
We are appealing to you in these difficult times,
As we find our happiness is gone.

Although Ranchod did not make any direct reference to earlier written commentaries about Dakore, it is certain that he and his supporters were well aware of the tax and the popular perceptions that were circulating in the area. In all likelihood, the individuals who had gathered at Ranchod's *mandwa* on December 9 would have been to Dakore at some point in their life. Ranchod's prophecy had appealed to all local communities for religious, political, and even economic grounds. While the specific details of his religious messages remain unknown, he nonetheless articulated a syncretic nature of local religion combining elite forms of "high" Vaishnavism with a local messianic *bhagat* tradition.[7] For example, the themes of the "flying" temple and lake were not specific to either the local form of the *bhagat* practices or the Vaishnavism centering on Ranchodji (Krishna) in Dakore.[8] Furthermore, the idea of a "flying" lake was certainly common to the local worshippers of Krishna, who were familiar with the story in which Krishna is said to have magically transported water from the sacred Ganges River to construct a lake known as the Radhakund near his birthplace of Vrindhavan. This story about Krishna is linked to Rupa Goswami's sixteenth-century text titled Upadeshamrita, but it is unclear if Ranchod was making a direct reference to this specific story or simply articulating another related myth that was part of the popular local imaginary.[9] However, at one point in Ranchod's court testimony, he remarked that his supporters had gathered to celebrate the birth of Ranchodji and "Gangaji": Krishna and the Ganges River, respectively.[10]

11 · THE KING'S PROCESSION

On January 9, 1898, Ranchod led a large procession in Chaklasi, in which he declared the end of the British raj and proclaimed himself king. He had expressed these ideas to his supporters at gatherings on earlier dates, but now Ranchod wanted to make a public announcement to all the residents in the village. Gema Mitha stated later in court, "The *Bhagat* started the procession to proclaim that the Raj of the Sarkar had gone. We believed the *Bhagat*."[1] Approximately five hundred to seven hundred Dharalas marched alongside three bullock carts through the village; Ranchod sat in the leading cart with Surta Ragha, who held an umbrella over Ranchod, and several leading supporters followed in the other two carts. Gema claimed, "Nobody went without an arm. There were three guns in the hands of Banna Khoda, Sura Surta and Salia Baji."[2] In court, Meru Mitha provided a more detailed description of the weapons: "Hema had a sword. Gopal Vira had a sword. Moti had a bow and Babar a spear. Ramtu Sura was walking with a gun. Dhula Ranchhod had a sword. Mawa Bawa also had a sword. Jibhai Kanka had a dharia [similar to a billhook]. Gela Khoda had a dharia."[3]

The procession started about midday and traveled from the *mandwa* to the village center; it grew in size as Dharalas from the neighboring villages of Devkapura and Raghupura arrived in Chaklasi and joined in. The procession passed by the village accountant's house and halted near a temple dedicated to Mahadev. Apparently, Banna Khoda fired a gun before the procession continued through the village. Ranchod then stopped in front of Kashibhai's home and challenged the *mukhi*'s authority. Meru also testified that Ranchod shouted, "If you want to try my power or to fight come out."[4] A Dharala named Rantu Sura also fired a gun to further threaten the *mukhi*. However, in court Kashibhai claimed that he was not concerned about Ranchod's declaration and did not even bother to step outside his house to view the procession. He stated, "I heard the noise of the drums when I was having my dinner: it passed by the back of my house. I did not go to see it."[5] The procession continued to the village center, where Ranchod made an additional challenge to Kashibhai: "If you want to take Government money[,] come to my mandup."[6] The Dharalas celebrated the demise of the British raj with the distribution of coconuts and sugar, and then returned to Ranchod's *mandwa*. The day ended without any direct conflict with the *mukhi*, fellow villagers, or colonial officials. Accordingly, for Ranchod and his supporters, this lack of interference with the procession was evidence that the British power in the village had indeed ceased.

Later in the day, Kashibhai went to investigate the activities in Chaklasi and secure further information about Ranchod. He testified, "Rawania Lala told me what had happened: he said accused No. 1 had told the people not to pay Government dues, but to pay ¼ of it to him[,] as a temple was to be built. Lala said that guns had been fired and the people had sticks, swords. . . . That day the Rawanias were afraid, and so I sent for no one."[7] Kashibhai had secured a bit of information that had not been revealed by any Dharala who had spoken in court: Ranchod wanted to construct a temple, but perhaps Kashibhai believed that this point was too obvious to discuss. For Kashibhai, the primary objective was to ensure that Ranchod's activities did not escalate into something larger that would lead to a "law and order" problem in the village; temple building was only a secondary concern.

Yet Kashibhai must have been aware that the presence of Dharalas armed with swords and guns was itself a violation of colonial legislation in the district. The government's policy of disarming Dharalas in the 1850s had worked for a time, but within a few decades the Dharalas were able to restock weapons in villages like Chaklasi. Kashibhai opted not to contact the district magistrate or the district police, as he had done during the full moon festival on December 9, but chose to speak to prominent Dharalas as a way to quell any further conflict. He further testified, "The next day I sent for the leading Dharalas. Manor Punja and Baber Jetha came and also Gudbad Kala: they said they had no objection to pay the Government dues."[8] The *mukhi* was satisfied with the assurances given by these individuals and expected the Dharalas to follow their leadership. However, in this instance, Kashibhai had underestimated Ranchod's authority and popularity, a decision that eventually cost the *mukhi* his job.

In court, Ranchod was also asked about the details of the procession. His responses were succinct, and they largely corroborated what others had said, except when he was asked to describe the types of weapons carried by his supporters.[9]

Magistrate: Did you take a procession at the Chaklasi Chowra *[chora]* on the 9th January last and proclaim there by words that the Government Raj was at an end and that Government dues should be paid at your mandwa?

Ranchod: Yes. I did take the procession to the village Chowra and had said that the Government Raj was at an end and that the Government dues should be paid at my mandwa.

Magistrate: You had sat in a cart in the procession and with an umbrella on your head?

Ranchod: Yes, sir.

Magistrate: What class[es] of people were in the procession and what arms [did they have] with them?

Ranchod: They were all Dharalas. Some might have wansle [agricultural implements] and sticks.

Magistrate: When [was] the mandwa . . . constructed and what was the object of constructing it?

Ranchod: The mandwa was constructed in my field one month before the procession[,] for praying [to] the god.

Magistrate: Who were the daily customers at the mandwa with you?

Ranchod: Surta Ragha, Gema Mitha, I, Malla Hallu, Dhula Ranchore, Shiwa Surta, my wife Bai Kanku, Shankara Dola, my nephew and other people used to come there.

Ranchod claimed that the Dharalas carried only sticks and agricultural implements during the procession, and he neglected to mention that others were armed with swords, knives, and bows and arrows. He must have been aware that an admission of having carried weapons would have provided sufficient evidence to convict himself and others of crimes against the government, even though there was no direct conflict during the procession.

12 · RANCHOD'S LETTER

On the day after the procession, January 10, Ranchod's first act as the new king was to issue a *patra* (letter) formally proclaiming his reign. It read:

> The temple of Ranchhodji is coming into existence in the middle of the lands of Chaklasi on the east side. The authority of the Government ceased from the full moon of Madgh-Samwat 1956. Therefore the satyug [age of truth] of Ranchhodrai has commenced. Therefore no one should tell a lie, or do a wrongful act. If anyone does so transgress[,] the wheel of Ram will pass above the ground and cut off the[ir] heads. [In the] *mandwa* a sugarcane press will be put up by Ranchod[ji,] and he who would pass through it and stand will rule. All people are hereby informed that no one should pay the Government instalment. The money is due by the command of Ranchodrai. Patel Kashibhai Ranchhodbhai is informed that—"If you want to inform your Government you may do so."[1]

Ranchod had dictated the letter to two disciples who served as scribes, while others were responsible for the delivery of the *patras*. When asked in court about the letters, Ranchod stated, "I can not read or write. . . . Teja Bama and Rama Nara used to write these letters."[2]

Gema Mitha added, "We returned to the mandwa and sat in council. Ranchod Bhagat said: 'Don't pay the Government assessment now; we shall pay it at Holi.' At the Bhagat's dictation, Teja Bawa and Nara Rama wrote a letter to the Mukhi of Chaklasi to say we would not pay the assessment. Dhula took the letter to the Mukhi."[3] Kashibhai does not appear to have immediately responded to the *patra*, echoing his reaction to Ranchod's oral threats during the procession. Over the next two days, Teja and Rama made many copies of the letter, which were delivered to Dharalas residing in twenty-one specified villages in Kheda district.[4] Gema further commented in his testimony, "These letters were given to the villagers who came to make darshan. In these letters the Bhagat said the assessment was to be paid to himself and not to [the] Government."[5] Ranchod's twelve-year-old grandson Shankaria also witnessed these events. He testified in court: "The people who came were given the papers to take with them to the village. . . . No one read the letters to me. I knew what was in them because they talked over them."[6]

The *mukhi* of neighboring Samarkha, Jhaverbhai Shivabhai, became aware that a *patra* had arrived in his village and began asking Dharalas for a copy. In court, he explained, "[Mathur Nara] brought a letter to my village. Hearing of it I asked him for it, and he said he had given it to the people who were there. He said he had brought it from Chaklasi from Ranchod the Bhagat. I could not find the letter."[7] But when the magistrate asked Ranchod if he had "sent the letters to the villagers mentioned in the list" read to him in court, Ranchod was evasive and took only partial responsibility. He stated, "Yes, I might have sent letters to the villagers mentioned [in] the list read over to me."[8]

As king, Ranchod chose to convey his message in written form at this juncture, rather than relying solely on oral transmission.[9] He appropriated writing to demonstrate his authority as the new leader, and to assert that elites and colonial officials no longer had a monopoly on written culture.[10] Ranchod's ascendancy signaled a change whereby even nonliterate peasants could engage in the production and circulation of writing. These were important concerns for his supporters, who were well aware of the significance of official documents in their everyday lives, and of the government's educational policies that had limited Dharalas' access to village schools, where they might have learned to read and write.

In 1884, the Education Commission had confirmed the implementation of a "permanent" levy to finance primary education in India, marking a shift from an 1850s policy under which peasants were asked to voluntarily add 1 percent to their respective rent rates to pay for additional village schools, teachers' salaries, and textbooks.[11] The early policy apparently had mixed results, as many peasants opted not to pay the extra levy or decided to send their children to "indigenous" or "religious" schools, which fell outside the jurisdiction of Bombay Presidency's Education Department.[12] The government's introduction of a permanent "education tax" in the 1880s raised the levy to 6¼ percent of the rent rate in the Bombay Presidency. The commission celebrated the increase and claimed that "the education of the masses was now finally secured."[13]

The new program for primary education posed many problems in the countryside, especially for groups like the Dharalas.[14] For colonial officials, educating Dharalas in the village school had one primary objective: to "improve" the children of those peasants viewed as "indolent" and "unthrifty." By establishing a link between education and "improvement," officials expected the village school to break the historical bonds that had led to Dharalas' subordination—namely, "indebtedness," "criminality," and poor agricultural techniques. Although, colonial offi-cials interpreted the "backwardness" of Dharalas as an innate character-istic, they promoted a new program designed to instill a work ethic and disciplinary order. There were strict limitations to the objectives of the actual education offered to Dharalas, which fundamentally differed in application from the education available to the children of dominant communities in village schools. Education for Dharalas was very basic and was never intended to create a class of teachers, clerks, or local government officials, as it was in the case of Patidars and Kanbis.[15] Instead, "the instruction given in schools attended by children of this class [was] nominally according to Rural Standards [and] nothing beyond a knowledge of the '3 Rs.'"[16] In fact, the government had been "under consideration . . . of further simplifying the Rural Standards" in its attempts to educate marginalized sections of the population that had not received even basic instruction.[17]

The Department of Public Instruction for the Bombay Presidency exacerbated the problem by classifying Dharalas as an "aboriginal and hill tribe," even while acknowledging the inaccuracy of the description: "The Kolis and Dharalas of the Ahmedabad and Kaira Districts are usually classed among the aboriginal tribes for the purposes of [the annual] report; it is doubtful whether the term can be fairly applied to them."[18] Nonetheless, the educational policies that were administered still reflected differences between "advanced Hindu castes" and "aboriginal and hill tribes." Whereas the former were encouraged to continue their education beyond the "vernacular final examination" or the "primary school leaving certificate examination,"[19] the latter could attend village schools only till the third standard, as the fourth and fifth standards were abolished by the Department of Public Instruction.[20]

For colonial officials, the education problem persisted even after the policy changes of the 1890s. Funds available to certain villages were unevenly distributed, leading the district magistrate to state: "It is[,] however[,] easy to show that Dharala villages by no means receive their just share in educational expenditure, proportionate to the cess they pay."[21] District officials also noted that many schools discriminated against Dharalas. One official reported that "a school master kept Dharalas from his school because he feared their admission would lower the daily average and the percentage of successful candidates from his school."[22] Another posited that "the education of Koli and Dharala boys is tacitly but persistently discouraged by the higher classes."[23] In one case, district officials insisted on the "recognition" and attendance of students from all communities in village schools. The response of dominant villagers was rapid and violent: "Five or six large schools [were] closed for years," and the huts and crops of the peasants were burnt in one village.[24]

13 · THE BOOK COLLECTION

Ranchod's *patra* symbolized a new beginning for his supporters. He had proclaimed that revenue payments were to be postponed for a period of two months and paid directly at his *mandwa* on the day of the religious celebrations of Holi at one-fourth the original rate. Gema testified in court: "We believed the *Bhagat*."[1] Within the context of Ranchod's world, it is understandable why he wanted to produce and circulate a letter that declared his authority as a way to end the subordination of Dharalas. Yet for Ranchod, the symbolic power of the *patra* was insufficient on its own. As king, he wanted to possess and control the written words found in official documents and religious texts. The following were found in Ranchod's *mandwa* upon his arrest:[2]

1. Gujarati first book [title not given]
2. Saragni Nisarni
3. Kelaiani Chopdi
4. Gyan Updesh
5. Manmera [pages five to twenty only]
6. Prabhatin [three pages only]
7. A book of bhajans [title not given]
8. A bundle of books related to Gopichand [Krishna; titles not given]
9. Two account-books
10. A bundle of account-books
11. Two books [titles not given]
12. Three letters [unspecified]
13. Two letters [Ranchod's *patras*]
14. A piece of paper bearing the date *Chaitra Vad*[3]
15. A list regarding the purchase butter
16. A list of 21 villages
17. 21 pieces of blank paper
18. A bond—attested by Teja Bama, dated *Bhadarwa Sudi* 2nd of 1947.[4]

Unfortunately, the list of Ranchod's books is incomplete. Officials did not provide any publication details for the books, nor did they bother to write down the titles for many of the books. Ranchod was not asked about his books during the trial, and it is impossible to know what he understood from these texts. It is not clear if his literate disciples like Teja Bama and Rama Nara read the books to Ranchod and others, or if Ranchod had simply chosen to collect them. The description "Gujarati first book" appears to refer to a primer used by children in village schools to learn Gujarati: perhaps Ranchod and others were learning to read. But the titles suggest religious themes, with the exception of the account books. Ranchod's adherence to religious thought related to Krishna, and Vaishnavism more generally, is indicated from the given titles and the reference to Gopichand. This religious focus appears to be consistent with Ranchod's own devotion to Ranchodji.

The details of the account books in Ranchod's possession are also incomplete. Officials did not state whether he confiscated them from moneylenders, the village accountant *(talati)*, or both. While peasants often destroyed account books that recorded debts, Ranchod made the decision to preserve them among his possessions. He might have claimed that as the king he would either eliminate Dharala debts altogether, or that the loans would be paid to him, possibly at a reduced rate. In addition, these account books contained information maintained by *talatis* about land payments and rent rates in the village—information that Ranchod needed for collecting taxes and monitoring the fiscal interests of his new polity.

14 · KASHI *PATRA:*
A CIRCULATING LETTER

Ranchod and his Dharala supporters were not alone in questioning the government's legitimacy to exist. And Ranchod's circulation of a *patra*, or letter, for purposes of political communication was not unique either.[1] In fact, in the years between 1896 and 1898 a countrywide disaffection with the government, largely corresponding to the emergent plague epidemic, had produced circulating letters popularly known as the "Kashi *patras*."[2] These letters not only established critiques of colonial power, but they also played a role in turning public opinion against domination by local officials and the government. *Patras* were successful in large part due to their underground status. The letters were often distributed anonymously and thus often proved difficult for colonial authorities to control. By the end of the nineteenth century, the government had made it a priority to monitor the circulation of seditious information: it was well aware of the ability of such information to generate countrywide disaffection, as was so clearly demonstrated in the rebellions of 1857–58.[3] Even officials who dismissed such phenomena as the product of an "ignorant" population were forced to contend with the potential for direct action, especially after confiscated *patras* revealed that their authors had predicted the end of the British raj, or that "white-faced people [would] soon be swept out of the land and there [would] be a period of general blessedness and comfort."[4]

The first Kashi *patra* was said to have fallen from the heavens to the Vishweshwaran Temple in Varanasi.[5] If the letter had indeed originated in northern India, it was likely written in Sanskrit or Hindi and then translated into several vernacular languages: Telegu, Tamil, Marathi, and Gujarati. The *patra* was constantly changing in form and content as it traveled throughout India. Certain elements remained constant, but other elements took on new meanings and reflected local concerns and customs. It is not only impossible but also inaccurate to understand the Kashi *patra*, in its various forms, as a single reified text. It was precisely the fluidity of the written word and the multifaceted way in which it was appropriated and disseminated that accounted for the *patra's* effectiveness as a medium of political communication.

One version of the Kashi *patra* made its appearance in Kheda district sometime in 1897.[6] Ranchod Vira was well aware of the *patra* by early December 1897, at which time he began prophesying miracles in Chaklasi. He acquired a copy of the *patra* as it circulated in the district, or he came into contact with someone who had acquired it while detained at the Anand Observation Camp, where it apparently was readily available. District Collector G. Carmichael confiscated a copy of the *patra* in the Anand Observation Camp in January 1898, while investigating that region in the aftermath of Ranchod's movement.[7] The path of the confiscated letter can be traced to south Gujarat, because the name Surat Sodapur Press was printed on the *patra.* It seems that Ranchod obtained the same version of the letter that Carmichael acquired approximately one month later.[8] Unfortunately, Carmichael did not enter a copy or translation of this version of the *patra* in the judicial records; however, he did provide a textual comparison with Ranchod Vira's rendition.

The Surat Sodapur Press, located in Rander (approximately ten miles from Surat) was responsible for printing at least five hundred copies of one version of the Kashi *patra.*[9] Jivanram Motiram, the acting manager of the press, when questioned by the district magistrate of Surat about his role in the printing and distribution of the *patra,* claimed to have no knowledge of it and attributed the entire incident to a worker in the press named Jaduram.[10] An investigation by the district superintendent of police revealed that a copy of the *patra* had also been printed in Karachi before it arrived in Rander, approximately five hundred miles away.[11] There were several versions of the letter circulating in Karachi in 1897 and 1898, and so it is difficult to uncover the full details of the *patra's* intricate path.[12] Moreover, any additional investigation of the *patra* would be hindered by the limited source material, as the district magistrate of Surat did not reveal any information about the printing of the *patra* or its trail before Karachi.

The *patra* that Ranchod initially came into contact with had probably taken the following path, covering a distance of nearly 650 miles: Karachi to Rander to Anand to Chaklasi. As a consequence of the proliferation of plague measures and limits placed on long-distance travel by colonial authorities, the postal service became the primary mode of disseminating the *patra* throughout the country.[13] In this instance the expansion of the postal service meant that underground writings could spread as rapidly as mail could travel from one locality to another. The establishment of a Branch Post and Telegraph Office inside the Anand Observation Camp may have been what linked Rander and Anand.[14] The arrival and wide distribution of the *patra* in the camp was facilitated by the large number of letter boxes, which were cleared twice daily.[15]

The case of the Kashi *patra* demonstrates the instrumental role played by the printing press and postal service in the production and distribution of knowledge and ideas in colonial India. The particular case of Ranchod Vira, however, illuminates the parallel ways in which information was produced and circulated by nonliterates, especially in rural areas, and without making use of the advances in communication technologies. Ranchod created and disseminated his own version of the Kashi *patra:* he dictated letters to Teja Bama and Rama Nara and relied on a system of runners to distribute his version to at least twenty-one neighboring villages.[16] It was reported that Ranchod's *patra* was seemingly different from those circulating in Rander and Surat. To begin with, there was no mention of imminent disaster or calamity. Rather, it spoke to local concerns with government revenue installments and simultaneously elevated Ranchod's own leadership status. On this point, the district collector noted in his report that Ranchod's *patra* was different from the ones originating in Surat: "[The Kashi *patra*] is to the effect that a letter fell in the temple at Benaras which said that the era of truth or *[satyug]* had commenced[,] and that the wind from the direction of the north would rule and the wheel of Ram would work. [Ranchod] repeated the whole of this to his followers and made additions. The wind from the north was turned into a large army of warriors and his king was to be he who should pass through a sugar cane press."[17]

Many of the same elements and signifiers of the Kashi *patra* of the north, as described by the district collector, are found in Ranchod's letters: the commencement of the era of *satyug,* the wheel of Ram, and the wind from the north, albeit changed to an army of warriors. What is significant, however, is that he made use of the form, content, and mobility of the Kashi *patra* for his own purposes: his *patra* was in the local vernacular, Gujarati; it incorporated symbols of power and authority recognized by local Dharalas, the *satyug* of Ranchodrai; and it reflected socioeconomic concerns having to do with the colonial state's revenue policies and the state's perceived interference with local custom. The government had stopped the *punem melas* at the temple of Ranchodrai in Dakore.[18] Thus, the reference to the temple can be interpreted as recognition of local irritation with this policy, and the declaration that the temple would miraculously appear in Chaklasi, a way of saying, symbolically, that a government policy would not interfere with local practices.

15 · THE PRACTICE OF CUTTING TREES

On January 11, Ranchod instructed his followers to cut babul trees in Chaklasi. This was a direct response to government land policies that banned such activities, and an assertion that Ranchod had reclaimed the right to use the land and trees based on local customary practices.[1] The bark of the babul tree was often used for medicinal purposes, but Gema Mitha claimed in court that seven or eight Dharalas cut the babuls for the making of a sugarcane press, which Ranchod stated in his *patra* would be set up. Gema said that "the Rawanias Lalo Jino and Remuda saw us cut the trees and went away," but noted there was no interference from any other officials.[2]

For Kashibhai, this was a fundamental violation of colonial land policies. In 1867, the government had sown babul seeds on nearly thirteen hundred acres of land in Kheda.[3] By the 1890s, it had planted additional unoccupied lands in the area with babul trees and placed the land under forest management for preservation and conservation purposes.[4] Kashibhai reacted quickly this time, rather than ignoring Ranchod's actions as he had done over the two previous days. He testified, "I heard that accused No. 1 was going to cut Government babuls. I sent Rawanias[,] but no one was found there and the babuls had already been cut. Then I got a report written to the Mamlatdar of Nadiad: the Rawanias refused to go as it was evening. So the next morning I took it myself. I gave it to the Mamlatdar. I went to the Chief Constable and told him what had happened. I also saw the Inspector and then returned to Chaklasi about noon."[5]

Ranchod's supporters used the wood from the three babul trees to construct a sugarcane press. Sugarcane was a minor crop in the locality, occupying less than 1 percent of the total cropped area during the nineteenth century.[6] For poor peasants, it was a difficult crop to cultivate as it required investments in large quantities of fertilizer and water and left the land virtually infertile for four or five years afterward.[7] Ranchod's reasons for constructing the press are unclear. Neither Ranchod nor his supporters explained in court the significance of the idea that any individual who "could pass through the press" would become king. However, it is possible to suggest that the reference does provide another allusion to Ranchod's supernatural abilities and, therefore, his strength as a leader. The mention of this instrument in Ranchod's *patra* symbolized for the peasants something significant about power and the authority of kingship.

16 · OFFICIAL BATTLE NARRATIVES

According to Chief Constable Surajram Mahipatram's testimony, on January 12 Kashibhai had reported that "there was a danger in the village."[1] By 2:00 P.M., Police Inspector Jagannath Sagun, Mamlatdar, Surajram, and eighteen constables departed from Nadiad to investigate the problem. The group arrived in Chaklasi around 4:30 P.M. and headed toward Ranchod's *mandwa*. According to Kashibhai, "The Chief Constable and the Inspector and Jamadar were all on horse-back, and the Mamlatdar was in a bullock shigram [carriage or cart] with the *Talati* and Kurnashanker the Karkun [accountant or clerk], and I was on foot following the shigram. The Police went on in front and we were behind."[2] In addition, the *mukhi* asked fellow Patidar Baji Bapu to assist the police, if necessary. The group was armed but was not expecting a battle.

Mamlatdar Naranshankar Manishankar explained that "when we got to the field we heard the drum being beaten and saw 200 or 300 persons assembled with dharias, sticks[,] and bows and arrows[,] and they were shouting. One man came up to the shigram with a bow and arrow and beads round his neck and asked me to go and worship the *Bhagat*. I refused."[3] Kashibhai corroborated: "Gema Mitha came up to the shigram with a bow and arrows and said to the Mamlatdar[,] 'go and worship the *bhagat*,' but the Mamlatdar refused."[4] Naranshankar and the others were unaware that this was a special request that had been made by Ranchod. Police Inspector Jagannath led the group into the field near the *mandwa* and noticed that some Dharalas had guns. He stated, "They were shaking their heads, and came towards us. I stopped the Police and gave my revolver to Hamid Dallu to load. . . . I also told the other police to load. There were 5 armed Police and about 12 others."[5]

Hamid, a head constable, loaded Jagannath's revolver with six cartridges. He testified that the inspector and the chief constable tried to persuade the Dharalas to stop, and stated, "One man came up and said[,] you are Government men and we will not let you go. . . . If you have anything to say[,] you can write it on a piece of paper and we will give it to the *Bhagat*."[6] Nearly all the members of this group testified in court about the sequence of events of January 12, and they largely agreed that they were attacked without provocation. These were the opinions of officials and village elites who viewed Ranchod as a peasant leader perpetrating crimes against the colonial government. Inspector Jagannath had wanted to arrest Ranchod as a way to diffuse the situation. Ranchod's claims of kingship were simply disregarded by Jagannath, but the Dharalas offered Jagannath a chance to reconsider his position. He explained:

> I signed to the people to be quiet, but when we had gone half through the field[,] some said I must not go and others said that if I came I must go alone. There were then about 300 or 400 people assembled at the sound of the drum and trumpet. They said "are you a topiwallah or a Gujarati?" and told me to write anything I had to say. I said I had no ink or pen[,] and if Ranchod Vira wanted to say anything he must get it written. Accused No. 5 pointed his bow and arrow at me and said I could come and see the Bhagat if I wished. I told the people I had nothing to do with them and only had business with the Bhagat and the rest should go away. While I was talking to the people[,] Baber Naba was trying to shoot an arrow at me, but others stopped him and said I should be heard. One man said he would get me the permission of the Bhagat[,] and he went off to the Mandva but he did not come back[;] and soon after I heard the sound of a trumpet and a drum being beaten near the Mandva. Then at the sound the people attacked us.[7]

Apparently, Ranchod had emerged from the *mandwa* and signaled his supporters to begin the battle against government officials. According to Kashibhai, the Dharalas "were throwing bricks and shooting arrows and shouting."[8] Someone attacked the inspector's horse, and a constable named Punja Dildar was struck in the head with a *dharia* and died. Inspector Jagannath testified, "There was much confusion, so I told Hamid to fire my revolver; hearing the sound of the shot[,] the armed police also fired. The revolver was emptied and Hamid had no more cartridges. . . . At that time there were about 500 or 600 Dharalas assembled. They were all armed. I could not see any of my police in the crowd."[9]

Chief Constable Surajram stated that the peasants were angered when the police began firing their guns: "All the people then attacked the armed police. Amin was the first to fall. . . . I was struck twice on the back with a stick, and my horse was struck in the foot with an arrow. . . . Then we all went back to the village; the people pursued us for half a mile."[10] The Dharalas then proceeded to strip the uniforms, belts, caps, and guns from the armed constables. Jora Meru stated, "I was struck on the hand and head with a sword. . . . My gun fell and then I fell as I was struck with a stick[,] and they stripped off my uniform."[11] Bhaiji Amtha claimed: "I was struck with an arrow on the chest . . . and with a dharia. In the riot I lost my cap, belt, and gun."[12] Satyanarayan Ajodhyaprasad reported, "An arrow struck me in the neck. . . . I was struck on the head with a dharia. I lost my cap, belt, and gun."[13]

Some Dharalas chased the police away from the *mandwa,* others simply ran away. Naranshankar was followed but managed to escape: "100 or 150 Dharalas ran after my cart. . . . My cart was struck on both sides with sticks. They left us within half a mile. Then the bullocks got tired, so I got on the Chief Constable's horse behind him and we came to the Chora."[14] The group met at the village center: five police constables were seriously injured, and Punja Dildar had been killed. The inspector sent a telegram to the district superintendent of police and the district collector. Both officials arrived the following day, January 13, along with two hundred troops of the Fourth Bombay Rifles from Ahmedabad.

17 · DHARALA BATTLE NARRATIVES

Approximately fifty of Ranchod's supporters were singing *bhajans* in the *mandwa* during the afternoon of January 12 before the police and village officials arrived. They all had weapons in their hands: most carried swords; others had *dangs, dharias,* bows and arrows, and sticks; one possessed a gun. Meru Mitha reported, "The police came [and] Ranchod *Bhagat* ordered the drum to be beaten. Batta, who was in the mandap, beat it, and the people collected to the number of 500 or so from the neighboring fields. They came armed. . . . I took an axe."[1] Ranchod's supporters were well aware of the signal to gather at the *mandwa*. Most Dharalas had abandoned their daily tasks and rushed with weapons in hand to support their new leader: the swordsmen were once again carrying swords (as well as other arms). They had obviously prepared for a violent encounter with representatives of the government.

Interestingly, Gema Mitha provided a different interpretation of the events, one that suggests the Dharalas had gathered for a meal rather than a battle: "Navla Amir came to invite the *bhagat* to dinner. There were about 50 men in the *mandwa* and they were getting ready to go. Then Teja beat the kettle drum. Hearing the kettle drum, about 500 men gathered, meanwhile the Mamlatdar and the Police arrived on the scene."[2] Yet Gema does not explain why the five hundred men arrived at the *mandwa* with weapons, or why he was carrying a bow and arrow. The *mukhi* even claimed that Gema had threatened the Mamlatdar: "He had fixed the arrow to the bow, and he had a red cloth tied round his head and a necklace round his neck."[3] Further, it was Gema who had prevented the inspector from seeing Ranchod by shouting, "You cannot go without the permission of the Bawa. . . . We won't allow you into the mandup. If you want to go you may write a letter."[4] This issue was not raised in court, and Gema did not offer an explanation. He probably wanted to avoid a criminal conviction, or his memory could have been fuzzy about the event after he was shot in the chest by a police constable.

He stated, "I was wounded by a stray shot. I became unconscious and was carried to the *mandwa[,]* where I sat."[5]

According to Surta Ragha, Ranchod "beckoned with his hand to the people and the fight began."[6] Gema added that Ranchod had ordered him to blow a *turai* (trumpet) as a signal to attack the police. However, most Dharalas claimed they did not actually participate in the battle and did not witness it. Some stated that they were in the *mandwa* and could not provide any details; others claimed they were not even in Chaklasi at the time. When Surta Ragha was asked "Did you take any part in the fight?" he replied, "No, I was in the *mandwa*."[7] Salia Baji stated, "I had been to Pallaia on that day to escort my uncle's daughter. . . . It is at a distance of 5 or 6 gaus."[8] Baber Mana claimed, "I had nothing with me. . . . I was near the Mandwa."[9] Meru Mitha testified that "about 1,000 Dharalas had collected in the fighting," but that he had remained in the *mandwa* and later ran away.[10] Mathur Nara stated, "I was at Samarkha."[11] Mala Halu said, "I was sitting in the Mandwa. . . . I had not got out of the *mandwa*."[12] Others repeated different versions of these explanations, but only Meru Mitha provided a detailed account of the events, including his weapon of choice:

> Gunna Surta struck a constable with a sword about the neck. The constable fell down. Gopal Vira struck the Inspector's horse with a sword. The horse turned round and went off. Four or five shot[s] were fired by the Police, who then fled, leaving their guns. I saw two guns. Sunna Surta was shot in the breast, and the bullet came out behind. He was carried into the mandup. I was standing close to where the police were attacked. I remained in the field, and about five hundred people followed the Police. Gema Metha, my brother, was struck in the chest with a bullet and was taken to the mandup. Baji Batta was wounded in the leg. Lalla Ranchhod got a bullet in the right leg. Rala Jalu was wounded in the right arm. I do not know who else was wounded. . . . I took my axe and returned to the village.[13]

Once the police and village officials had departed from the site of the battle, the injured Dharalas were taken to the *mandwa*. Ranchod had acquired a reputation in the area as a medicine man and had claimed that he would be able to treat his injured supporters. However, Ranchod's skills were limited in this instance, and he was unable to help those who had suffered bullet wounds. Surta testified, "[Sama] was wounded with bullets in two places on the chest. . . . His wife and I brought him into the *mandwa* and asked the *Bhagat* to heal him. He burned incense and threw ashes over the wounds. Afterwards Ranchod went away. We carried my wounded son to my own field. At nightfall we carried him near a tank as we felt afraid of the S[a]rkar. On the evening following he died, and we burned his body."[14] Meru had a similar report: "Ranchod burned incense near the wounded and said he would cure them. They did not get well, and Gunna died that night. The people dispersed about 8 or 9 P.M., leaving in the mandup the wounded and Ranchod *Bhagat*" and eleven others.[15]

18 · THE ARRESTS

On the day after the battle, January 13, Ranchod was captured in a field close to the *mandwa*. In all, the government arrested eleven individuals. Several Dharalas ran away and went into hiding in neighboring villages; some were caught within a few days, but others evaded capture for a few months. Constable Punja Dildar's body was found under a tree near the *mandwa*. Inspector Jagannath, the district superintendent of police, and the district collector proceeded into the *mandwa* and gathered Ranchod's belongings, which included the book collection, papers, one police belt, one police cap, a bow and three arrows, a bayonet sheath, and a blood-stained cartridge.

Over the next several weeks, an extensive search for further evidence was conducted throughout Chaklasi and neighboring villages. Government officials were aided in this by Patidar elites, who identified themselves as members of the *panchayat*—the village or caste council. This was to be expected in a Patidar village, especially following a serious violation of the law, but it is unclear why the *mukhi* Kashibhai did not turn to the members of this institution before the battle. According to District Collector G. Carmichael, the *mukhi* and the *talati* were at fault for not alerting either government officials or village elites. He noted in his report on the incident: "The village officers of Chaklasi are primarily responsible for this mistake and they will be dealt with."[1]

It appears that officials turned to the *panchayat* members as "native informants" who could provide detailed information about the village and about possible hiding places for Dharalas. After all, these Patidar men would have had either direct dealings with the wanted Dharalas or some knowledge of where to locate family members for additional information. The officials' assumptions were correct: the Patidars assisted the police in making crucial arrests. Jhaverbhai Shivabhai testified, "I was a member of the Panch [*panchayat*] when the house of the father-in-law of Salia Baji was searched three or four days after the riot. Salia Baji was arrested from an earthen grain-jar in which he was hidden[,] and a bow

and arrow and country fiddle were found in the house."[2] Jivabhai Mithabhai followed with additional details: "I was a member of the Panch in
whose presence a gun was produced by Mathur Nara, from some straw
in the field of Bana Khoda, where it was concealed. I was also present
when another Government gun was produced by Bhatta Detar, from
near an earthen pot of grain in his house."[3]

Officials were pleased with the quick end to the peasant movement.
The troops stationed in Chaklasi prevented further disturbance, and
intensive surveillance in the area continued until officials were satisfied
that the primary Dharala perpetrators had been arrested. Colonial power
had prevented the further development and strengthening of Ranchod's
alliance with fellow Dharalas in twenty-one villages in Kheda district, or
so it seemed at the time. However, Carmichael was aware that the mechanisms of information-gathering and policing of the countryside had
proven to be ineffective in preventing Ranchod and his supporters from
violating colonial law. He blamed "village officials" for the delay in circulating information to the district-level officials, yet he was willing to
acknowledge that Ranchod's "influence was astonishing" even beyond
his Dharala supporters in Chaklasi.[4]

Carmichael's own investigation in Chaklasi was based on extensive
interrogations of Dharalas who had been present at the *mandwa* on the
day of the battle. He cited specific factors that "influenced" Dharalas to
support Ranchod—"the loss of rent-free service lands," "the plague
operations," the "closing of the Dakore temple," and "the guarding of
the Mahi" River. But it seemed impossible to Carmichael that Ranchod
could have developed his own ideas about the impact of colonial policies
on Dharalas.[5] He stated that Ranchod was "inspired" by the Kashi *patra*
but also noted that Ranchod's own letter differed from any other version
of the Kashi *patra* circulating in Kheda district. Unfortunately, it is
impossible to know how Ranchod understood the Kashi *patra,* but it is
clear that his letter spoke to specific concerns directly relevant to his
Dharala supporters. Ranchod did not have an opportunity to respond to
the claims made by Carmichael, but on May 17, 1898, Ranchod finally
explained his side of the story to Magistrate J. Becharlal in the town of
Kheda, albeit in an obfuscating way.[6]

19 · RANCHOD'S TESTIMONY

Magistrate: How many Dharalas were there at the time of the rioting?

Ranchod: There were about 400 or 500 Dharalas.

Magistrate: Did you call Mamlatdar on the day of rioting to pay respects to you?

Ranchod: Yes, I had sent to call Mamlatdar one Gema Mitha and Shana Surta.

Magistrate: And you refused the Inspector and the Police to see you?

Ranchod: Yes, because they had seen me before.

Magistrate: What arms were with the Dharalas collected at the mandwa at the time of rioting?

Ranchod: I have not seen any Dharalas' arms[,] as the lamp in the mandwa [had] been extinguished.

Magistrate: Is it true that fighting took place between the Police and the Dharalas[,] and some policemen were killed and wounded?

Ranchod: Yes, fighting took place. Ganu Surta on my side and one police peon [were] killed[,] and accused Gema Mitha and Baja Bhathi of my side were wounded[;] and I cannot say how many persons of the Government were wounded.

Magistrate: Is it true that a dead body of a police peon was found from near your mandwa the next morning?

Ranchod: Not from near my mandwa, but from near a peepul tree, which is at a distance of 50–60 hands from my mandwa.

Magistrate: You were at the head of all these people?

Ranchod: Yes.

Magistrate: Where were you on the night of the rioting?

Ranchod: I was at the mandwa.

Magistrate: Is it true that these papers were found from your Chowra by the Police?

Ranchod: Yes, when the Saheb came to catch these papers[,] they were in my mandwa[,] and so these were found from it.

Magistrate: Why had you collected Dharalas at the mandwa when the Police came there?

Ranchod: The men were naturally collected there.

Magistrate: Were you punished before?

Ranchod: No.

Magistrate: When did you see the dead body of the police peon near your mandwa?

Ranchod: At the time of the sunset.[1]

20 · THE KINGSHIP

In his brief but evasive testimony, Ranchod provided answers to the magistrate's questions in his first appearance in court. (But from Ranchod's perspective, did a king really have to explain himself?) The magistrate simply asked about the basic details of the events of January 12, without demanding a complete explanation. The magistrate was required to document the facts of the case as government evidence. A full interrogation of all the accused took place in the Sessions Court in Nadiad in the presence of Judge E. H. E. Leggatt.

Officials were perplexed by Ranchod's order that the *mamlatdar* "pay his respects" or "pray" to Ranchod in the *mandwa*. Yet there is no explanation of why a visit by the *mamlatdar*, rather than any other government official, was so important to Ranchod. He did not want to see the police inspector or the constables, but specifically asked for the *mamlatdar*—a district-level revenue official responsible for maintaining accounts and administering a sizeable staff of clerks and inspectors who monitored the records and activities of village accountants and documented regular land reports. Ranchod had explained that the policemen "had seen me before." But what did he mean exactly? This may have been a reference to an earlier encounter with the police or was perhaps simply a king's right of refusal. It is possible that Ranchod would have allowed Jagannath a viewing if the inspector had provided a written response to the query about identifying himself as a Gujarati or *topiwallah*. Yet to complicate matters even further, Ranchod claimed that it was difficult to see anything inside the *mandwa* as the "lamp was extinguished." Ranchod stated that he could not see if any of the Dharalas carried weapons. Of course, he was not completely truthful in his response. Moreover, he offered no explanation about why the men had collected at the *mandwa*, except to say that they were there "naturally."

On May 20, Ranchod was brought in front of the magistrate for a second time to answer only one question: "What have you to say to the charges framed against you?" Ranchod replied, "I have nothing to say."

Perhaps Ranchod avoided answering the magistrate's question to avoid further implicating himself and his supporters; this might explain why he did not discuss the details regarding weapons. Yet his brief testimony, and that of those who spoke in his defense, suggests a far more developed understanding of power, authority, and kingship than could have been imagined by government officials at the time.

To begin with, Ranchod's selection of dates for any activity was carefully planned, especially the battle on January 12. This specific point is not explored in any of the government reports, but statements made during the trial reveal important clues that were completely ignored by all the local officials. These were comments made in passing and which never became central to the case, despite their significance to Ranchod and his supporters. Baji Bapu, for instance, was the only person who commented on the fact that the battle between the Dharala peasants and the police took place on the day that land rents were due: "On the day on which Government dues were to be paid, I was coming home from the fields in the evening. On the way I met the Inspector, the Chief Constable and the Mamlatdar: the Mukhi called to me to go with them."[1] This helps to explain Ranchod's request to see the *mamlatdar*, a revenue official who could interpret the information contained within the pages of the account registers in Ranchod's possession.

Revenue was typically collected in January and March or April. *Mamlatdars* throughout the area had acquired a reputation for using extra-economic coercion to extract the entire annual payment in January as a way to guarantee that peasants would not default on the second part of their rent in March or April. Consequently, peasants often were forced to take out loans from local moneylenders to make these payments, or they simply had to abandon the land. What makes Ranchod's request difficult to understand in this case is that Mamlatdar Naranshankar Manishankar stated that he was "new to the district" and "could not recognize anyone" in Chaklasi, including Ranchod.[2] Ranchod wanted the *mamlatdar* to "worship," or "pay his respects," as a way to acknowledge the new king, who now had the jurisdiction to collect revenue from peasants. It is not likely that Ranchod sought the *mamlatdar* to administer land revenue, but he may have wanted to inform him that the British raj had ended and that payments were reduced and postponed for two months till Holi—a holiday that typically took place in March.

However, Ranchod may have been interested in Naranshankar for a completely different reason, one that had more to do with the fact that

Naranshankar was a Brahmin than with his official government position. How would Ranchod have known the *mamlatdar's* caste? The posting of a district official would have been known to all the village officials, and the information certainly would have spread throughout the villages. Peasants would want to know what to expect from the new official, especially since the January payment date was quickly approaching. But more specifically, the *mamlatdar's* name—Naranshankar Manishankar—revealed a great deal about his background, including his caste. Naranshankar was not the only Brahmin outside the *mandwa* just before the battle; Inspector Jagannath Sagun and Constable Satyanarayan Ajodhya-prasad were there that day too. But Ranchod could not have known in advance that these two would show up.

Brahmins had played an indispensable role in the ritual confirmation of kingship throughout India. These individuals performed ceremonies that validated a new king's ascendancy to power by establishing that the king was a direct descendant of one of the two great deities of Hinduism—Vishnu or Shiva. (In this case, Ranchodji was a manifestation of Krishna and an incarnation of Vishnu.) In return, kings fulfilled their royal duties and further established their authority by providing Brahmins with endowments of land, money, and gifts. Could Naranshankar have been the Brahmin selected by Ranchod to authorize the king's sovereignty? Possibly, but it is difficult to know what Ranchod expected from an encounter with Naranshankar, especially since Ranchod's request was simply refused. Ranchod never explained his motives to Magistrate Becharlal or other government officials, and his desire to have the *mamlatdar* pray inside the *mandwa* was probably linked to other unknown factors. Yet even in the absence of more complete details, Ranchod's practices suggest an understanding of kingship in western India.

Ranchod Vira was ritually ambitious: he had proclaimed his own era, symbolically established divine authority, and produced a *patra* that served as a royal edict.[3] He led a procession through Chaklasi celebrating his coronation, in which he reproduced one of the primary symbols of Hindu kingship, the imperial umbrella.[4] By positioning himself under the umbrella during the ceremonial journey, Ranchod laid claim to a traditional emblem that had been used by the most powerful of Hindu kings in India. His pursuit of authority included building a divine throne that served as a seat of power *(gadi)*, where he could hold meetings and ceremonies *(durbar)*. Within this context, the *mandwa* served not only as a sacred space but also the central headquarters for Ranchod's polity, where peasants publicly discussed issues of dominance and the policies of the colonial government, performed rituals, and celebrated Ranchod's ascendancy.

Ranchod's decision that Dharalas would arm themselves and gather on January 12 was related to the fact that land rents were due that day; in particular, he would have anticipated the arrival of government officials to collect their payments. However, the day was significant for another reason as well: it was Uthran,[5] one of the most auspicious days of the Hindu calendar year.[6] Ranchod and his followers were certainly aware of the importance of the day, which symbolized the end of an inauspicious period and the start of a favorable one. The fact that the government had decided to collect rent on that day probably exacerbated the situation. Yet the statements that Dharalas made in court about the day were not given serious consideration by the government. For officials, Ranchod and his supporters had violated numerous laws and had to be prosecuted. This no doubt was seen as a harsh resolution by many individuals in the area, especially those who embraced the principles of the holiday, described in court by Mansi Natha: "Uthran [is] a day for giving charity."[7]

For Ranchod, the impending collection of rent payments was an important consideration in establishing his authority. At one level, popular belief held that "good" kings simply would not collect land rent during a period of crisis. By reducing and deferring rent payments until the Hindu festival of Holi, Ranchod was perhaps fulfilling his obligation as a proper leader. Historically, the day was celebrated to mark the ritual beginning of a new year, but it also signaled the symbolic inversion of all social relations, much like annual carnivals in other parts of the world do.[8] Although, Holi was a one-day celebration, it appears to have been ritually significant for peasants who had survived the plague epidemic, especially because specific prayers recited during the festival were meant to ward off the onset of disease and famine.[9]

At another level, Ranchod's reduction of land rent rates was a form of charity for Dharalas unable to pay the full amount, but it also suggested a desire to reestablish norms of kingship that had existed in western India for centuries.[10] By deciding to collect only one-fourth the rate set by the government, Ranchod sought to reinvent the practice of *chauth*—a traditional revenue claim that had been central to the construction of kingship within the Maratha polity in the seventeenth century.[11] *Chauth*—literally "one-fourth"—was a tribute paid directly to kings to maintain order within the polity. Even though Ranchod never discussed in the official record why he had proposed the idea of *chauth*, his supporters would have been well aware of this legacy.

Fulfilling the duties of a good king, Ranchod began his reign by eliminating peasant debts and setting new, reduced land revenue rates. His possession of account books *(bahis)* and a loose bundle of account registers suggests that, within the new polity, all old debts incurred by peasants would be either negated or reduced.[12] Typically, peasants would go to moneylenders for loans during periods of crisis, such as the plague, and, as noted, to borrow money for making rent payments.[13] By confiscating the *bahis*, Ranchod was denying the fundamental authority of the institution to exploit peasants by charging exorbitant rates for loans.[14]

21 · FRIENDS AND ENEMIES OF THE KING

One matter that remains unclear is how Ranchod defined political relations between Dharalas and others in the locality. While there is no direct articulation by Ranchod or any of his supporters on this point, there is a small, but interesting clue: the reference to a dialogue between some Dharalas and Police Inspector Jagannath Sagun before the battle. Recall that, as Jagannath approached Ranchod's *mandwa*, he was stopped and asked if he was a Gujarati or a *topiwallah*.[1] As Jagannath did not answer this question, resulting in Ranchod's decision to attack, it is fair to assume that he was identified as a *topiwallah*.

What did this identification signify in the locality? *Topiwallah*, literally "hat wearer," was a reference to Europeans recorded as early as the 1780s, in contrast to "Indians," who were referred to as *puckery wallahs*, or turban wearers.[2] By the end of the nineteenth century, the concept of the *topiwallah* had changed. It was no longer a reference to Europeans, but to all individuals who were classified as "government men," or those working for the colonial state.[3] This is explained by the fact that, as colonial networks and institutions expanded through the nineteenth century, Indians were recruited as part of the state apparatus and consequently became "government men." Indian *topiwallahs* often became targets of anticolonial sentiments in various parts of the country, especially during periods of crisis, when strict policy measures were implemented. For example, in Chaklasi in 1898, the police inspector and constables identified as *topiwallahs* were attacked by Dharalas in the village, and in Bengal the same year, colonial doctors and health care workers were subjected to the same treatment.[4] For Ranchod, his Dharala supporters, and others throughout India, the *topiwallah* was the enemy.

The Gujarati, in contrast, was a friend. But how was a Gujarati defined in the countryside in 1898? And how was Gujarat spatially conceptualized by peasants like Ranchod and his supporters? Unfortunately, the answers to these questions are difficult to uncover, especially when treating the ideological concerns of nonliterate peasants. The Dharala peasant's question addressed to Jagannath about his identity offers some additional clues. Ranchod's supporters were aware that Jagannath was a police inspector, since he arrived on horseback wearing a uniform signifying his rank, and he clearly commanded the group of police constables. Yet he was still offered the opportunity to declare his allegiance: friend or enemy. Why? Although it was evident that Jagannath worked for the government, he could have abandoned his *topiwallah* identity and declared himself a friend of the new polity. This would not mean that Jagannath would necessarily have to become a member of the polity. Rather, the Dharala peasants wanted him to accept its legitimacy and Ranchod as the leader, and to defy the rule of law defined by the colonial government. By accepting these terms, Jagannath would have identified himself as a Gujarati and a friend.

This point is also supported by the fact that, when peasants captured some of the constables during the battle, they only removed their police uniforms and did not violently attack them: this was a literal removal of the symbols of *topiwallahs*. Jagannath maintained his official standing as a *topiwallah*, and when asked to identify himself during the trial, he said, "I state on solemn affirmation that—My name is Jagannath, my father's name is Sagun, my age is 40, my religion is Hindu, my caste is Brahmin, my profession is Police Inspector."[5]

For Ranchod, political relations were determined by social and strategic concerns when it came to formally interacting with government officials and fellow Gujaratis. His internal relations with his peasant supporters were primarily based on kinship. Ranchod did not declare the end of the British raj throughout the entire countryside, but specifically in Chaklasi and twenty-one other villages. His network consisted of scattered villages throughout the locality; some were only a few miles from Chaklasi, and others were as much as twenty miles away. Even so, Ranchod included in the polity only those fellow Dharala peasants who were the initial recipients of his *patras*. Presumably, the other villagers were to be treated like Gujaratis, as long as they accepted Ranchod's legitimacy and did not collude with the enemy, the *topiwallahs*.

Because of the paucity of information, understanding Ranchod's concept of territoriality is a more difficult task. The villages were not contiguous, but neither were territories of other princely states in the area—

Baroda, for example—or throughout India. Ranchod's conceptualization of territoriality would not have been based on demarcating boundaries predicated on a fiscal calculus, as in the model of the colonial government, but on a formulation of legitimate social relations derived from the shared bonds of poor Dharala peasants.

22 · SYMBOLS OF LEGITIMACY

Ranchod's ascendancy to power in Chaklasi was explained by his ability to legitimize a political order through symbols of authority well known to and accepted by Dharalas.[1] The *patra*, for example, was a "text of legitimation" used by kings for declaring the beginning of a new era, or *satyug*.[2] Ranchod made such an assertion in his *patra* by stating that Ranchodji's *satyug* had started with the full moon in December 1897—the day of the prophesy. By implication, he was also confirming that the *kaliyug*, or age of darkness associated with the British raj, had finally ended.[3] The *satyug* was considered to be the age of truth and an auspicious time for a king to establish a new mode of governance.

One of the first acts for a king was to construct a temple in order to assert his sovereignty over the polity and provide a sacred space for the performance of all royal rituals. For Ranchod, this was an important consideration. His *patra* begins with a reference to the Ranchodji temple, echoing the prophecy of December 9. It is unclear whether Ranchod was speaking of another supernatural event with a flying temple, or whether he wanted to construct a temple dedicated to Ranchodji in Chaklasi, as mentioned by Kashibhai. The *mandwa* was already functioning as the inner chamber of a temple despite the fact that it was made of millet stalks. However, Ranchod had ambitions for a larger, more permanent building. Perhaps he hoped to, like earlier kings, provide priests with land and money for the construction and maintenance of a temple. Within the ritual domain of kingship, a king could assert himself as a direct descendant of either Vishnu or Shiva. Furthermore, the *patra* suggests that Ranchod saw himself as the controller of the "wheel of Ram," which was also known as the *chakravartin*. This was perhaps Ranchod's grandest claim of all: the *chakravartin* was the universal monarch who had sovereignty over the earth.[4]

In the traditions of kingship, Ranchod had to establish himself as ritually homologous with Ranchodji—a manifestation of the deity Krishna. If we read Ranchod's *patra* within this context, his declarations refer to the symbols associated with Krishna found in the Srimad Bhagavata Purana Book X—the principal text for the stories of Krishna for the past thousand years or so. Lord Krishna, the universal monarch, is said to have inaugurated the present age, or *yuga*. In fact, the anonymous narrator of the Bhagavata Purana claims, in part 1, chapter 1, that the "narration of [Krishna's stories] can destroy the sins of the age of *kali (kaliyug)*. He introduces Krishna as "the wielder of the discus" and later points out that the "Lord's weapon is the disc," with which Krishna "sliced off the head" of an enemy.[5] Krishna's powers are recounted in numerous places throughout the text and assert the benevolence of the great king:

> This Krishna is the beginning and the end
> to all living beings in this world,
> as he is their protector.
> No one prospers who disregards him.

Ranchod probably was not familiar with the details in the voluminous Bhagavata Purana, nor did he make such a claim. However, like other disciples of Krishna, he interpreted the stories and made them relevant for the particular circumstances of his time, especially his declaration of the beginning of a new era. In addition, he used the emblems of Krishna and Vishnu during his brief reign: conch, disc, sword, club, bow, kettledrum.[6] How was it possible for a nonliterate peasant to incorporate such stories into his own discourse? To begin with, Ranchod and most Dharalas would have visited the Ranchodji temple in Dakore at some point, where oral narratives of the Krishna stories were constantly recounted by disciples. Further, Krishna, in the form of Ranchodji, was the primary deity worshipped in the region and was celebrated monthly during the full moon festivals. His visual images featured the emblems cited in the Bhagavata Purana.

Ranchod's religious identity seems to have been largely associated with Vaishnavism linked to a form of Krishna worship performed in Gujarat. Yet significant differences within these complex traditions distinguish Ranchod and his Dharala followers from other disciples of Krishna. Ranchod was trained as a *bhagat* by his teacher, Bama Kuberdar, presumably a high priest in the area. He learned to perform special rituals, including a variety of supernatural skills for warding off diseases and illnesses. Like other *bhagats*, he may have specialized as a spirit-medium, or he may have had a background in narrating folk stories and *bhajans*. *Bhagat* traditions varied from one area to another: some priests specialized in particular practices, depending on their training; others saw a convergence of

ideas between *bhagat* practices and Vaishnavism and identified themselves as "Vishnu *bhagats.*" It is difficult to know exactly what would
initiate an instance of specialization, departure, or incorporation of ideas
in *bhagat* ideology, especially since information about the practices was
kept under the strict control of *bhagats* and their disciples by means of an
oral tradition.

Ranchod both promoted *bhagat* practices among his followers and
adhered to the Vaishnavism that elevated Ranchodji. Like Bama Kuberdar, he had a group of disciples, whom he had trained in Chaklasi. And,
like Kuberdar, he had adopted the practice of presenting a *kanthi mala*,
or necklace made of beads from the *tulsi* plant, to his disciples. The *kanthi mala* became one way for colonial officials to identify Ranchod's key
supporters in the aftermath of the battle. In court, Surta Ragha testified
to the significance of the necklaces: "My son Saina had been his disciple
and had tied his *kanthi [mala]*. Ranchod and I had been the followers of
the Bama Kuberdar of Sarsa, who had tied the necklace on us." Ranchod
did not specifically comment on his *bhagat* disciples, but additional statements by Surta and Gema Mitha suggest that Ranchod had brought
together a large number of *bhagats,* who were at the center of all activity.
Surta claimed that the *bhagats* permanently remained in the *mandwa* and
participated in the procession and the battle. But Gema testified, "The
bhagats cut three Government *[babuls]* to make the pressers." In fact,
following the end of the battle on January 12, only *bhagats* were arrested
and prosecuted for crimes against the government. Other Dharalas were
simply released, but it is not known how many *bhagats* actually had
gathered to support Ranchod.

The fact that these *bhagat*s carried arms can be understood as a sub-
version of the 1850s colonial policy that outlawed the possession of
weapons by Dharalas in Kheda district, but it also harks back to an earlier time when religious men had the right to bear arms. Throughout the
eighteenth century, Vaishnava priests in India carried arms to protect pilgrimage routes and served in the armies of land magnates and local
kings.[7] Many of these priests became central to the fiscal calculus of
regions, especially as they provided security on roads connecting temple
complexes, which also served as sites for commerce. In return for their
services, these armed religious men were afforded rent-free land, weapons, and endowments by their respective patrons. However, with the
arrival of the British and the expansion of commercial interests, the
armed priests were forced out of religious centers by a stronger military
and excluded from their former responsibility to provide protection. In

addition, the British also reduced or completely eliminated the perquisites that had been given to the priests for their services.

Over the nineteenth century, similar processes affected the status of Dharala *bhagats,* resulting in their loss of rent-free lands and their swords, leading many individuals to question the legitimacy of colonial authorities. In fact, one of the earliest *bhagats* to declare the end of the British raj was Govindas Ramdas (literally, the "slave of Krishna and Ram"). On March 17, 1826, he led five hundred armed men into Thasra, a town near Dakore, and proclaimed himself king. A British official noted, "His followers thought Govindas a saint and believed him endowed with supernatural powers."[8] Little else is known about Govindas, but it is difficult not to speculate on the numerous connections between him, Ranchod, and other armed *bhagats*. After all, Ranchod and his followers may have carried weapons as a way to assert their rights as armed *bhagats* in a new era in which a Dharala could be king.

23 · ORAL CULTURE AND WRITTEN CULTURE

Ranchod's *patra* was an encounter between the written word and an oral culture.[1] Ranchod certainly did not develop the ideas in it by simply reading texts and then reinterpreting them for his own purpose. It was an oral culture that helped him to formulate his ideas—that is, if we are to believe that he dictated the *patra* on his own. District Collector G. Carmichael suggests he did not, arguing that Ranchod was influenced by the ideas articulated in the Kashi *patra*. But although Ranchod's letter follows the form of the Kashi *patra*, it does not mimic its content. He radically altered its symbols to make it comprehensible and relevant to Dharalas.

How was this actually accomplished? Presumably, Teja Bama, Rama Nara, or some other literate Dharala read a version of the Kashi *patra* to Ranchod and others at some point in late 1897. Ranchod could have then constructed a set of ideas, either on his own or in consultation with his supporters. (This was not the first time a Dharala had questioned the authority of the British raj: earlier that year, all the Dharalas in Chaklasi had protested the new land policies.) Ranchod would have then dictated his thoughts to his disciples. Meru Mitha confirmed that this happened: "I saw Bhagat Ranchod dictating a letter which was written by Teja Bama." Gema Mitha corroborated it: "At the Bhagat's dictation, Teja Bawa and Nara Rama wrote a letter."[2] Other Dharala supporters took copies of the handwritten letter to twenty-one specific locations in the district, and the letters were read aloud to Dharalas in the villages. The details of Ranchod's message were discussed among the villagers present and told to those who did not hear the public reading.

Ranchod's encounter with writing did not exist in a vacuum; it represented the important presence of the written word in the everyday life of peasants at the end of the nineteenth century.[3] This is not to say that peasants in India were unaware of the power of writing before this time. In fact, historically, Brahmins had prevented peasants like Ranchod, and Dharalas more generally, from seeing or touching specific religious texts, as this was a privilege of Brahmins only. Peasants had not even been allowed to hear the words read aloud. Moneylenders had prevented peasants from holding account registers that recorded their debts, for fear that peasants might destroy them. Government officials maintained an enormous bureaucracy with archives and document rooms that were impervious to peasants. Even if peasants had possessed these texts, most would not have been able to read them. But this was not always a problem. Peasants often asked others to read texts to them. By the end of the nineteenth century, not only were most peasants aware of official documents and accounting books, but most had had some close contact with them in their everyday lives. The introduction of village schools had provided some peasants further access to the written word by teaching them to read and write.

Ranchod's desire to circulate his own *patra* and collect books, and his demand that Inspector Jagannath write him a letter, suggests an acknowledgment of the power of the written word. But even though his words had been written down on paper, Ranchod's ideas were primarily transmitted through an oral culture. Ranchod's case is unique because, not only was he king, but also he apparently wanted his followers to possess his letters as auspicious texts relevant to their future well-being. The letters were powerful because they were sent by Ranchod and each was inscribed with a statement of legitimacy from Ranchodji. The Dharalas could keep the *patras* for themselves—as Ranchod had held on to his books—and orally transmit the ideas contained in them.

Local newspapers represented another convergence of the written word and the oral culture. It was common for literate individuals to give public readings of newspapers in village centers as a way to disseminate news and information. These gatherings also provided an opportunity for discussing and debating issues relevant to their audiences. Presumably, some of these ideas were then circulated to others by word of mouth. Newspaper publishers were aware that their papers were consumed within villages, but they also actively participated in reproducing the oral culture. Rumors circulating within a newspaper's subscription area were collected and printed along with the daily news. Peasants would be aware that their ideas and thoughts that were informally discussed could also find their way into print. It is likely that newspaper editors sent reporters to villages and the public readings as a way to collect new rumors that would be of interest to their subscribers.

For the colonial officials, rumors posed a problem for governance, whether they were circulated orally, handwritten in the form of *patras*, or printed in newspapers. They were impossible to control, and it was impossible to know which ones actually posed a threat to the stability of the countryside. Memories of the rumors associated with the rebellions of 1857–58 were very much alive for British officials, and they remained on guard against the circulation of any idea that questioned the authority of the government. Any potential threat needed to be monitored, but for officials the question remained, which of the rumors actually had the potential for creating a legitimation crisis?

Carmichael's investigation into the emergence of Ranchod's movement led him to a weekly newspaper called the *Svadesh Bandhu and Cambay Gazette*, published in the town of Mahuda, approximately fifteen miles from Chaklasi. Carmichael was informed that the January 5, 1898, issue of the newspaper included a section on local rumors that might possess crucial information about the Chaklasi case.[4] He immediately wrote to Maneklal Khusaldas Desai, the manager, asking for a copy of the paper and full details of the rumors. Maneklal responded, "I printed the rumors as I heard them from the people. To show this expressly I have headed the article 'It is heard.'"[5] The manager was adamant that his decision to print the rumors had nothing to do with any seditious activity, and that the article was meant to be a service to the people who read his paper and to provide the government with total access to the ideas circulating within Kheda district. Maneklal continued: "Sir, many such rumours get their origin among the people often times. Afterwards some of them turn out to be true and some false."[6]

The article speculated that the government was planning to increase the number of troops in the locality for the purpose of preventing "fanatic people" from "committing mischief." It also suggested that the troops were meant to stop individuals from traveling from Baroda and to monitor the Anand Observation Camp. Carmichael did not find a specific connection between the article and Ranchod's movement, but he was concerned that the general public was questioning policies related to the plague epidemic, and that it believed the government was using excessive force or intimidation. Carmichael speculated that these same concerns had influenced Ranchod's thinking. The convergence of the written word with oral culture made it more difficult to control the spread of information, a fact that peasants like Ranchod were fully aware of.

24 · THE CRIMINAL CASE

Criminal Sessions Case Number 61 of 1898, *Imperatrix vs. Ranchod Vira and Others,* began on July 5, 1898, in Nadiad, before Judge E. H. E. Leggatt of the Sessions Court. Ranchod was identified as "Accused Number One" and was charged with numerous crimes under the Indian Penal Code:

> Accused Number One[,] with the conspiracy to commit offences of waging or attempting to wage war, or abetting waging of war against the Queen, excited disaffection, rioting, armed with deadly weapons, being a member of unlawful assembly, guilty of offences committed in prosecution of common object, voluntarily causing grievous hurt to deter [a] public servant from his duty, and murder, in that at Chaklasi, taluka Nadiad in the district of Kaira, on or about the 9th day of January 1898, he went in a procession of Dharalas with arms to the village chowra of Chaklasi and there proclaimed by beat of drum (Nagara), &c., that the Government raj was at an end and the Government dues should not be paid[,] but its chowth (¼ portion) should be paid at his *mandwa* thenceforward; also circulated seditious letters to the same effect in the surrounding villages, collected Dharalas with deadly weapons at his *mandwa* on the 12th January last, and when ordered by the police officers to disperse, attacked them, which conduct of his resulted into the death of one police officer, Punja Dildar, on the spot, and the serious injuries caused to one Mustafabeg Husenbeg ended his life on the next day and four Police officers were seriously hurt.

Ranchod responded to the charges by stating that he was "not guilty." His testimony from May 17 was presented to the court as evidence of Ranchod's participation in the crimes against the government. The government's case was solid. It was based on the evidence and testimonies given by the *mukhi* Kashibhai, Inspector Jagannath, Mamlatdar Naranshankar, and the constables involved in the battle on January 12. Witnesses had corroborated the reports given by the government officials, but the case against Ranchod and the other accused Dharalas was sealed with the confessions of four of his closest supporters: Meru Mitha, Gema Mitha, Mala Halu, and Surta Ragha. However, Ranchod was given another opportunity to speak in court on July 7; it appears that the defense lawyer, Shri Chhotalal, wanted Ranchod to have an opportunity to retract some of his earlier comments.

> *Chhotalal:* Did you take a procession through Chaklasi, and say that the British Raj was at an end?
>
> *Ranchod:* I did take the procession, but did not say the British Raj was at an end. Those with me may have said so.
>
> *Chhotalal:* Did those with you say so or not?
>
> *Ranchod:* No.
>
> *Chhotalal:* Were you at the *mandwa* when the riot took place?
>
> *Ranchod:* Yes.
>
> *Chhotalal:* Did you come out of the *mandwa* and lift your hand and tell the drum and trumpet to sound?
>
> *Ranchod:* No.
>
> *Chhotalal:* Did you send letters to the villagers saying the British Raj was at an end?
>
> *Ranchod:* Letters were written. I only said that whoever was King would take the assessment, but they may have put in the rest. I can't read.
>
> *Chhotalal:* Did you make the statement which has been read over to you?
>
> *Ranchod:* Yes.
>
> *Chhotalal:* Is it true?
>
> *Ranchod:* Yes.
>
> *Chhotalal:* In that statement you said that it was you who said the British Raj was at an end, and who wrote the letters, is that so?
>
> *Ranchod:* No.
>
> *Chhotalal:* What was the procession and assembly at the *mandwa* for?
>
> *Ranchod:* The assembly was for praying, and as I wanted to go into the village I went in a cart and I could not help the people following me.
>
> *Chhotalal:* When the riot took place, did you give the signal for attack?
>
> *Ranchod:* No.
>
> *Chhotalal:* Have you anything else to say?
>
> *Ranchod:* No.[1]

Ranchod's comments were obfuscating yet again. He refused to corroborate his earlier testimony, despite the fact that it was read for everyone to hear in the courtroom. He no longer took sole responsibility for declaring the end of the British raj but attributed the claim to others. He maintained that letters were written, but he attributed their contents to his literate disciples. He claimed that Dharalas had "followed" him, suggesting that the gatherings had much more to do with a large number of peasants who were protesting colonial power than with him as a single individual. He explained that the gatherings at the *mandwa* were only about "praying."

Perhaps this was the only way for Ranchod to escape a long prison sentence or the death penalty. He may have been responding to the confessions of his closest supporters, who had blamed their leader. Although Ranchod appeared to contradict himself about the statement regarding the end of the British raj, he maintained that the Dharalas "may have said so." Thus, while claiming that he was not the author of the ideas, he acknowledged these ideas were circulating, nonetheless. It may be true that Ranchod did not ask the Dharalas to follow him, and that it was their own choice to participate. The emphasis on "praying" was also correct, but the activities in the *mandwa* symbolized a far more complex world of ideas for Dharalas and the armed *bhagats* than was perceived by Judge Leggatt and British officials. Ranchod certainly retracted his earlier statements, but he understood that his ideas about legitimate authority and government echoed in those of his supporters: it was equally powerful whether he had stated that the British raj had ended, or other Dharalas had made the claim.

On July 9, 1898, Judge Leggatt sentenced Ranchod to fourteen years "rigorous imprisonment" for "rioting," "conspiring to overawe the Government by show of criminal force," "of attempting to excite feelings of disaffection to Government," and "voluntarily causing grievous hurt to a public servant."[2] Salia Baji was found guilty of murder and sentenced to be hanged; the others were convicted of "rioting" and "carrying deadly weapons" and sentenced to up to two years of "rigorous imprisonment." Ranchod was placed in Ahmedabad's Central Prison to serve out his prison term. However, in October 1898, he filed an appeal asking the government for a commuted sentence, stating, "I have not committed the offences of which I have been convicted by the High Court."[3] Ranchod claimed his innocence in the appeal, but he was willing to acknowledge that the colonial government maintained a different interpretation. The request was denied.

Despite the successful convictions of Ranchod and the others, the government maintained that the Dharalas posed a threat to the stability of the countryside. The acting district superintendent of police, H. R. Hume, noted that there was "general rejoicing" at the sentences, and that the "Dharala community . . . thought that the accused would soon return to their homes where they would be looked upon as heroes and martyrs."[4] He was convinced that all Dharalas had aided Ranchod because they belonged to the "same caste." He argued that Dharalas continued to pose a problem in Chaklasi and throughout the district and neighboring territories. He stated that "they are extremely excitable and ever ready for a faction fight[,] and that they do not require any lengthened plans or preparations, that in a thickly populated Dharala neighbourhood, an hour would suffice for a very large and dangerous assembly to collect."[5] Hume resolved that government should keep Dharalas "in awe," especially since they were forced to submit to "unsavoury plague measures." Ranchod probably would not have been surprised by Hume's analysis. It was continuous with British claims about the necessity of subjugating Dharalas. Ranchod would have maintained that the age of darkness should be ended, if not by him, then by someone else.

25 · THE AFTERMATH

It appears that Ranchod died in prison shortly after the appeal. There is no known report confirming this fact; instead, an official simply wrote "died" next to Ranchod's name in a copy of the 1899 issue of the court proceedings. However, even after Ranchod was arrested, British officials noted, his *patra* was still in circulation. It was reported that people were making copies and forwarding them to other villages. According to H. R. Hume, "wide-spread" rumors about Ranchod had traveled throughout Kheda district—well beyond the twenty-one villages—and into neighboring "foreign territories," a direct reference to princely states like Baroda, Cambay, and the Kanthas. As late as 1907, officials noted that versions of the Kashi *patra* were still in circulation in India: some may have provided the inspiration for other movements.[1] The convergence of the written word and oral culture helped to disseminate Ranchod's ideas beyond what the *bhagat* had imagined. Moreover, his kingship provided a way for peasants to contribute to the making of a political community and participate in the functions of statecraft. For most peasants it was evident that colonial rule would not end easily. The political future was unclear at the turn of the century.

PART TWO

26 · **POLITICS CONTINUED**

News of Ranchod's death probably circulated as widely as his message. There is no way of knowing how such information was received by his supporters and others who may have been inspired by his ideas, or even how his detractors in the locality may have interpreted his message of anticolonialism. Ranchod was aware that he was not alone in establishing a critique of colonial power and offering, at the turn of the century, an alternative political future. And officials knew that peasant movements had the potential to grow and harness wide support. In the words of Judge Leggatt, who convicted Ranchod for sedition, they "excite feelings of disaffection to Government."

Central to the ongoing debates in cities and villages throughout India was a concern about how the land and people should be governed. The circulation of ideas within agrarian society, for example, had conditioned the political culture of the countryside, especially concerning the ways in which individuals were thinking about the nature of the colonial state. The subsequent emergence of conflict had much to do with the fact that figures like Ranchod did not want to cede statecraft to the colonial authorities or allow elites like the Patidars to further establish their dominance. Ranchod's death did not signal the end of politics among Dharalas in the locality. Rather, other peasant movements would soon follow.

The second part of this book considers the continuation of peasant movements led by Dharalas in the first half of the twentieth century. However, writing such a history is not without problems, especially in relation to sources. Dharalas typically appeared in documents when officials became concerned about problems with law and order in the countryside. The attention of the colonial state at this time was turned to the emergent nationalist movement, which was viewed as a greater threat. Yet when Dharalas began organizing large meetings where peasants questioned the nature of colonialism and nationalism, the response from the authorities was quick and led to application of the Criminal Tribes Act.

What remained possible, in light of this and the accompanying increase in surveillance, were strikes and underground movements. However, Dharalas were also aware that open protests or attacks involving large numbers of Dharalas would be quickly stopped by the police or military. The colonial government had already demonstrated its power in how it dealt with Ranchod and his supporters. Evidence of later peasant movements that still remains in the official record is incomplete and fragmentary, especially concerning movements that occurred during the rise of mass nationalism. As a result, the histories of Dharala politics discussed in this part of the book appear fragmentary. I bring together a series of peasant movements that took place during a period of great transformation in colonial society as a way to show that Dharalas were fighting for greater access to the means of production within the agrarian economy. Equally, Dharalas were engaged in debates on the politics of identity, asserting claims for a political community which challenged the idea that all subjects of the British raj would become "Indians" in a post-colonial nation.

27 · AGE OF DARKNESS

The small world that Ranchod had left behind changed forever shortly after his death. In the years 1899 to 1901, nearly 20 percent of the agrarian population in Kheda district perished (approximately 155,257 individuals) in the most devastating famine to affect western India during the nineteenth century.[1] The summer monsoons had failed to deliver adequate rainwater throughout the region, especially in the British-controlled districts north of the Narmada River in Gujarat. Kheda, for instance, received only 6.05 inches of rain in 1899, compared to 30.63 inches the previous year; the districts of Ahmedabad, Bharuch, and Panchmahals experienced similar patterns.[2] For the government, the onset of the famine in late 1899, following the plague epidemic, signaled a further decline in the agrarian economy. Peasants had complained of a systematic decline in the availability of well water and stated that it was becoming difficult, if not impossible, to cultivate agricultural lands.[3] Crop failures were reported throughout the district, with officials recording a 55 percent decrease in the total output of crops between 1898 and 1900.[4] In addition, Kheda's cattle population was decimated, as 234,000 of the 418,000 cattle died in 1899 alone, the first year of the famine.[5]

Yet in the midst of such conditions, the government was determined to avoid a fiscal crisis by securing land revenue payments from peasants based on rates set in the mid-1890s. In December 1899, peasants began sending large numbers of petitions to the district collector complaining about their circumstances. The petitions were ignored on the grounds that they were copies of a "stereotyped form" and provided a generic description of famine conditions, rather than detailing the specific concerns facing each cultivator or village community.[6] A *mukhi* named Narotamdas Venidas and forty-five other villagers responded by writing to the viceroy and governor-general of India explaining their circumstances:

> Owing to the failure of rain last year[,] there has been a famine in our village. The kharif [monsoon] crop has totally failed[,] and the rabi [winter] crop is expected to be only about one anna in the rupee. Large numbers of

our cattle have perished[,] and [the] few that have survived are not likely to live long. The Government of Bombay [has] issued an order to recover the land assessment for the current year, but neither the rich nor the poor are able to pay it. We submitted petitions to the Collector and the Commissioner, Northern Division, praying for remission of the assessment, but without avail. We, therefore, pray that it may be ordered to be remitted and that the order may be communicated to the Mamlatdar of Mehmedabad.[7]

It is not known how the government responded to Narotamdas and the others. However, officials maintained that they would not grant remissions, believing that peasants had the resources to recover from a year or two of failed rains by using their capital reserves.[8] If necessary, peasants could borrow from moneylenders or simply sell their possessions to make their payments. Revenue officials traveled throughout the district in the early months of the famine to ensure that village headmen and accountants were making adequate collections. These officials did not hesitate to use threats or violence to extract payments when peasants resisted the revenue demands.[9] Within a few months after declaring the famine, the government realized that such efforts were futile. In May 1900, the collector reported that "there remains a very large number of cultivators, chiefly of the Dharala class, from whom it will be impossible to recover, and . . . the total realizations will not come up to the anticipations of Government."[10] And the following month, he noted that "coercive methods have now been practically stopped," as most peasants were "without means of immediate subsistence."[11]

Officials reported that the greatest impact of the famine was experienced by Dharala peasants, who simply forfeited their possessions and land and began wandering the countryside in search of food and water. In May 1900, the district collector reported that "the large majority of persons, who now swell the death-roll, are Dharalas, a caste of Kolis."[12] In response, the government created famine relief camps, where individuals could receive a daily wage in exchange for work.[13] Officials captured thousands of Dharalas and forcibly placed them in famine relief camps based on the government's policy of "compulsory detention of destitute persons."[14] Others arrived in these camps voluntarily, having no other options available to them.

A strict disciplinary regime was enforced in the camps, where individuals were required to submit to physically demanding public works projects, like the construction of roads, tanks, and canals.[15] Officials noted that most of the workers were "fatigued" and "starving" and were not familiar with the rigors of the projects. In addition, it was suggested that the workers' wages were insufficient to purchase adequate quantities of food. Large numbers of Dharalas died in these camps as a result of exhaustion and malnutrition, but others also perished from communicable diseases like cholera and dysentery. Many who survived the relief camps simply preferred to return to their respective villages during the famine as a way to escape the labor demands established by the government.[16]

While throughout the nineteenth century colonial officials had claimed that the Patidar-controlled villages of the Charotar tract were "immune" to famine, many Patidars were on the verge of complete fiscal collapse at this point. *Narwadars* had collectively filed petitions with the collector claiming that they had no resources to make land payments. Large numbers of families opted to sell their personal jewelry and household utensils as a way to avoid the famine relief camps.[17]

However, the government had a different strategy for dealing with many Patidars in the Charotar tract. Rather than forcing individuals to work, the government suspended land payments in some cases and allowed a payment deferral program. Government loans were granted for making investments in the means of production, such as purchasing cattle and constructing wells, with the hope of encouraging a recovery from the crisis.[18] Lands that had been abandoned by Dharalas during the famine, especially in the Mal tract of the district, were offered to Patidars following the earlier nineteenth-century policy of colonizing wastelands. Yet despite such incentives, there was a severe labor shortage throughout the area, especially as nearly seventy thousand Dharalas died at the end of the 1890s, and others abandoned their villages to go in search of food and water. As a way to counter the problem, many Patidars removed Dharalas from famine relief camps and forced them to work in their fields.[19] For the district collector, the famine had a positive outcome: "The Dharalas . . . changed for the better: it may be inferred that the discipline maintained on the works in 1901–1902 had done them good."[20] For Dharalas, the nightmare of the *kaliyug* continued.

28 · DADURAM

In 1901, a *bhagat* named Daduram arrived in the town of Dakore with his daughter, having come from the village of Chalali three miles from Chaklasi.[1] He may have traveled to Dakore in search of food and water like many other Dharalas, and it is possible that he was captured and placed in one of the famine relief camps in town (in Dakore alone there were more than 24,374 such workers).[2] However, Daduram may have arrived in Dakore for other reasons, such as to be with his teacher, a Brahmin priest, who resided in the town.[3] Apparently, Daduram met the priest, about whom nothing is recorded, on a visit to Dakore during one of the full moon festivals to honor Ranchodji. He soon became a disciple of this individual and began a study of religious texts.

The fact that Daduram was unable to read or write suggests another convergence between oral culture and the written word, in which the priest read the texts and Daduram learned to recite them from memory. But why was this significant for the priest and his disciple? Apparently the Brahmin was training Daduram to become a priest, or at least introducing him to practices that had long been inaccessible to Dharalas. Such practices were traditionally limited to Brahmins, who maintained the most sacred of texts in their possession. Most castes were not allowed to touch or even see these texts, let alone hear them.

The relationship with this priest appears to have led to a significant transition in Daduram's life: he stopped consuming alcohol, opium, and meat. To what extent Daduram attempted to adopt the customs, rituals, and ideology of his teacher, or Brahmins more generally remains unclear.[4] Yet Daduram was certainly not the only person in the region, or in this period, to make such changes. In the late nineteenth century, Vaishnava priests often adopted "pure" lifestyles as a way to gain respectability, not simply to emulate Brahmins, but also to argue for religious and political transformations for marginalized communities in agrarian society.[5]

Daduram constructed a temple in Dakore, where he began giving discourses on Dharala reform. Initially, these meetings attracted small numbers of individuals, but they quickly grew in size. By the time Daduram had attracted the attention of colonial officials, in 1906, it was reported that the gatherings were characterized by an "uproarious" and "enthusiastic" quality and often attracted up to several thousand individuals.[6] The district magistrate began an inquiry into Daduram's background to investigate whether he posed a threat to the stability of the countryside. Since Daduram was a *bhagat* who originally resided in the village of Chalali, the magistrate first assumed he had a connection with Ranchod. Chalali was only a short distance from Chaklasi and was among the twenty-one villages that had received one of Ranchod's *patras*. Ranchod had organized many *bhagats* from neighboring villages to participate in the activities in his *mandwa,* and it was plausible that Daduram had attended one or more of these gatherings. The magistrate's concerns became heightened when he learned that several Dharalas who had been arrested with Ranchod had recently completed their sentences and been released from prison. However, the magistrate was unable to establish any connection between Ranchod and Daduram, and he concluded, "I have had enquiries made whether Daduram took any part in that outbreak, but it doesn't appear that he did."[7]

Daduram began traveling to villages throughout the locality in order to spread his message of reform. He required that his disciples vow to stop drinking alcohol, eating meat, lying, and stealing.[8] Individuals who agreed to follow Daduram's reforms were given necklaces made of wooden beads from the sacred *tulsi* plant. However, it was reported that Daduram was often known to scrutinize and interrogate individuals wearing the necklace as a way to ensure that his disciples properly understood the reforms. (Ranchod had provided his disciples with similar necklaces.) Officials soon noted the proliferation of Daduram's necklaces throughout Kheda and parts of neighboring Ahmedabad district. Apparently, entire villages agreed to Daduram's pledges, and they were identified by officials as "communities of necklace-wearers."[9] However, the district magistrate noted that Daduram did not simply accept all Dharalas in his reform movement: "He is not indiscriminate with villages any more than with individuals: he will ban a whole village and refuse to initiate a single member of it until they give proof of general amendment."[10]

Daduram's meetings were carefully planned affairs. Apparently he personally traveled from village to village to invite individuals to attend a function at a select location, usually a village with a large Dharala population. Thousands of peasants would travel from villages far and near to assemble for a couple of days at gatherings that resembled festivals with music and *bhajans*. There were other attractions as well for Dharalas: Daduram served unlimited amounts of food on these occasions while publicly discussing and debating issues about the dominance of local elites and Indian nationalists. He required that peasants contribute money to fund the meals based on their financial resources, but in many instances Dharalas were too poor to pay. This was to be expected, especially following a devastating famine and the ongoing period of scarcity, drought, and disease. Any surplus funds that remained after a meeting were simply set aside for the construction of Daduram's temple in Dakore.

By 1906, Daduram had assumed the leadership of one of the largest and most influential peasant movements in the locality. While Daduram may not have formally declared himself a king (or at least colonial officials never noted that he had), he functioned like one in providing charity and assuming the role of authority to protect Dharalas from starvation following a period of crisis, something that the colonial state had neglected to do during the famine and plague years.

29 · **SURVEILLANCE**

Daduram relied upon the local oral culture for spreading his message about Dharala reform. He was a composer of *bhajans* recited at all the gatherings, which quickly circulated from village to village. The district magistrate noted that many disciples had learned Daduram's *bhajans* and were introducing them to other Dharalas in the locality: "Daduram's propaganda also [has] spread with growing rapidity. . . . His necklaces are to be met anywhere."[1]

Many Dharalas who had received Ranchod's *patra* probably also came to know about Daduram, and some Dharalas likely accepted both leaders. The district magistrate may be correct in claiming that Daduram did not have any direct connection with Ranchod and his disciples, but it is unlikely that Daduram was unaware of Ranchod. He probably knew Dharalas who had participated in Ranchod's procession or battle, and probably had an opinion about Ranchod's claims regarding authority and legitimate government. However, these are speculations. The oral culture of Daduram's world (and Ranchod's) allowed for the quick transmission of information, but this culture also made it difficult, if not impossible, for elites and officials to understand the nature of Daduram's ideas and sentiments. This strategy allowed specific thoughts to reach the intended audience and, at the same time, shielded their content from intelligence agents trying to document information for the government. Hence, based on surveillance reports, the district magistrate concluded that Daduram was a "moral teacher . . . with the object of converting his whole tribe to better ways."[2] He observed that "Daduram's doctrine and methods alike, in short, bear a remarkable likeness to those of Evangelical Christianity, though he has never come under Missionary influence. . . . In other respects his gatherings are like Salvation Army or Revivalist Meetings."[3]

Daduram's message and methods were more acceptable to the government than Ranchod's. He neither carried weapons that threatened law and order in the countryside, nor declared the end of the British raj.

He advocated social and religious reform among peasants who had long posed a problem for the colonial government. In fact, the magistrate was deeply impressed by what he called Daduram's "moral teachings" and claimed that Daduram was "perfectly loyal and non-political."[4]

By May 1908, the district magistrate had set up an intelligence network to monitor Daduram's everyday activities. The example of Ranchod's movement had convinced the magistrate of the need for a preventative measure such as this. With the increased surveillance, the magistrate could report on Daduram's habits and appearance to his superiors while also commenting on Daduram's movements or how he spent his money.

The magistrate, for example, knew that Daduram had been a "hard drinker" for many years, and he commented that Daduram had "a very good face."[5] He secured a plan of the layout of Daduram's temple in Dakore and was aware of Daduram's movements within Kheda district. However, the magistrate became suspicious of Daduram once the latter began claiming supernatural powers. He was skeptical of Daduram's miracles and linked them to "the hot weather" and "excessive *ganja* smoking."[6] At this point, the magistrate noted that Daduram's appearance had changed for the worse and attributed this to the negative influences of a "gang of Brahman and Bania [merchant] parasites," who, he claimed, were actually responsible for the "bogus" and "wretched" miracles.[7] He was also concerned that Daduram was performing rituals that resembled "Brahmanical formalities." However, it is unclear why he raised such objections. In addition, it is not possible to determine whether one of the Brahmins associating with Daduram at this point was his teacher, or whether Daduram was in fact engaging with other priests at this point.

Despite his concerns, the magistrate maintained that "[Daduram's] influence . . . is still entirely to the good." He added, "When he came to bid me goodbye the other day, he produced a bag of silver and poured it out on my table as a present! A man who combines so much ignorance with so much influence is well worth watching and attaching to our side."[8] A few weeks later, on June 5, 1908, the magistrate's opinion of Daduram changed dramatically, when new surveillance suggested that Daduram was frequently intoxicated. The magistrate declared: "His day is over, but in his day he has done good."

30 · THE POLITICS OF FOOD

The district magistrate's assessment of Daduram's demise was premature.[1] Official reports from neighboring areas claimed that Daduram's movement was rapidly spreading beyond Kheda and into the villages of neighboring districts and princely states.[2] In fact, it was also reported that other peasant communities had been influenced by Daduram's ideas and had started similar reform movements of their own.[3] News of Daduram's activities became a topic of discussion within the emergent public sphere in Gujarat.[4] Reports claimed that Daduram was responsible for "purifying" and "uplifting" Dharalas, especially by encouraging peasants to give up the consumption of alcohol.[5] Daduram's ability to organize meals for every individual who attended his gatherings, even meetings lasting a couple days, became a curiosity for colonial officials and the local media. On May 7, 1908, the *Gujarati Punch*, a newspaper published in Ahmedabad, reported that a sadhu named Daduram was performing miracles in Pasataj village by "feed[ing] multitudes of people with the quantity of food which he has got in a small vessel and which does not become exhausted."[6]

Daduram's special powers were very specific and centered on the idea of providing unlimited food to peasants who had survived a plague epidemic and famine. Droughts, scarcities, and famines were typically considered to be signs of "bad government or no government."[7] As a matter of principle, the rulers of a territory were expected to suspend the collection of land revenue during a period of crisis and provide their peasants with food for subsistence. Yet the colonial state opted to forego such customary practices, despite the district collector's claims that "the worst off are absolutely without food[;] . . . the best off have a little grain left, but only enough to feed for a month or two."[8] By serving food in the aftermath of a crisis, Daduram assumed the responsibilities of a proper government or king, which explains his popularity among peasants who had lost access to their means of production and subsistence. It is possible that the miracle described in the *Gujarati Punch* reflected a belief that

Vaishnava priests, or even village *bhagats,* possessed the ability to use miracles to help the poor.[9] The narrative of Daduram's miracle bears a striking resemblance to one depicted in Jan Gopal's seventeenth-century text titled *Life Story of Dadu Dayal:*

> The Andhiya garden was like a bazar,
> crowds lined up to see Dadu.
> To the beat of drums they sang his praises,
> everybody was able to see Dadu.
> Realizing food-supplies were getting short,
> Madhav Kani informed Svamiji [Dadu],
> who replied: "Do not worry
> know that the Indweller is present."
> Plates full of food were brought
> and Svamiji distributed the meals of Hari [Krishna].
> *Sacred offerings were collected in vessels,*
> *and the saints witnessed an endless supply.*[10]

It is difficult to know if there was a direct connection between the two stories, but this one suggests similarities between Daduram and the sixteenth-century saint Dadu Dayal (who was also called Daduram).[11] Daduram may have been aware of Dadu Dayal's life story and may have attempted to replicate his power to provide food. For centuries, Dadu Dayal's disciples had promoted Vaishnava principles of equality and social reform among peasants in western and central India. It is possible that Daduram was influenced by the contemporary followers of Dadu Dayal and adopted his name, or it is simply a coincidence that the two shared a name and adopted a similar religious ethos of providing feasts for peasants. Although, there are no complete answers to these concerns, both individuals gained authority, in part through the distribution of food.

In Daduram's case, there was an additional dimension to the food issue that related to the context of the colonial economy. The food problem had worsened in western India with the application of the Mahua Act of 1892.[12] The mahua flower was a staple food consumed by poor peasants during the summer months of April and May, especially during periods of scarcity, and it was also the key ingredient for the production of a popular country liquor.[13] The new legislation imposed restrictions on the cultivation and collection of the mahua flower by peasants as a way to prevent the production and distribution of the country liquor. By creating greater restrictions on peasants, the government established control of the alcohol market in the countryside and was able to generate revenue from an excise tax on alcoholic beverages. In many instances peasant distilleries were destroyed by officials and their liquor agents; in others, peasants were arrested or beaten for collecting the flower. Most peasants found the government-produced alcohol simply too expensive and refused to pay the new levies. But more significant, the act worsened the food problem in western India by making it illegal for peasants to consume mahua.

Daduram's decision to give up alcohol took place after the implementation of the Mahua Act. He may have decided to stop drinking alcohol as a direct consequence of the Mahua Act and the legislation's impact on Dharalas. He may have even decided to distribute food as a way to assist those who could no longer rely upon mahua for subsistence. While no direct articulation by Daduram on this issue is recorded, it is worth considering whether Daduram was protesting restrictions on the customary uses of mahua and the controls imposed on alcohol. In fact, the district magistrate had noted that the Barber community, which was influenced in part by Daduram's ideas, also had stopped drinking alcohol.[14] He observed that "they can no longer buy the cheap liquor which [Dharalas] used to distil."[15]

The district magistrate's initial celebration of Daduram's prohibition on alcohol became muted when he learned that Daduram and other Dharalas consumed large amounts of ganja (marijuana). He stated, "It is the one vice that [Daduram] permits himself."[16] For the magistrate, Daduram's smoking habits were immoral and inconsistent with the idea of not drinking alcohol. Yet the Indian Hemp Drugs Commission of 1893–94 claimed that ganja was preferred by poor peasants in Kheda as a consequence of their material conditions and the increases in alcohol prices.[17] The change in stimulant-consumption patterns—from alcohol to ganja—in Kheda were attributed to the government's new control of the production and distribution of alcohol. But Daduram's desire to consume marijuana may have had nothing to do with the increased costs of alcohol. In fact, Desaibhai Kalidas, a public prosecutor, had testified to the Drugs Commission that "in Dakore almost all the sadhus . . . smoke ganja."[18] Daduram certainly may have been one of these individuals: he may have simply enjoyed the intoxication, or he may have used ganja as part of a *bhagat* ritual. Even Ranchod had claimed at one point that he "smoked ganja" with his disciples.[19]

31 · "THE DIGNITY OF LABOR"

The transformations in everyday life articulated by Daduram's popularity among Dharalas and other peasants can be further understood by examining his reform message on the question of labor rights. This theme was common among Vaishnava reformers throughout India. Daduram wanted to make Dharala labor more respectable, especially in the aftermath of a demographic catastrophe. The decline in the Dharala population meant there were fewer peasants who could work on Patidar lands in Kheda, but equally it signaled a moment of "peasant freedom" for Dharalas.[1] Peasant mobility increased in this period, as many individuals simply left the agrarian sector for higher paying jobs in the mills of Nadiad and Ahmedabad.[2] With the ensuing scarcity in labor supply, Patidars were forced to negotiate with the surviving Dharalas for the types of services they would be willing to perform, and to end the existing surplus-extraction relationship of imposing levies and demanding gratuitous services. Dharalas also demanded new contractual agreements for payments in cash that reflected the transition from customary patron-client bonds to the commodification of labor power.

For Daduram, this historical conjuncture marked the end of the Patidar ability to use extra-economic coercion to control Dharala mobility and labor services. But it also allowed Dharalas to redefine physical labor on their own terms rather than on those dictated by elites.[3] Daduram argued for a total ban on menial and domestic service in Patidar homes and demanded an increase in wages for agricultural laborers.[4] In addition, he proclaimed that peasants should accept only cash for their services, not payments in-kind. Daduram's message was influential, as many Dharalas stopped working in low-status jobs, and wages for agricultural laborers increased by 25–33 percent in 1907–08.[5] District Collector A. Chuckerbutty noted that this period marked a transformation in the wages set according to "caste rules" (unfortunately, he did not explain the nature of these "rules"). He concluded, "The dignity of labor is beginning to be acknowledged."[6] Not surprisingly, the district magistrate reported some resistance from local elites: "Most Patidars and men of substance welcome and countenance the movement[,] . . . but they are uneasy at the prohibition of menial service."[7]

32 · THE BARAIYA CONFERENCE MOVEMENT

In 1906, a small group of educated men, who were apparently influenced by Daduram's activities, founded an organization known as the Baraiya Conference Movement (BCM).[1] Garbadbhai Motabhai Parmar, the head of the organization, initially held informal meetings with Dharalas in villages to discuss topics related to caste identity and reform. Parmar and others in the organization identified themselves as Baraiyas rather than Dharalas. This was a shift away from a Dharala identity that government had associated with the characteristics of "criminality," "indolence," and "thriftlessness," and it simultaneously reclaimed a respectable status for Baraiyas in local society. Officials like the district magistrate already had acknowledged Baraiyas as the "highest class of Dharalas," but the BCM was interested in reinventing a Baraiya identity that celebrated its past. The organization believed that Baraiyas needed to adopt customs, practices, rituals, and ideologies that reflected their position as Kshatriyas— the much celebrated martial caste of warriors, princes, and kings.[2]

The BCM published a monthly journal, *Baraiya Hittechu and Kshatriya Vijaya*, which included discussions of official caste rules and guidelines; it also proclaimed that Baraiyas were the "original Kshatriyas of Gujarat," and that they needed to "reconquer the lost status."[3] The organization's first formal meetings, held in April 1909, were well-attended events with twelve hundred to fifteen hundred Baraiyas.[4] One of the primary functions of these early conferences was to instruct fellow Baraiyas about the changes in caste rules while advocating reforms within the community. Pamphlets were published and circulated among those who attended the meetings to encourage discussion. Interestingly, the district magistrate claimed that the police and judicial authorities had actually used coercive tactics to force the peasants from more than three hundred villages to attend the meetings; however, it is unclear why these officials were interested in using draconian methods to ensure the organization's success.[5] British officials described the BCM as an "organised and secular movement in favour of social elevation" that strictly regulated its followers.[6]

According to local officials, Daduram denounced the BCM and objected to the claim that Baraiyas were Kshatriyas. He considered it "preposterous and somewhat inflammatory," and he "repudiated" the organization.[7] It is possible that he rejected it because it welcomed the patronage and financial contributions of local Patidars.[8] For Daduram, this symbolized a continuity of the patron-client bonds that he was contesting. Daduram also opposed the idea of claiming a higher caste status, especially since he was promoting ideals of equality and social reform within specific Vaishnava traditions, which were opposed to the caste system. Colonial officials stated that the BCM had achieved local prominence "partly because the ground [was] well prepared by Daduram," but they noted a fundamental difference: the BCM was interested in forcing "the whole community into line through its caste-organization, wielding powers of fine and excommunication."[9]

Daduram stood out as a peasant leader who had influenced public opinion on questions of everyday life. His ideas and strategies had been well received by peasants and elites and helped to shape the dialogues and debates of his world. In fact, he may have forced the BCM to reconsider its own ideas about caste reform.

33 · CONTESTING NATIONALISM

In 1908, Daduram also engaged in public protests against the emergent nationalist movement in western India led by the political extremist Bal Gangadhar Tilak.[1] There is no explanation of why Daduram chose to challenge Tilak, but it signaled a new direction in his role as a public figure. In the 1890s, Tilak had successfully organized large Hindu processions using symbols from local folklore that attracted large sections of the agrarian population.[2] In the years between 1905 and 1908, he had achieved national prominence for leading large anticolonial protests and strikes, but also for harnessing a pan-Hindu movement in western India.[3] However, Tilak was a socially conservative Brahmin who opposed any politics that questioned the structure of the caste system.[4]

Colonial officials interpreted Daduram's protests against Tilak as a sign of his ignorance and irrationality as a peasant, but stated that it was unclear what motivated him to take up the issue. According to the district magistrate, Daduram "girt up his loins, mounted his pony, and rode all around the Charotar in the wet denouncing Tilak and his admirers."[5] Daduram's critique probably originated in a popular belief in western India that nationalists like Tilak promoted conservative, high-caste politics and wanted to establish their dominance in the countryside. Daduram had already opposed the Baraiya Conference Movement's claims for higher caste status, and he may have been active in challenging Tilak for similar reasons. However, Daduram's response to Tilak was likely influenced by the reception of his nationalist ideals within Kheda district. Tilak was celebrated as a "popular hero" in schools and had acquired a significant following among many Patidars.[6] Although, Daduram's position on the topic of caste is not clear, he may have opposed Tilak for promoting the continuity of caste hierarchies that had historically marginalized Dharalas.[7]

34 · PEASANT FREEDOM

Daduram died suddenly in 1909, and it is difficult to map out the details of the peasant movement after that point. His name did not enter the official record again, but this was to be expected. The district magistrate concluded that Daduram's movement had ceased to exist after his death, claiming that "Daduram has no lieutenants or apostles and no Elisha."[1] Officials simply lost interest in Daduram's legacies and turned their attention to more pressing concerns, those that posed a direct threat to the functioning of the agrarian economy.[2]

In the aftermath of the demographic crisis in Kheda district at the turn of the century, in which nearly 20 percent of the agricultural labor population perished, peasants began demanding greater rights to their means of production and a transformation of the political order in the countryside. Peasants pressed for a radical increase in compensation for their labor power, rejected menial occupations, and wanted new terms for land possession. For Patidar landholders, freedom for Dharala tenants, servants, and agricultural laborers from traditional patron-client bonds posed a direct threat to the functioning of the agrarian economy.[3] It was no longer possible to squeeze poor Dharala peasants in order to extract a surplus to help cover the revenue payments owed to the government. Officials noted in this period that village headmen who had attempted to use extra-economic coercion or demanded the payment of informal levies were frequently attacked and murdered by Dharalas.[4] For a state facing a fiscal crisis, violence against its revenue-collecting agents, especially in the most highly taxed agricultural tract in the Bombay Presidency, became an issue of great administrative concern.

35 · POLICE REORGANIZATION

By the late nineteenth century, an informal system of surveillance was already in existence at the village level: *mukhis* were responsible for supervising "bad characters" in the village by "writ[ing] up registers" with the names of individuals viewed as threats to the district's stability.[1] The headmen were also required to ensure regular roll calls for miscreants and arrange for village watchmen to go on night rounds.[2] As the colonial state simply did not have the resources to monitor every village in the countryside, it had legislated the Village Police Act of 1867 to force village officials to participate in the state's attempt to create stability in the countryside.[3] The system, however, was not without problems, since the *mukhis* were considered inefficient and unreliable in executing their police duties. Some *mukhis* were viewed as collaborators with criminals, and were believed to have often "assisted bands of dacoits" (bandits) or "misled the police instead of helping them."[4] Other *mukhis* simply did not take roll call with regularity or monitor the movements of select individuals.

While officials declared village policing a "farce,"[5] they maintained that the village headmen were "useful" to the functioning of the district police in Kheda: "[The *mukhis* are] no doubt inefficient[,] but at the same time it must not be forgotten that without their cooperation the District Police would be paralyzed in detecting offences."[6] The informal system of surveillance under the jurisdiction of the village headman was considered insufficient, and proposals were introduced for granting the district police legal authority to "control and watch movements of bad characters."[7] In 1909, the commissioner of the Northern Division of the Bombay Presidency declared that "special measures for the repression of crime in this district may be necessary before long."[8]

Police posts with armed constables were established in Kheda district with the intention of monitoring peasants and punishing the village police when necessary. The police posts provided a temporary solution to curbing the crime rate, but they were unable to prevent the rise of train

robberies and the organized Dharala raids on villages.[9] The *mukhis'* inef-
fectiveness in monitoring peasants raised concerns about the future of the
institution. After the murders of some village headmen, officials were
forced to reassess the district-level policy on crime.[10] In addition the
government was also interested in protecting the Bombay-Baroda and
Central India Railway line as a way to generate profits from the sale of
trees in Kheda district.[11] The Department of Forestry had sanctioned the
annual sale of five hundred tons of wood from land newly confiscated
from peasants who lived near the railway lines.[12] The problem, however,
was that many Dharalas who had apparently lost access to their means
of production as a result of government land policies had begun robbing
the trains and further threatening the rule of law. The violent attacks
raised questions about the economy and the stability of the locality that
led to the reorganization of the police.

In 1911, the inspector general of police introduced new reform measures for policing the district, which included the addition of two subinspectors and sixty constables (and reduced the number of head constables by ten), with the largest restructuring taking place in the Charotar
tract.[13] As a consequence of fiscal constraints, the government opted to
make policing more efficient by opening outposts and placing policemen
in sensitive areas of the district, rather than substantially increasing the
total number of staff.[14]

In less than a year, however, the reorganization of the district police
was declared a failure, as "serious crimes" continued to be perpetrated.
The district superintendent of police stated that "the [1911] police reorganization scheme, while it aimed at better distribution of the existing
strength, could bring about no improvement because the total strength
was not increased, whereas a considerably increased staff was and still is
a real necessity."[15] Another reason for the failure, according to police officials, was the "injudicious handling" of "true cases" by district policemen.[16] The prevalence of police violence against sections of the population, and torture of individuals, had been an issue of great concern in the
district since the late nineteenth century.[17] While the reorganization
scheme was intended to make policing more efficient, the outcome
demonstrated that internal police corruption was rife and inhibited the legal processes in the district. The frequency of peasant raids and robberies
intensified the problem, leading officials to declare that all Dharalas residing in Kheda were culpable for the crimes against the state.

36 · THE CRIMINAL TRIBES ACT

In 1911, the entire Dharala population of nearly 250,000 individuals in Kheda district was declared a criminal tribe under Act III of 1911, the Criminal Tribes Act.[1] The original CTA of 1871 had been applied in parts of India for the purposes of registering, monitoring, and controlling nomadic communities in order to convert them into settled peasants.[2] In the case of Dharalas in Kheda district, the new legislation had a different purpose. It was not meant to direct Dharalas away from any peripatetic tendencies that posed law and order problems for colonial officials, because by the mid-nineteenth century most Dharalas had already settled and become small peasant cultivators. In fact, one official commented that "criminal tribes in Kheda are different from the rest of India, in that they are not nomadic and rarely leave their own district."[3]

Rather, the CTA provided a legal means of controlling and disciplining Dharalas at a time when peasants were not only demanding labor and tenure rights but also disrupting commerce on the railway lines and using violence against the revenue-collecting village headmen. Sections 26 and 27 of the CTA authorized every village headman and watchman, and "every owner and occupier of land," to monitor "any persons who may reasonably be suspected of belonging to any criminal tribe."[4] Furthermore, the failure to inform police at the nearest police station about suspicious characters became "an offence punishable under . . . the Indian Penal Code."[5]

Although the act criminalized the entire Dharala population in the district, the CTA was initially enforced in fifty-five select villages, the majority of which were Patidar-controlled villages in the Charotar tract, close to the railway line in the *talukas* of Nadiad and Anand.[6] Interestingly, not all the villages were considered to be threats to the stability of the district, and in fact some villages were selected for extra enforcement because they were "good." Officials wanted to "induce forms of communal punishment" by forcing peasants to attend daily roll call in villages that did *not* have a crime problem.[7] By punishing innocent peasants for the actions of others, it was thought, they would resolve the crime problem internally, within the community, through the traditional pressure of caste norms.

The registration process was first introduced on December 18, 1911.[8] It required individuals to have their fingerprints recorded and to fill out a standardized form with basic details such as name and age, plus their caste affiliation and the "reason for registration."[9] There was a paradox within the system of registering criminal tribes. The argument put forth by colonial officials for implementing the CTA was based on the communal nature of criminality in the district, or what they labeled "collective criminality." Crime was committed by the entire community of Dharalas, and not by its individual members. Hence, all Dharalas were complicit in crimes committed by even one individual and the entire community must be held responsible.[10] But the actual process of registering criminal tribes involved individualizing each member of the community to make him or her "identifiable" and "controllable."[11]

Colonial administrators saw the Dharalas' propensity for crime as a consequence of a poor work ethic that allowed for "leisure time": if the rhythms of everyday life could be monitored and controlled, then the crime rate would decrease.[12] Only select individual officially registered as members of the criminal tribe were required to attend *hajri* (roll call) twice daily: at sunrise and at eight o'clock in the evening. They could no longer travel outside the boundaries of their respective villages without a registered pass authorized by the *mukhi*. To ensure that these individuals were complying, *mukhis* could perform random searches, especially at night.

There appear to have been mixed opinions about how aggressively to implement the new law. Its application was not limited to individuals, but extended to the family and village community. Women and children were not exempt from the registration process or the daily roll calls, even though public opinion on this issue "consider[ed] the application of the CTA to women degrading."[13] And, it was believed that both boys and girls of marriageable age would have difficulty in finding partners, as the stigma of attending roll call had created a group of social outcasts. Dharala men also protested that, "in having their thumb-impressions taken for registration purposes[,] their women had to be touched by strange men."[14] In justifying the position of the administration, A. Chuckerbutty, the district magistrate of Kheda in 1912, stated that "women should not be exempted[;] though they don't commit crimes, they serve as agents of disposing stolen material. . . . Exemption of families can not happen[,] because in a district like Kheda [it is] extremely difficult to find who is law abiding and who is not."[15]

By 1914 marriage patterns in the district had already changed: J. Ghosal, the new district magistrate, acknowledged that "no one of a respectable [Dharala] family would give their daughters in marriage to families whose members are on the *hajri* list."[16] The potential implications for the family life of those on the registration list were severe. In addition to requiring children to attend roll call, colonial officials proposed forcibly removing children from their families and placing them in schools. It was argued that "this removal of children ought to have a great deterrent effect[,] . . . [and] it is desirable[,] if this method is to be adopted[,] to remove the children as far as possible from the neighbourhood of their parents or family."[17] In other instances, officials such as E. E. Turner, the district superintendent of police in 1913, proposed removing entire families and "tak[ing] them far away from their home, where they would have little influence on forty per cent of the district population."[18]

Colonial administrators were vexed with the daily problems of gathering information about local society. Peasants maintained silence and were simply unwilling to cooperate with police officials investigating problems in a given village. Intimidation by *dacoits* was one important reason for the silence. In fact, informants were brutally attacked and killed in many instances for offering information to the police.[19] In other cases, silence served as a collective weapon against the indiscriminate colonial policing practices, leading the commissioner of the Northern Division to claim that "this co-operation is denied to the police in Kheda in a degree unknown in other parts of the Presidency."[20] Colonial officials expected individuals, who technically were criminals by association, to offer information on other community members. But since punishments were applied to the community rather than the individual, those providing information were unlikely to sacrifice their own well-being for the benefit of the government.

Police officials viewed villagers' silence as an admission of complicity in crime. Collective silence became collective guilt. For example, in cases where a member of a criminal tribe was indicted for a serious offense, such as murder, and information about the crime was suppressed, then the village's entire population was placed on *hajri*.[21] Furthermore, for colonial officials, the question of whether villagers were unwilling or actually unable to provide information about crimes became superfluous, as Chapter VIII of the Criminal Procedure Code allowed the police to arrest individuals without evidence. In 1917, A. C. J. Bailey, Kheda's district superintendent of police stated that "the Magistracy should vary accordingly their requirements as regards proof of bad characters and not insist on the amount of evidence which might be desirable in other places."[22] Guilt had acquired a new meaning: since an entire community could be held accountable for the actions of a single individual, the main objective for colonial officials was to identify the criminal's community identity.

Chaklasi, the village at the center of Ranchod's movement in 1898, experienced the most extensive application of the CTA in Kheda district.[23] Although it was not explicitly stated in official correspondence, the specter of Dharala peasant defiance in Chaklasi apparently prompted the high degree of surveillance in the village. Ranchod and ten of his supporters had been prosecuted for crimes under the Indian Penal Code in 1898;[24] according to the CTA, all Dharalas in Chaklasi were culpable for Ranchod's movement against the state. Consequently, the entire population of five thousand Dharalas was officially registered in Chaklasi; two thousand were forced to attend roll call.[25]

Typically, *hajri* was held at the *chora* (village center); however, because Chaklasi was spread out, several sites had to be established to facilitate the *hajri*. Some Dharalas, whose agricultural fields were located on the outer boundaries of the village, were forced to walk two miles to attend. Headmen often waited for all the Dharalas to arrive before beginning the roll call, leading officials to complain that "agriculturalists have . . . to waste hours waiting."[26] G. K. Parekh, in a report on the working of the CTA in Kheda, provides further details on the loss of time: "They go to the chora at about 6 P.M., and the hajri is not taken till 9 P.M. Most of these people are detained at the chora for nearly three hours, and there is much time lost in going from the field to the chora and return. So a man loses on average from four to five hours daily in complying with the hajri requirement."[27] The *hajri* had a direct negative effect on the village economy, because the rhythms of daily work patterns changed. Peasants were not able to graze their cattle effectively or to irrigate agricultural lands properly.[28] Other Dharalas either lost jobs as servants or were forced to take reduced wages because of the long periods of absence resulting from the *hajri* process.[29]

In places where registration and surveillance were not implemented, Patidars became interested in expanding the scope of the CTA. The unintended consequence of the act, however, was an increase in the exploitation of Dharala labor: dominance acquired a new face in the countryside.

The threat of registering Dharalas who refused to comply with orders to work as servants or agricultural laborers provided a new way to threaten peasants and to extract a surplus from the village population. For example, the Patidars of one village, with the support of the headman, circulated a petition to district officials requesting that their village be included on the *hajri* list. After an official investigation, it was revealed that the Dharalas of the village were considered "harmless," but that the headman and the Patidars wanted to use *hajri* as a way to control Dharalas in their village.[30]

37 · UNDERGROUND ACTIVITIES

One of the outcomes of the Criminal Tribes Act was a series of migrations from villages in Kheda district to other parts of the British territory and Baroda State.[1] The quickest way for Dharalas to escape their criminal classification was to take up residence in one of the neighboring princely states, where the CTA did not apply.[2] In other instances, Dharalas from villages where the CTA was rigorously enforced opted to move to another village within the district that was not subject to registrations and roll calls, or even into other British-controlled districts where Dharalas were not classified as a criminal tribe.[3] The latter options could work only if the peasants were able to evade the notice of colonial officials.

The lands outside of Kheda's boundary initially provided refuge for the migrants, especially as many Dharalas had some kinship ties with others outside the district who could provide assistance and a place to hide. However, the government imposed a new policy that provided legal means to formally force escaped Dharalas back into the district.[4] An agreement was struck with the authorities of neighboring Baroda State that permitted the official return of registered criminals: Baroda police officials, supplied with a list of registered criminals from officials in Kheda, were authorized to enter specified villages with the intention of capturing the migrants.[5]

While the CTA was intended to rid the district of criminal activity, many Dharalas who opted to live outside of British jurisdiction had gone underground and began participating in organized crime—raids, robberies, and attacks—that not only brought hundreds of Dharalas together to contest local power but also posed further problems for the colonial state. The CTA made certain that Dharalas were subject to surveillance and repression, and peasants could no longer have *bhajan mandlis* (groups who sing devotional songs) and public meetings in the form popularized by Daduram. Ultimately, the government resolved that any political advances made by the peasant movements had to be reversed to ensure that Patidars could control the means of production in the agrarian economy.

38 · "MY LAND CAMPAIGN"

In 1914, District Collector Jyotsnanath Ghosal began an aggressive program to suppress crime in Kheda. He acknowledged the problems of police corruption, especially at the village level, and proposed creating a "more workable system of regulations" that would control criminal tribes.[1] At the center of Ghosal's agenda, which he called "my land campaign," was a plan to colonize and transform parts of the district that he identified as wilderness or wasteland.[2] He argued that Dharalas who had committed crimes and who wanted to evade the application of the Criminal Tribes Act were living in parts of the Mal tract in the Thasra and Kapadvanj *talukas* that were accessible only to "criminals and a few wild animals."[3] These were the same areas that had troubled colonial authorities when Koli chieftains were attacking British-controlled territories in Gujarat at the beginning of the nineteenth century.

Ghosal began the campaign by having forest contractors cut several thousand babul trees, thereby clearing large areas of land. He argued that Dharala hideouts would be exposed and that the newly opened land could be cultivated to generate additional revenue for the government. Ghosal was applying tactics used by early colonial officials in forested areas where tribals and peasants often hid to avoid arrest.[4] In the process, Ghosal provided special incentives to Patidars to settle the newly opened areas, explaining that he was following the "policy of giving out large waste areas to well-to-do agriculturalists for cultivation."[5] He invited "Patidar experts" to test and analyze the soil and provided a special lease for Dadubhai Desai, a Patidar landlord and prominent politician from Nadiad, to pursue cotton cultivation experiments.[6] (Interestingly, during the 1930s, Desai actively led nationalist politics in the locality as the president of the Kheda District Congress Committee.) Initially, eight hamlets were established with approximately 550 peasants, but a total of 82,051 acres was eventually distributed.[7] Ghosal wanted to ensure the success of the newly opened territory by reserving small areas of each village for "local demands," presumably so that peasants could have access to common land. Further, in order to maximize cultivation, he guaranteed that peasants would have sufficient grazing land based on the number of cattle in their possession.

The land campaign, which brought in an additional Rs. 176,075, quickly accomplished the goal of increasing annual revenue for the government.[8] Moreover, Ghosal pointed out, the newly colonized lands had "miles and miles of undulating crop with new hamlets scattered all over instead of the wilderness impossible alike for horse and man."[9] He expected that the new Patidar settlers would inculcate a work ethic in local Dharalas by providing proper training to cultivate the land. However, this was not to be. Despite the transformation of the landscape, the plan of eradicating criminal activity among Dharalas proved ineffective, leading Ghosal to argue for stricter enforcement of the CTA to further restrict the mobility of Dharalas.

39 · THE LABOR STRIKE

On September 17, 1916, a number of Dharalas from villages in the Thasra and Kapadvanj *talukas* met in the village of Fagwel to discuss the colonization of wasteland by the new Patidar settlers, who were called *lotwallahs*.[1] Two central issues were raised at the meeting that directly affected the Dharala population. First, land that had been used as communal property in the locality had been permanently handed over to the settlers by the Bombay government. Second, Dharalas were expected to work as agricultural laborers for the *lotwallahs* in the opening up of the wasteland. According to District Collector Jyotsnanath Ghosal, the Dharalas "were very much put out at all the waste lands being given away[,] as it deprived them of their . . . profits from such land."[2] These Dharalas typically had supplemented their income by selling grass and natural fertilizers collected there, in addition to generating revenue by allowing herdsmen from neighboring districts to graze their animals—cattle, sheep, and camels—on the land. For Dharalas the problem was further exacerbated by the idea that colonial officials no longer viewed their use of the land as legitimate.

As a way to resist colonial land policies, Dharala peasants formed alliances with other peasants, workers, and local landholders who feared losing their means of subsistence to the Patidars. All agreed to boycott the Patidar *lotwallahs*: "They ruled that no one should work for the [Patidars] and that no carpenters, blacksmiths, barbers, et cetera, should keep any connection with them."[3] The primary objective of the boycott was to push out all the *lotwallahs* who had recently arrived to take advantage of government incentives.

The labor strike against the *lotwallahs*, which had initially raised concerns particular to the wasteland in the Mal tract, spread rapidly throughout the district and to neighboring areas, incorporating a wider spectrum of political demands as it spread. Within a few weeks, laborers in about 240 villages had stopped working, forcing officials to worry about the impact of this movement on the agrarian economy of Kheda.[4]

The government began introducing new agricultural laborers into the Mal tract as a way to break the strike, but this strategy was unsuccessful. Ghosal reported that "agriculture began to suffer[,] as the imported labor was not enough to cope with the situation."[5] The government also adopted a second strategy: namely, it prevented Dharalas from generating any revenue by selling grass or fertilizers. This action produced the desired result, as Dharalas agreed to negotiate with the Patidars when, as noted by Ghosal, "the loss of wages began to have an effect."[6]

The strike lasted nearly a month and affected almost half the villages in the district, leading the collector to state that it "was fairly well organized and threatened at one time to be a serious affair."[7] Later in the year, a second strike emerged at Naika village in Matar *taluka,* spreading to two neighboring villages. The government's response was quick and powerful with the implementation of "strict measures," leading to the rapid "collapse" of the movement.[8] Once the government had imposed interventionist policies ensuring that peasants could no longer have an income during the strikes, the movement came to a quick end. In addition, new police stations were opened to protect the new settlers, further ensuring that the Patidar *lotwallahs* could cultivate the area with the support of the colonial state.

40 · THE KHEDA *SATYAGRAHA*

Although the government had increased its revenue as a result of Jyotsna-nath Ghosal's campaign to transform the landscape in the Mal tract, it was facing a serious fiscal crisis. Following the plague and famine years at the turn of the century, the productive forces in the agrarian economy had not recovered, and the entire population was facing a series of ongoing problems: crop failures, inconsistent rainfall, a recurrence of the bubonic plague, a partial famine, flooding, an outbreak of cholera, and a devastating influenza epidemic.[1] Further, Britain's participation in the Great War had led to inflationary prices for subsistence foodstuffs and basic commodities throughout India.[2] While some individuals were able to consistently make their land revenue payments during this period, the vast majority of peasants—Patidars and Dharalas alike—simply did not have sufficient resources to do so.

In 1917, political activists in alliance with the Home Rule League—a nationalist organization working for political change in India—began a petition campaign to protest the government's revenue demands that addressed the poor conditions facing peasants in Kheda district.[3] Approximately twenty-two thousand signatures were gathered by the end of the year and forwarded to government headquarters in Bombay for consideration.[4] The activists also consulted with Patidar elites, members of the Bombay Legislative Council, and the district collector to express their concerns about the state of the peasantry.[5] While the collector had cut revenue payments in half in select villages, village officials refused to administer the changes and continued to demand full payment from peasants.

Perhaps such difficulties emerged from the contradictory guidelines set by the government, as colonial officials had also authorized the use of extra-economic coercion in villages to extract land revenue specifically from Dharalas. F. G. Pratt, commissioner of the Northern Division, noted, "There was an appreciable increase in the number of coercive processes issued in Kaira district[,] which is accounted for by the fact that nearly two years['] land revenue had to be recovered during the year. . . .

Greater use of compulsory processes had to be made [against] Dharala cultivators in that district."[6] However, the use of force had limited results in securing total payments, leading the government to approve stricter measures to collect land revenue from the entire agrarian population, including Patidars.

Activists also sought the help of M. K. Gandhi, asking him to assist the peasants of Kheda district in his capacity as the president of the Gujarat Sabha, a welfare organization based in Ahmedabad.[7] He had recently returned from Champaran, in northern India, where he had successfully led a political campaign for peasants' rights.[8] Gandhi arrived in Kheda with the plan to survey villages in order to understand the concerns of peasants before approaching government officials. He reported: "I have made enquiries into the crops of about 400 villages. . . . I saw that many of the ryots [peasants] had no money, and that the granaries of many were empty; further that many poor people were importing maize wholesale from outside in place of grain grown in this district and living on that. I even saw this, that whenever the people had paid up the Land Revenue they had done so through fear."[9] Gandhi communicated his findings to colonial officials in Kheda and Bombay, stating that under the present conditions peasants could legally call for a suspension of the revenue assessment stipulated in the government's Land Revenue Rules.[10] However, the government refused to investigate Gandhi's claims and was unwilling to change its position on land revenue payments, saying that the district collector had already provided relief for many peasants.[11] After negotiating for several months without any productive results, in March 1918 Gandhi finally launched a "no-revenue campaign" against the government—a political movement that famously became known as the Kheda *satyagraha*.[12]

While Gandhi had expressed the fact that the district was "approaching famine," and noted that this affected the entire agrarian population, his efforts specifically centered on assisting the Patidars.[13] For Gandhi, it was the Patidars, not other peasant groups, who were primarily involved in demanding that government payments be suspended for the year. Consequently, he traveled from "village to village" explaining the principles of his message of *satyagraha* to Patidars.[14] By April 1918, the "no-revenue campaign" had spread to seventy villages in the district, with peasants making the following pledge:

> We . . . requested the Government to postpone collection to the next year, but they did not do so. We the undersigned therefore solemnly declare that we shall not pay the assessment for the year whether it be wholly or in part;

we shall leave it to the Government to take any legal steps they choose to enforce recovery of the same[,] and we shall undergo all the sufferings that this may involve. We shall also allow our lands to be confiscated should they do so. But we shall not by voluntary payment allow ourselves to be regarded as liars and thus lose our self-respect. If the Government would graciously postpone for all the remaining villages collection of the balance of the revenue, we, who can afford it, would be prepared to pay up revenue, whether in be in full or in part. The reason why the well-to-do amongst us would not pay is that, if they do, the needy ones would, out of fright, sell their chattels or incur debts and pay the revenue and thus suffer. We believe that it is the duty of the well-to-do to protect the needy against such a plight.[15]

For Gandhi it was crucial that wealthy Patidars who could afford to make the revenue payments support their less fortunate kinsmen by refusing the government's demands. In the Charotar tract, such collaboration was already present for most of the nineteenth century, especially in *narwadari* villages. In addition, colonial officials had encouraged rich Patidars to settle lands in the Mal tract along with Patidar cultivators as late as 1917. However, the district collector issued a notice allowing officials to confiscate the property (e.g., land, cattle, crops, jewelry) of any cultivator unable to make the government payments.[16] Gandhi knew that it was necessary to promote Patidar solidarity for the *satyagraha* to have any long-lasting impact.

Despite the emergence of the peasant movement, the government was able to collect nearly all its payments for the fiscal year. According to Gandhi, the "well-to-do" Patidars paid their taxes, while the "poorer" Patidars were finally granted a suspension by the government.[17] News of the *satyagraha* had circulated widely throughout India and had elevated Gandhi's position as a major nationalist figure despite the limited impact of the "no-revenue campaign" on the government. While it was uncertain if those Patidars who had agreed to collaborate with Gandhi were actually convinced by his principles of *satyagraha,* it was clear that the Patidars of Kheda were celebrated in the public sphere for their efforts in contesting colonial power in one of the first organized movements for nationalism. Patidar solidarity had grown in the midst of the peasant movement, and new political alliances with Gandhi were formed that would help guide the direction of future anticolonial struggles in the locality.

Gandhi had acknowledged the contribution of the Patidars by stating that the Kheda *satyagraha* was "an awakening among the peasants of Gujarat" and "the beginning of their true political education."[18] However, the long-standing efforts by Dharalas on similar political issues against colonial policies were simply ignored by Gandhi and the print media at this point. Even the small number of Dharalas who agreed with the demands of the "no-revenue campaign" were never mentioned. While Gandhi and his Patidar supporters were claiming that the colonial government was unjust and unethical for demanding full revenue payments from peasants during a period of crisis, there was no discussion about the impact of the Criminal Tribes Act on one-third of the district's agrarian population. In fact, there was no mention of how the CTA had worsened the condition of Dharalas during the second decade of the twentieth century. However, on May 20, 1918, during the Kheda *satyagraha*, District Magistrate J. C. Ker made the following observation:

> One of the principal difficulties in working the Act is that it has to be done through the [headmen] of the villages[,] most of whom are Patidars[,] and between the Patidars and Dharalas there is a constant tug-of-war. Very few [headmen], it is to be feared, attempt to carry out their duties solely in the public interest; the Act is regarded more as a means of getting Dharalas under their control, and it leads to many abuses. . . . In many cases the threat of the Act is employed in order to put pressure on the Dharalas so as to get the better of him in some dispute, or even to make him perform petty tasks.[19]

Ker's report on the working of the CTA raised an important unintended consequence of the legislation. Because the government had authorized the use of coercion against all peasants, the CTA further worsened the situation for Dharalas by allowing Patidars a means to extract a surplus from the poorest section of the agrarian population in areas where Dharalas had the strongest political organization and where the nationalist movement had its greatest support. Dharalas were increasingly aware of the daily use of extra-economic coercion, especially where Patidars maintained control in villages. But more important, the "no-revenue campaign" provided Dharalas a glimpse of how Patidar solidarity would function during nationalist politics in the locality. The question that remained unanswered was how Dharalas would respond to the new political crises in which their subordination by both the nationalists and the colonial state was assured.

41 · STRIKES AND RAIDS

In May 1918, twelve Dharala peasants met at the village center in Chaklasi one night and fired a few rounds from their guns.[1] They proceeded to the *mukhi's* house to express their grievances against him and then fired their guns once again in protest. Later they broke into to the police constable's residence in the village and stole his uniform and a sword. Police officials labeled the group the "Chaklasi *badmashes*" (outlaws) and stated that "these incidents are in themselves of no outstanding importance."[2] Shortly after leaving Chaklasi, the twelve Dharala peasants "brutally murdered" the village headman of neighboring Andhari-Amli for providing information about their activities to the government. Little else is known about this group, except that, according to District Superintendent of Police A. C. J. Bailey, the Dharala peasants who remained in the villages supported the Chaklasi *badmashes:* "[They] were looked up [to] with boundless admiration by the Dharalas and were regarded as mighty heroes."[3]

Officials claimed that many Dharalas believed that British rule had weakened in 1918 as a direct consequence of the "no-revenue campaign," leading peasants to challenge the rule of law in the countryside. But the government's explanation about the events in Chaklasi on the fateful night in May 1918 neglected to note the similarities between the actions of the twelve peasants and Ranchod Vira's supporters in the same village twenty years earlier, in 1898. Nor does it mention that the peasants were responding to the fact that Chaklasi had the most rigorous application of the Criminal Tribes Act in all of Kheda district. As Patidar solidarity had strengthened during the "no-revenue campaign," many of the Dharala peasants who were subject to continual coercion and violence took up arms and began underground strikes, raids, and murders.[4] Bailey noted that a growing collaboration among Dharalas throughout the district was a direct response to the rise of Patidar power: "Dharalas who now learnt the value of unity . . . make use of this to punish the Patidars against whom they have many scores to pay off. . . . Murders still occur[,] and these must be expected as long as the Patidars' greed for land and grain exists."[5]

By August 1918, the number of Dharalas involved in raids increased dramatically. The first raid, on August 11, 1918, involved a large group of Dharalas who robbed Patidar homes in the village of Surasamal in Nadiad *taluka*.[6] Over the next two weeks, raids were reported in twelve other villages in the district, and these fell into a similar pattern: between 150 and 500 Dharala peasants armed with guns, bows and arrows, and spears would descend upon a selected village at night and plunder the crops and houses of their chosen victims.[7] In most instances the attacks were perpetrated against Patidars, but some targeted villages associated with the Irish Presbyterian Mission.[8] Organized raids such as these had not occurred in the locality since the early decades of the nineteenth century, and colonial officials were forced to determine the factors related to their reemergence. Bailey had acknowledged that the events of August 1918 were politically motivated, saying that the raids "may justly be described as an 'Uprising' or 'Revolt.'"[9] Bailey further suggested that, given the rumors of Britain's demise in the Great War, perhaps the "Dharalas thought that the day of the British Raj was over and that there was now nothing to prevent them acting according to their own will."[10] He also, however, subscribed to the idea that every Dharala "was a potential criminal," and that the raids were part of a larger outbreak of lawlessness associated with the emergence of nationalist politics in the district.[11]

If indeed Dharalas thought colonial rule had ended, the widespread emergence of raids in this period signaled a return to a practice of statecraft that had long been prevented by the British in western India. As early as the eighteenth century, raids had been part of a complex interdependence between polities in western India, in which plunder functioned as a type of tax collection.[12] They were an accepted, ethical form of action that allowed political power to be negotiated between weak and strong polities, typically taking place during periods of scarcity.[13] By all official accounts, the raids during the month of August were collaborative efforts by Dharala peasants and *talukdars*, local landholders considered to be the direct descendants of the early Koli chieftains residing near the Mahi River on the borderland between Kheda district and Baroda State.[14] At the same time that many Dharala peasants had lost access to their means of production during the late nineteenth century, the status of the Koli chieftains had also declined with the colonial expansion into the inner frontier. But more important, the application of the CTA had eroded Dharalas' attempts to hold organized political gatherings and public discussions. If Dharalas needed to meet in large numbers to discuss any grievance or concern affecting their lives, they would have to get the permission of the village headman, local landholders, and the district police. Rather than facing certain persecution, arrest, and violence for their politics, many Dharalas opted for underground movements in solidarity with other Dharalas in Kheda.

According to the deputy district superintendent of police, N. V. Trivedi, both peasants and *talukdars* had privileged two factors in explaining the raids: "While one of the reasons . . . was and is their poverty, the other is the spirit of awakening which is generally felt all round and which, in the case of the Dharalla and *[talukdars]*, has taken the shape of revenge on the Patidars and the Banias who, they think, have brought about their present low state."[15] Trivedi's explanation sheds light on why the raiders attacked Patidar homes, but it does not address the attacks on the Christian hamlets run by the Irish Presbyterian Mission. Bailey stated the following on this point: "[An] interesting feature of the raids was the quite disproportionate number of Christian villages which were attacked. This is probably due to the fact that no Dharalas were to be found in them and the knowledge that the Christians would always be on the side of law and order. These Christian settlements had to suffer great hardships. . . . I speak of the Irish Presbyterian Mission[,] which suffered the most."[16]

For the officials, the raids on the Christian villages were acts of immense "cowardice," as mainly women and children were present in the hamlets. Most of the young men had joined the army to fight in the World War.[17] It is certainly possible that the Dharala raiders were targeting the Christian hamlets as a quick revenue-generating strategy, or that they had developed antipathy toward "untouchable" converts belonging to the Dhed community.[18] Crimes against Christians had been reported as early as 1891 in the neighboring village of Vishampur in Baroda State, where Robert Boyd, an Irish Presbyterian missionary, had filed a complaint against Kolis who had attacked some Dheds.[19] A more contemporary example is that of Reverend J. Umbricht of the Roman Catholic Mission in Anand, who in 1918 filed a complaint with the district collector against seven Dharalas from neighboring villages who had stolen items valued at Rs. 118 from a teacher and his family.[20] However, a further inquiry into the links between Patidars and the Irish Presbyterian Mission reveals another facet to the story. Like the many Patidars who were given land with special incentives, the mission too was granted land: more than a thousand acres of wasteland in Thasra *taluka* in 1881.[21] The news of the end of colonial rule meant that official land policies that had allowed for the colonization of Dharala lands could be reversed. The raids signaled a way to push *all* settlers off the land with the aim of reestablishing Dharala control over the territory.

42 · NATIONALIZING DHARALA RAIDS

During the "no-revenue campaign," Kheda district acquired a reputation as a center for rural nationalism in India.[1] But, equally, it was identified as one of the most criminal districts, as raids continued well into the 1920s without showing signs of subsiding.[2] In addition, officials had noted that peasants from other communities were actively participating in the raids, thereby exacerbating the problem of lawlessness.[3] The two most prominent raiders in this period, Babar Deva and Alimiya Sadak, emerged from the Charotar tract's Borsad *taluka*. Babar Deva, a Patanwadia from the village of Golel, first began his activities in 1919 and was celebrated in villages for helping poor peasants, but he also was notorious for numerous violent attacks against village headmen, watchmen, informants, and Patidars.[4] Between 1918 and 1924, Alimiya Sadak was equally prominent for protecting poor peasants and murdering his enemies.[5] It was reported that he was responsible for nearly thirty-five murders and fifty-five raids.

In 1920, A. C. J. Bailey, the district superintendent of police, argued that the crime rate could be reduced only with a stricter policing of the countryside, and he proposed opening new police stations throughout the district, especially around the village of Chaklasi, where the *bad-mashes* were continuing to obstruct the rule of law.[6] Bailey also noted persistent problems in areas where Patidars had recently received land as part of Ghosal's campaign: "I would also like to see a new Police Station opened near Khadgodra for the protection of the leaseholders of the newly opened waste land. The Dharalas bear a grudge against these people for the wrong they imagine they have suffered by being deprived of the land for grazing purposes[,] and do everything in their power to drive them out."[7]

The wave of raids in the 1920s had an impact that went beyond the locality. Regional and national newspapers that had finished covering Gandhi's role in the "no-revenue campaign" turned their attention to the raids in Kheda, searching for answers to the local problem.[8] While some reports claimed that the raids were "crimes of poverty," others supported the official government's position by linking "lawlessness" to the emergence of the nationalist movement. Yet, the explanation by the district superintendent of police, which attributed some of the violence to the recent colonization of Dharala land by Patidars and the Irish Presbyterian Mission, was largely ignored.

Gandhi, too, offered an explanation. In a speech to twelve thousand nationalist supporters in Ahmedabad on September 30, 1920, he denounced the government's suggestion that the increasing criminality in Kheda district was a result of nationalist agitations. Rather, he claimed, these were specific crimes committed by the poor. In an appeal to his primary constituents, the Patidar peasants, he made the following proposal: "I advise the brave men of our community to *control* the Dharala and dacoity [banditry]. They are our brothers, and if they have no food, clothes, etc., give to them and tell them to beg rather than plunder. Tell them that insignificant persons take advantage of this to curb us if they commit such offences; but if they refrain from doing so[,] we will be able to remove the strain and control of Government."[9]

In spite of Gandhi's efforts, his message further alienated the Dharalas from the nationalist agenda and failed to acknowledge the alternative ways in which Dharalas and others were interpreting the implications of the end of colonial rule. Not only were Patidar elites using the Criminal Tribes Act for extracting a surplus by coercion and violence, but now Gandhi himself was advocating that further controls be imposed. Perhaps the Dharalas were not interested in adopting poverty at a time when their access to the means of production was being eroded by colonial policies and by the emergent nationalist program led by local Patidars in alliance with Gandhi. In any case, Dharalas had little recourse at this time when the colonial state and the nationalists were advocating greater controls over them.

43 · A SECOND "NO-REVENUE CAMPAIGN"

The Dharala raids were posing serious problems for the nationalist program after the Kheda *satyagraha* in 1918. Patidar elites had even suggested abandoning their attempts at future anticolonial campaigns in Kheda, fearing that Dharalas would not only disrupt the efforts of the Patidar nationalists but also would further draw attention to the high crime rates that colonial officials had associated with nationalism. Instead, it was argued that future campaigns should be moved to south Gujarat—specifically Surat district—an area without serious problems of "lawlessness," because local Patidars had long established firm control of the patron-client relationship with bonded laborers.[1]

Gandhi, however, was not fully convinced that the efforts in Kheda should be abandoned, and he encouraged nationalists to pursue direct engagement with Dharalas concerning education and social reforms as a way to prevent further raids. As part of this endeavor, Gandhi held a large meeting in the town of Vadtal on January 19, 1921, to convince Dharalas that they should abandon all vice, including drinking alcohol and stealing, and take up a proper education and religion.[2] Gandhi readily accepted the claim that Dharalas were Kshatriyas (an idea he would later modify), but argued that the members of the community in their present condition had "fallen away from their ancient manhood" because of Dharalas' willingness to support raids.[3] He proposed that Dharalas come together with other nationalists in the ongoing Non-cooperation Movement against colonial rule.

However, the raids persisted in 1921, and Dharalas offered little support for nationalist politics.[4] After much deliberation regarding the problems with Dharalas, Gandhi decided to launch a second "no-revenue campaign," on November 23, 1921, as part of the larger all-India Non-cooperation Movement initiated in 1920. Approximately fifteen hundred landowners signed petitions stating that they would refuse to pay land revenue to the government, and forty village headmen and *matadars* (heads of a Patidar lineage) offered to resign their official posts in solidarity with the movement.[5] Interestingly, the most significant support for the second "no-revenue campaign" came from four Patidar villages where the Criminal Tribes Act was fully enforced.[6] While many nationalists feared further Dharala raids, others were concerned that the government would confiscate the property of the protesters and sell it to other villagers. Colonial officials also threatened *mukhis* who had resigned, stating that their posts would now be occupied by Dharalas in the village. Nationalist volunteers belonging to the Congress Party began their own efforts to convince Dharalas that it was in the interest of the "no-revenue campaign" that Dharalas not take up the protesters' land or official posts if these were offered to them by the government.[7] Not surprisingly, many Dharalas refused to cooperate with the nationalists.

In the end, the colonial government's tactics convinced most protesters that they would lose their property to Dharalas and others willing to purchase the land. While some Patidar nationalists threatened to murder any individual who accepted the government's offer, Gandhi chose to call off the Non-cooperation Movement in February 1922, when a group of peasants decided to take revenge on local oppressors in the north Indian town of Chauri Chaura by killing twenty-two policemen.[8]

44 · DEPORTING DHARALAS

As part of the plan to reform criminal tribes, the government began sending Dharala families outside of Gujarat in August 1923 to a reformatory
settlement in Bijapur, claiming that "the Dharala problem in Kaira [was]
becoming more acute."[1] J. W. Smith, the district magistrate, declared
that the district, especially in Borsad and Anand *talukas*, was facing a crisis, as serious crimes were rapidly spreading, and that "police resources
were almost strained to a breaking point."[2] The settlement in Bijapur
was chosen as the site for relocating Dharala families for a period of up
to five years, because it not only permitted the government to remove
individuals and their families perceived as "the worst and most dangerous" to areas outside of Gujarat but also served as a deterrent to others
in the district.[3] Officials argued that "deportation [was] a means of striking terror" in Dharalas and "frighten[ing them] out of crime,"[4] despite
the fact that the government considered it imprudent to place individuals
outside of their own "language area" or in a part of the country considered "foreign."[5]

The nearly eight hundred individuals who were viewed as the most
dangerous threats to their respective districts of the Bombay Presidency
were relocated to Bijapur.[6] This was done in accordance with the guidelines of the Criminal Tribes Act, which stated that a "criminal tribe shall
be restricted in its movements to the area specified or shall be settled in
the place of residence specified."[7] Approximately one hundred Dharalas
were forcibly placed in the Bijapur settlement as a way to "wean [them]
from criminal courses and convert [them] to habits of industry," along
with a mixed population made up of Kaikadis, Chhapparbands, Haran-
shikaris, and Bhats.[8] The government's primary aim in placing presumed
criminal tribes in a controlled environment was to introduce a disciplined
and rigorous work ethic for the purpose of securing extracriminal
employment. While attempts to establish control in the countryside were
unsuccessful, the settlement provided a space where individuals could be
strictly monitored. They were subject to roll calls twice a day, typically at

6 A.M. and 8 P.M., and at night they were required to remain in a location in the settlement specified by the district magistrate.[9] The following rules, which were posted in the settlement in English and vernacular languages, detail some additional rules in the settlement:[10]

1. A registered member of a criminal tribe which [has] been settled in a place of residence shall not refuse to work when any suitable work is provided for him.
2. He shall not obey the calls of nature in or near the Settlement buildings, except in places prescribed for the purpose by the person in charge of the Settlement.
3. He shall not drink to intoxication or cause disturbance by quarrelling.
4. He shall be bound to give a true account of his movements to any person in charge of the Settlement.
5. He shall not neglect or refuse to send to school his children who are of a suitable age.

For the colonial administration, the creation of the settlement served fiscal interests: the settlement required a smaller investment than jails, and it provided an inexpensive and disciplined manual labor force for developing Bijapur's local economy.[11] After spending a minimum of two and a half years in the reformatory settlement, some individuals were allowed to take jobs as unskilled or semiskilled workers in the town's industrial settlement.[12] They could find jobs in industries such as the cotton ginning mills or in the Public Works Department.[13] However, the tenure at Bijapur provided Dharalas with few skills that would enable them to find employment in Kheda district.

All the Dharala families deported to Bijapur came from the Charotar tract, specifically Borsad *taluka*—an area perceived to have the highest concentration of serious crime. The failure of the intensified armed patrol units of the police in the area had persuaded colonial officials to look to more extreme measures to curb the crime rate. Suggestions that the armed police force be increased had been rejected because of fiscal constraints.[14] The government never intended to send large numbers of Dharalas to the settlement, but argued that the idea of deportation would create a culture of fear. However, the Criminal Tribes Settlement Officer in Bijapur, while acknowledging that threats of deportation could "restore law and order," argued that the "Dharala question" would not be resolved by simply forcing a selected number of families to move.[15] In fact, some people believed that public opinion would turn against the government if such a policy were implemented broadly.[16]

45 · THE PUNITIVE POLICE TAX

In October 1923, shortly after instituting the plan to deport Dharala families from Borsad *taluka* to Bijapur, the government imposed a punitive police tax. The purpose of the new levy, which amounted to Rs. 2–7–0 for every adult living in Borsad *taluka* and in selected villages of Anand *taluka*, was to pay for more than three hundred extra policemen to capture criminals and prevent raids.[1] Local nationalists strongly opposed the new tax, claiming that the police were exacerbating the criminal problem by actually assisting the raiders. Equally, there was discontent over the fact that the police tax coincided with the thirty-year cycle of land resettlements, in which the government had substantially increased its fees for each cultivator. The land rates, originally settled by the government in the 1860s, were adjusted in the 1890s and then again in the 1920s.[2] Individuals circulated petitions from village to village pointing out that, not only was the tax unjust for suggesting that all residents of the locality were guilty of crimes, but also it was sanctioned during a period of scarcity resulting from a poor harvest.[3]

It appeared that, in levying the police tax, the government was specifically targeting Dharalas and Patidars residing in the two *talukas*, with the view that both communities were complicit in criminal activity: Dharalas for harboring and actively supporting the raiders; and the Patidars for participating in nationalist politics, which were interpreted as tacitly encouraging lawlessness.

In early December 1923, local nationalists agreed to participate in protests against the police tax.[4] Individuals traveled to over one hundred villages where the tax was imposed to garner support for the campaign against the government, later known as the Borsad *satyagraha*. Village elites throughout the locality were reported to have passed resolutions stating that any individual who opted to pay the government would be fined and possibly forced to leave the village. The strongest opposition to the tax came from Patidars, who later claimed that their solidarity as a community was largely responsible for the success of the movement.[5]

Colonial officials were unable to secure adequate payments because of the united response from the villages, leading the government to cancel the tax altogether on January 7, 1924.[6]

While the Borsad *satyagraha* succeeded in preventing implementation of the police tax, the government agreed to pay for the extra policemen and opted for drastic measures to enforce the rule of law. J. W. Smith, the district magistrate in 1924, proposed that the regulations of the Criminal Tribes Act and their enforcement against the Dharalas of Kheda "should be abandoned" and replaced by "the use of overwhelming physical force."[7] In addition, officials advocated arresting and prosecuting Dharalas under Chapter VIII of the Criminal Procedure Code, which allowed them to bring criminal charges against an individual or a group without direct evidence.[8] Police posts were reestablished in villages as a way to maintain police authority in the countryside, and the police developed a special intelligence branch and "a striking and patrolling force" in the district to capture criminals.[9] The impact of the policy changes was immediate: several prominent raiders were caught or killed. Officials further encouraged both the district police and the village headmen to continue using intimidation, violence, and physical force to control Dharalas and eradicate crime altogether.[10]

46 · "TO FORGET PAST ENMITIES"

Local nationalists started organizing large-scale meetings in Kheda during the 1920s following Gandhi's attempts to persuade Dharalas to take up education and social reforms.[1] The meetings were primarily led by Patidar elites who wanted to persuade Dharalas to stop committing crimes and give up any associations with the raiders for the betterment of the nationalist movement.[2] In fact, members of the Patidar community even offered to support Dharalas' grievances against government policies on the condition that Dharalas abandon all criminal activities.[3] Vallabhbhai Patel, a prominent leader of the Patidars, offered to accept Dharalas' claims of a new political identity if Dharalas would end their interference with the nationalist movement: "When your actions are those of Kshatriyas, I shall be prepared to stand by you and see that you are borne on the Government record as Kshatriyas and not as Dharalas."[4] But there was discontent among many Patidars—those who supported the nationalist movement but opposed any strategies that required negotiating with Dharalas and abandoning the use of force to stop the support for the raiders.

It was clear that the persistence of the raids had effectively contested local power and forced Gandhi and the nationalists to consider alternative modes to address the problem of social relations with Dharalas, who had made clear that they were not interested in the nationalism of the Patidars. The meetings, organized by the Indian National Congress—the leading political organization fighting for India's independence—were large events at which thousands of peasants gathered. Local nationalists were encouraged by the Dharalas' interest in attending the meetings, but it was apparent that many individuals had arrived for the purpose of publicly opposing the measures legislated to control Dharalas and to challenge the nationalists. In addition, many individuals used the opportunity of the large gatherings to declare a new "Baraiya-Kshatriya" identity that moved away from the official criminal-tribes classification attached to all Dharalas, with the aim of harnessing further support for alternative politics.[5]

Figure 1. M. K. Gandhi with workers in Kheda district, 1929.
Copyright © Vithalbhai Jhaveri/GandhiServ.

What remains unclear is which section of the Dharala population initiated such a debate, and why individuals were asserting a "Baraiya-
Kshatriya" identity, rather than a "Kshatriya" identity. It is possible that
the Baraiya Conference Movement, having raised an earlier claim to
Kshatriya status in Kheda, was at the forefront of these arguments.
However, the political climate had changed in the aftermath of the implementation of the Criminal Tribes Act, shifting the internal debate among
Dharalas. Daduram and his followers had rejected the BCM's argument
for declaring all Dharalas to be Kshatriyas, but Dharala peasants appear
to have offered little resistance during the 1920s to accepting the new
classification as Kshatriyas. Daduram had mounted his protest against
the Kshatriya identity before the criminalization of all Dharalas in
Kheda; now people felt a political necessity to get rid of the criminal-
tribes label. The resolutions offered by the nationalists at the meetings,
however, were far from satisfactory from the perspective of Dharalas, or
the Baraiya-Kshatriyas, who felt that the Patidar nationalists had only
created additional policies allowing for the continued extraction of surpluses from Dharalas. The meetings led to official measures by some
nationalists who had "decided to use the weapon of caste and social boycott to wean Dharalas [from criminality]," while others passed resolu-

tions allowing Patidars the right to fine Dharalas between five and ninety-nine rupees in cases of robbery, theft, or arson.[6]

Gandhi, who initially had accepted the Kshatriya identity for Dharalas, changed his position at a meeting in 1923: "Dharalas have now come to regard themselves as Baraiya Kshatriyas. If, however, I may advise them, I would ask them to stick to the name Dharala and sanctify it. No purpose is served by changing a name. Status is not gained by assuming the name but only by acting in a manner benefiting Kshatriyas."[7] Gandhi's reluctance to accept the new identity raised concerns about his preference to align with Patidars over Dharalas yet again. Not every Dharala was interested in moving outside the district boundaries or participating in raids as a way of challenging colonial legislation and Patidar dominance. Some individuals were even sympathetic to the issues raised by the nationalists after the success of the campaign to reject the police tax.

However, for Dharalas, the primary concern seemed to be the criminal tribes legislation and its constant abuses. While local nationalists had offered to assist Dharalas in challenging colonial policies, the resolutions at the meetings appeared to further strengthen the dominance of Patidars through the application of informal levies and punishments. Even Gandhi publicly noted the role of Patidar dominance in the locality: "Patidars tyrannize over lower communities, beat them and extract forced labor from them."[8] But his resolution did not involve an appeal to Patidars to stop applying violence or extra-economic coercion for the betterment of the nationalist movement. Rather, he requested that Dharalas forgive Patidars for the cause of the nation: "Many of our Dharala brothers have taken to a wrong path. The Government often extends to them the law pertaining to criminal tribes. I appeal to you to use your courage to die, without killing anyone, for the sake of the country. I beg you to forget past enmities and remove your neighbour's fears by adopting peaceful ways."[9]

Gandhi's pleas demonstrate that the idea of the nation required Dharalas not only to abandon their own claims about the past—as the descendants of kings, princes, and warriors—but also to actively ignore the everyday forms of violence perpetrated by Patidars. For Dharalas, the task was clear: to become national required silencing the past. Most Dharalas, or Baraiya-Kshatriyas, were unwilling to cede their demands for the sake of the nation. Their struggles continued, but time was running out for political alternatives.

47 · RAVISHANKAR VYAS

While Gandhi's statements appeared to further alienate Dharalas from the Patidar-led nationalist politics, Ravishankar Vyas, one of Gandhi's disciples, began a grassroots campaign to reform Dharalas and encourage civil disobedience following the Borsad *satyagraha*.[1] He had regularly attended the Congress-sponsored meetings in Kheda,[2] and he was actively involved in Gandhi's *satyagrahas* in Gujarat.[3] However, unlike other nationalists, including Gandhi, Vyas argued that the "disorder" and "unrest" in the locality were not the result of a Dharala propensity toward crime but instead a response to the conflicts in social relations. He was not interested in disciplining or punishing Dharalas, because, he claimed, the main problem in the district lay with the *mukhis* and the communities that had supported the exploitation of Dharalas in the first place.[4] He pointed out that the application of the Criminal Tribes Act had actually led to an increase in the number of raids in the locality, as few Dharalas had the ability to challenge the power and authority of village elites.

Vyas pursued an extensive reform program that involved traveling to villages and convincing individuals to adopt Gandhi's principles of passive resistance and *satyagraha*.[5] He explained that he would support Dharala grievances if the community agreed to give up supporting the raiders and drinking alcohol, as part of a long-term program for "social upliftment."[6] But more important, he agreed with peasants about the necessity of adopting a Kshatriya identity.[7] Vyas helped organize small, village-level protests to challenge the injustices of local landholders, arguing that such problems would cease once India had gained its independence from colonial rule. Many Dharalas welcomed Vyas's messages and were willing to consider participating in the nationalist movement, especially in villages where Patidars did not dominate social relations.[8]

Yet, many Patidars active in the local nationalist movement resisted the reforms because they directly challenged Patidar authority in the villages. Greater involvement of Dharalas in nationalist politics would also

alter the direction of debate at the public meetings, forcing all nationalists to consider the problems of abuse and exploitation facing most
Dharalas. Perhaps the Patidars were not only concerned with the fact
that Dharalas would demand more rights; they may have also been wor-
ried by the implications of Vyas's interpretation of the problem in the district. Vyas had made it clear that he attributed the criminal problems to
those who were abusing the CTA.

48 · THE LAST "NO-REVENUE CAMPAIGN"

The onset of the Great Depression in 1929, and a further downturn in the economy during the early 1930s, served as a background to the emergence of the final "no-revenue campaign" in Kheda and the beginning of the Civil Disobedience Movement against government taxation throughout the country. Gandhi had decided to specifically protest the application of the salt tax by organizing a march from Ahmedabad to the Arabian Sea that would cross through the villages of Kheda district. He argued that it was important to raise the issue of the salt tax because it affected the entire population of India and had the potential to harness wider support for the main objective of the nationalist movement in the 1930s—to remove the colonial government. While Gandhi encouraged all government workers in Kheda, including village headmen and police officials, to resign from their posts and join his march, he was less enthusiastic about raising another "no-revenue campaign" in Kheda, as he considered it a local issue. But peasants who had experienced three consecutive poor harvests, a bad monsoon season, and a crop failure in 1929–30 demanded that the government suspend its land revenue collection for the year.

Patidar nationalists were once again at the forefront of the protests in Kheda. However, their grievances against the government centered on the fact that, in March 1930, the district magistrate had arrested one of their leaders in the village of Ras without cause.[1] As news of the persecution quickly spread, greater numbers of Patidar villages agreed to suspend their land revenue payments. Gandhi's presence in Kheda encouraged nearly half of all *mukhis* to resign from their posts, and perhaps more significant, the Dharalas who had worked with Ravishankar Vyas were also protesting the salt tax.[2] But the vast majority of Dharalas were hardly sympathetic to the "no-revenue campaign," which effectively became another effort in which Patidars asserted their power. Dharala raids reemerged shortly after the start of the campaign in 1930.[3] A violent protest was also recorded in Od—one of the original fifty-five villages in which the Criminal Tribes Act was fully enforced—where three thousand armed peasants attacked the district superintendent of police and sixty policemen.[4]

The nature of district policing had changed because of the lack of financial resources available to the government, with the most significant changes appearing in the "retrenchment of police stations and outposts, [and the] rigid curtailment of patrolling."[5] This period also witnessed a large-scale withdrawal of the district police, which led to village headmen having even greater powers in the countryside. As had happened after the 1911 attempts to improve policing, all efforts to reorganize the police were abandoned.[6] Instead, the government reinstated capital punishment as a way to deter serious crimes.[7]

The government was most concerned at this time by the Patidars' participation in the "no-revenue campaign." The protesters were aware that, if they refused to pay land revenue, their property could be confiscated by the government and sold. Many Patidars opted to take their personal possessions out of the village altogether, moving them to the homes of relatives living in Baroda territory, where the British authorities had no jurisdiction.[8] Others threatened to kill any individual who might purchase confiscated property that was originally owned by a Patidar. District Collector Alfred Master, however, was not deterred by the Patidars' organized response, which spread to nearly one hundred villages. Earlier colonial officials had protected the *narwadari* villages controlled by Patidars in the Charotar since the early nineteenth century, but new land policies set in place in 1930–31 finally abolished this special shareholder system of land tenure.[9] Master not only began his own campaign to confiscate and redistribute Patidar land, but he also encouraged other peasants to occupy the positions of *mukhi* and *talati* with the protection of the district police.

The government sold prime Patidar land to Dharalas at reduced rates in various villages in the district.[10] The most significant transformation took place in Ras, the village where Patidars first began organizing the "no-revenue campaign," when a Dharala occupied the position of village headman and many Dharala peasants purchased land that the government had recently confiscated from Patidar families.[11] The new *mukhi* started to transform the landscape of the village by cutting down babul trees and hedges planted by Patidars.[12] He ruled with a heavy hand, often resorting to violence and abuse against the Patidars who remained in the village. The world was beginning to turn upside down as Dharalas became possessors of Patidar lands and began assuming local positions of authority. The news of Ras quickly spread throughout India as reports circulated that Patidar nationalists protesting the imposition of land taxes were under attack by the colonial government and by Dharala criminals.[13] The *mukhi* not only was believed to have direct contact with raiders but also was blamed for the looting and burning of Patidar homes.

Gandhi was in regular contact with his Patidar supporters in Kheda, who asked for assistance in the conflict with the new *mukhi* of Ras. Gandhi agreed that the *mukhi* was responsible for crimes and abuses in the village and demanded that the district collector find a replacement.[14] But more important, Gandhi wanted the Dharalas to return the land they had purchased from the government at a discounted rate, even if the Patidars could not afford to reimburse the new owners. He was concerned that the government was interested in confiscating Patidar land rights as a way to disrupt the nationalist movement and punish individuals protesting colonial policies.[15] Gandhi claimed that he wanted to protect Patidars from Dharalas for the cause of the nation. In the end, he further alienated Dharalas, who clearly had not received any of Gandhi's protection from Patidars.

49 · THE COMING OF THE POSTCOLONIAL

Any Dharala victories were short-lived. Gandhi and the nationalists forced Dharalas to abandon *mukhi* positions they occupied, and negotiated with the government to pass legislation that would formally return lands to Patidars through the Forfeited Lands Restoration Act.[1] As the Patidars worked alongside Gandhi, their solidarity became publicly more pronounced and their ability to wield power increased. This had much to do with how Patidars maintained control over Dharalas. Gandhi's call for the British to "quit India" in 1942 generated support from Patidars.[2] Most Dharalas, however, remained reluctant to participate alongside Gandhi and his primary supporters in Kheda, and some chose to continue the raids and obstruct nationalist politics. New leaders emerged, like Fulsingh Dabhai, demanding that Dharalas be "removed from the declaration as a Criminal Tribe" and be officially identified as Kshatriyas.[3] In the run-up to India's independence, the making of a new order was begun, one in which the bonds of the British raj would be broken but the structures of agrarian dominance would remain.

Dharalas did not fail to resist the nationalists or the coming of the nation-state. Their strikes, protests, and attacks shaped the direction of the Patidar-led nationalist movement in Kheda by ensuring that the process was full of conflict. Despite the use of force by Patidars, most Dharalas refused to abandon their strategies for the cause of the nation. Nor were Dharalas convinced that they should forget their past as prescribed by Gandhi. The Patidar nationalists did not exclude Dharalas *from* the nation, but wanted to ensure that the Dharalas accepted their subordinate place *within* the nation. The nationalists were not interested in ridding the new nation of the structures of dominance, despite the rhetoric of "freedom" that was central to a universalist ideal of nationalism. But the subordinate subjects of the British raj were well aware that the nationalists were arguing for a freedom from colonialism, not necessarily a freedom within the boundaries of the nation.

As national citizens, Dharalas were forced to engage with their new identity as Indians. This did not mean they simply accepted the idea of India without further critique or resistance. The fact that the nation maintained the Criminal Tribes Act was further testament that their struggle against forms of power had to continue. Dharalas' conflicts with Patidars were not forgotten. These conflicts persisted well into the twentieth century and took on different political forms in the postcolonial era.

50 · BECOMING INDIAN

All Dharalas gained a new identity on August 15, 1947, by becoming citizens of the Indian nation, but they continued to be classified as members of a criminal tribe till 1952—the year the Government of India finally banned the criminal tribes legislation. As citizens, the poor, the nonliterate, and women were all given the right to vote, to choose their representatives in local, state, and national elections in independent India. However, the point is not that all politics became electoral politics with the creation of a democratic nation but that historically oppressed groups gained the potential to share governmental power in a way that had not been available under colonialism or even before.[1] At an earlier time, figures like Ranchod had attempted to control statecraft, but colonial power had ensured that such ideas and practices propagated by peasants were quickly stopped. The nationalists had secured control of the "material" domain, only to discover that those who had been marginalized from the nationalist movement quickly figured out that they could outnumber those in power.

The idea of the imagined community, which seemed so alienating for so many, suddenly had promise. (Or did it?) The coalition of oppressed groups in India was one unintended consequence of the nation-state for those nationalists who had imagined a nation in which they would continue to dominate.[2] The contest over the control of statecraft took on a new character following Indian independence. The founding of the Gujarat Kshatriya Sabha in 1950 was an attempt to create a pan-Kshatriya alliance between Rajputs who were large landholders and the tillers of the land identified as the descendants of Kolis.[3] While all official forms of kingship formally came to an end in independent India, those who identified themselves as descendants of kings, princes, and warriors asserted a claim for Kshatriya status.

Although there was no agreement on the question of identity at the beginning of the twentieth century, there was, among the descendants of Dharalas, a greater awareness of the need to maintain respectability within the nation by renouncing all associations with criminality, and an awareness of the need to work within a broader coalition to defeat local power brokers. The pan-Kshatriya campaigns in Gujarat during local and national elections were a way to target Patidars and to secure entitlements promised by the leaders of the new nation. However, Kshatriya elites in power often did not side with their poor Kshatriya constituents, especially when it came to land reform.[4] Kshatriya elites who had gained power in postcolonial India had secured land rights, like their Patidar counterparts, while Kshatriya tillers had not.

Today, most descendants of Dharalas continue to be aware that their material conditions in everyday life are threatened, especially as land has remained a primary area of conflict in the locality. While the Government of India legislated land reforms in Gujarat in order to place ceilings on the size and number of holdings and to redistribute land to the tiller, the implementation of such policies has been limited at best. Land reforms were meant to protect peasants who had suffered during colonial rule, but the main beneficiaries of postcolonial land policies have been Patidars, who have maintained strong communal networks that allow many individuals to control power in the area.[5] Not surprisingly, government reports state that Kolis—a term that continues to be used in official discourses—have not made substantial gains in their means of subsistence since independence.[6] Individuals and groups who may have forgotten how British land policies and Patidar dominance functioned in marginalizing Dharalas (or Baraiyas, Kolis, and Kshatriyas) in colonial India now could witness it firsthand within the postcolonial nation.

PART THREE

51 · SMALL DISCOVERIES

I might have written a very different story of the past had I not come across Ranchod and Daduram in documents in the archives in Bombay. Ranchod's name appeared by chance in 1996 while I was looking at a Judicial Department file in the Maharashtra State Archives in Bombay (now Mumbai) for 1899.[1] I was looking for revenue documents relating to the devastating famine of that year, when I came across a reference to a "riot" led by a peasant named Ranchod Vira. This hardly surprised me, since I knew there had been at least 110 documented peasant rebellions (riots or insurgencies, according to government officials) during the "long nineteenth century" in colonial India.[2] I noted the reference and immediately requested the file, as I was unaware of this particular movement. The file arrived on my desk late in the afternoon, shortly before the reading room was to close. I quickly scanned the many pages, learning that Ranchod Vira was no ordinary peasant: he not only declared the end of the British raj but also proclaimed himself king. What intrigued me further was the fact that he had dictated a letter to his disciples, despite the fact that he was unable to read or write.

I copied the letter by hand but was unable to decipher its contents. The file also contained detailed testimonies by Ranchod, his supporters, family members, and witnesses to the "riot." At the time, I believed this to be a somewhat rare find. I left the archive for the day, realizing that I had stumbled across something fascinating. Later that night I showed Ranchod's letter to a couple of friends who specialized in languages and literatures of western India, but they were unable to explain the significance of the letter. The references to the sugarcane press, Ranchodji, and government dues seemed too unrelated to make sense. I spent the next few weeks pursuing the clues in that one file and located more files that spoke of the Ranchod case, until one day there were no further leads to follow. I frequently looked at the letter and showed it to others, but without any resolution. I returned to other concerns about colonial power and agrarian politics in Gujarat, but kept the notes of Ranchod's story with me in case any new clues might emerge.

Approximately five or six months later, I consulted another archive, one administered by the Central Intelligence Department Office in Bombay. I was interested in looking at a very specific set of documents known as the Secret Abstracts of Police Intelligence. Most scholars who had consulted this series were primarily interested in surveillance reports filed during the rise of nationalist politics from the 1920s to the 1940s. I suppose my interests were also drawn in a similar direction, not least because I had no idea of what to expect in looking at these documents.[3] Compilation of the Secret Abstracts begin in 1888, and they cover reports on a variety of topics ranging from traveling mendicants, to suspicious-looking peasants, to crimes of sedition, to full-scale rebellions. The volumes covering the nationalist movement are by far the most comprehensive. However, I soon noted that, in the volumes for 1897 and 1898, British officials throughout India were reporting the presence of circulating letters that posed a threat to the stability of the countryside from Bombay to Madras, and from Bengal to Punjab. Officials included either the full contents of the letters or summaries. It quickly became clear to me that Ranchod's letter was somehow connected to these other letters. Ranchod also made an appearance in these reports for leading armed peasants against government officials and for possessing copies of the circulating letter.[4]

In all, I was able to locate approximately one hundred references to these letters and related rumors that had caught the attention of intelligence officials. It is unclear to what extent the circulation of such information had actually led to a crisis of legitimation in the colonial state, but for Ranchod the British raj had ended. I realized that Ranchod's movement, albeit short-lived, was significant for contextualizing the rise of anticolonial ideas and sentiments in an area that would become one of the centers for peasant nationalism and Gandhian politics in the early decades of the twentieth century.

Unlike Ranchod, I had read a brief account of Daduram in a history book.[5] I was aware that he was a *bhagat* who had helped to reform peasants in the first decade of the twentieth century, but I knew nothing else about this figure. There were passing references to Daduram's activities in several files in the Maharashtra State Archives. Other records that may have contained relevant information about Daduram were apparently missing or misplaced at the time when I was doing my research. But given my first impressions, I began to wonder if there were any connections between Ranchod and Daduram: both were *bhagats*, both were

Dharalas, both were poor peasants, both appeared to be political. Once again, however, disappointed with the limits to the sources available to me, I had no choice but to turn to other concerns: the stories about Daduram and Ranchod that I found were certainly pertinent, but were incomplete at best.

I turned to a topic that at first glance appeared to be unconnected to either Ranchod or Daduram: the Criminal Tribes Act of 1911. But it quickly became apparent that Ranchod had left a deep impression upon British officials, who had decided to "criminalize" the entire Dharala population in Kheda district, nearly 250,000 individuals. The most severe application of the act took place in Chaklasi, where Ranchod had organized his movement. What appeared to be more important was the fact that Kanbis and Patidars were required to monitor the application of the act in the villages of the Charotar tract to ensure that Dharalas were behaving in accordance with the legislation. It was no surprise that a British police official had noted that the *mukhis* in these villages were abusing the Criminal Tribes Act as a way to control Dharala labor. But what did catch my attention was the possibility that this abuse was being perpetrated in 1918 by the same Patidars who were participating in the first peasant nationalist movement in Kheda district, led by Mohandas K. Gandhi. I was not sure how Daduram fit into these events, but it appeared more than a coincidence that the Criminal Tribes Act was applied only two years after Daduram's death.

Once again, my desire to continue with this line of inquiry came to a sudden end. Most of the Judicial Department records for the years following 1911 appeared to be missing from the State Archives without explanation. The old handwritten indexes, for example, list the files, volumes, and compilations detailing the Criminal Tribes Act, but these entries did not appear in the new, typed indexes. I suspected that the records were probably moved to another location for review and had not been returned; hopefully, they have not been destroyed. (I later consulted the summaries and abstracts of some of these reports now kept in the Oriental and India Office Collections of the British Library in London.)

My turn to the Secret Abstracts proved far more fruitful than I could have imagined when I first consulted the intelligence reports. Much to my disappointment, there was minimal discussion of the Criminal Tribes Act; however, in the 1908–09 volumes, the entries for Daduram were by far the most comprehensive I had come across for a single peasant. The idea that colonial officials had collected surveillance information about Daduram was in itself extraordinary, but the type of information included in these reports provided new possibilities for the research project that I could not have anticipated. It became apparent that I was not the first to speculate about a connection between Daduram and Ranchod; in fact, the district magistrate had unsuccessfully pursued this line of inquiry in 1906.[6]

However, I was not convinced by the magistrate's explanation, because he neglected to consider the intellectual, political, and ideological links that could have existed between the two men. I was equally intrigued by the fact that Daduram not only had influenced other peasants to lead their own political movements but also appears to have inspired educated, middle-class men to enter public life as well. Daduram was engaged in public debates about nationalist figures like Bal Gangadhar Tilak, he demanded that Dharalas get paid in cash and not in-kind by their Patidar patrons, and he distributed food to peasants in the aftermath of a famine. My initial thoughts regarding the application of the Criminal Tribes Act in 1911 seemed to be substantiated, as it began to appear that any political advances made by Daduram's movement stopped shortly after his death. The colonial state was involved in this process, and so were peasant nationalists. However, it was becoming evident that I could no longer simply go from one archive to another, or one set of documents to a different set of documents, whenever I had reached the limits of official reports.

These surveillance documents, court testimonies, and administrative reports served very specific purposes in asserting colonial power in the countryside. The government had demanded their production to ensure that necessary measures were in place to maintain law and order and to provide regular accounts of the agrarian economy. During periods of great turmoil, like the famine and the plague epidemic, official concerns about the dangers of a fiscal crisis of the state were heightened even further. The Secret Abstracts were full of problems that began at the moment a decision was made to gather information about a particular individual or group. Such information was not neutral, nor could it ever be.[7] Officials were not only creating categories and stereotypes in the process of collecting information about peasants, Dharalas, *bhagats*, and Patidars, for example, but they were also reproducing earlier stereotypes that were widely circulated within officialdom.[8]

The information was gathered and reported to a government official, who then recorded it in some file and forwarded the file to another official, who either read the file or simply sent it on to others in the government. At some point the information was collated, typed, copied, bound, and distributed to other officials as part of the Secret Abstracts of Police

Intelligence. If a serious problem was identified, then the appropriate institutions were notified to investigate and arrest the troublemakers. Officials were often susceptible to bad surveillance information. Sometimes they anticipated the emergence of a popular uprising, only to realize that their sources were faulty. In the case of numerous circulating letters that obviously questioned the legitimacy of the colonial state, officials simply did not know whether these were real threats or not. In other instances, surveillance practices did not serve the government's purpose, because rebellions occurred without officials knowing in advance about the independent initiative among peasants. However, peasants were also aware that they were being observed, and they developed strategies to avoid the detection of their ideas and sentiments.

In Ranchod's case, the village *mukhi's* delay in relaying information upward to district officials was considered the single greatest mistake that could have prevented the violent conflict between the police and peasants in Chaklasi. In Daduram's case, a vigilant district magistrate monitored the daily activities of Daduram for three years with the specific aim of preventing another uprising. However, since Daduram did not call for peasants to carry weapons, and he argued for reforms, the district magistrate did not consider Daduram a threat. In addition, he relied upon his assistant for further details specific to Daduram. In the records, he stated: "Mr. Joshi, the First Class Magistrate, helped me watch these movements."[9] He was probably correct in his assessment based on the criteria used by the government, especially since there were no crime problems in Kheda associated with Daduram's movement, despite the fact that thousands of peasants would come together in one village after another. However, it appears that Daduram circulated many ideas and raised public debates that influenced a large number of individuals and groups in the area, even beyond the borders of the district. Yet the district magistrate simply viewed Daduram's activities as the expressions of an "ignorant," "non-political," and "loyal" peasant. It is not clear whether Daduram somehow prevented the discovery of his ideas by Mr. Joshi and the district magistrate, or these officials simply were unaware that Daduram could formulate a political agenda.

In reading the surveillance reports, I often hoped that somewhere Daduram would speak, and speak at length. I realized that it was unlikely this would happen, and that if it had, it might have put Daduram in some peril. But more likely, officials would have simply ignored the speech as the rants of a peasant. Of course, Daduram's words would have been filtered and distorted in the best of circumstances, but such obscured visions of the past were preferable to no vision at all. Even if the magistrate had noted Daduram's comments, it would have been unclear whether Daduram was actually speaking or whether he was responding to the questions under coercion by a colonial official. I suppose my interests were similar to those of the district magistrate: I wanted to learn more about Daduram—his background, his thoughts, his ideas, his family, his friends, his allies, his politics, and his consumption of ganja—but for very different purposes. However, it is also necessary to point out that there is a basic contradiction in relying on these reports, because more comprehensive surveillance practices often resulted in the production of more thorough reports, irrespective of whether the surveillance was "flawed." The fact that the magistrate came to know so much about Daduram over a three-year period implies the use of some level of extra-economic coercion by colonial officials.

In fact, at least two Dharalas made such claims in their testimonies at the end of the trial, *Imperatrix vs. Ranchod Vira and Others.* When Judge E. H. E. Leggatt asked Meru Mitha "How is it that you gave a full account of the riot to the District Magistrate?" Meru replied, "Because I was afraid. I was beaten."[10] Gema Mitha made a similar claim: "I made the former statement, as I was beaten."[11] Ranchod and the others who had testified did not make such claims, but this does not mean they were not coerced. The fact that these comments about police brutality were even entered into the official record is an indication that the judge and the colonial legal system accepted such abuses. Simultaneously, it is an official rejection of the claim made by Meru and Gema that such evidence was invalid in explaining the "true" events of the case.[12] This was not considered a contradiction. The questions put forth by the judge and the government's prosecutors did not usually elicit lengthy answers. Responses were often repetitive, and in most instances they were simple reiterations of the prosecutor's questions: "Were you present in the mandwa during the riot?" "No, I wasn't present" or "Yes, I was present." Yet in contrast, government officials were required to speak at length to solidify their case against Ranchod and the other Dharalas.

Despite these problems, there are moments captured in the pages of the court trial that provide great insights into the world of Ranchod and his supporters. These moments may not have had relevance for a government interested only in prosecuting a group of peasants for "sedition," "murder," and "a public disturbance," but for the historian these distant voices of peasants provide possibilities for reconsidering the beliefs, thoughts, and practices of the past.

52 · CHAKLASI

As a result of my small discoveries in the archives, I traveled to rural Gujarat in 1996. Since Ranchod's extraordinary case had played such a central role in allowing me to consider the alternative ways in which peasants were thinking about their world, I had decided to travel to Chaklasi. I wanted to meet the descendants of those who had participated alongside Ranchod. While Chaklasi is still officially classified as a village, its population exceeds twenty thousand.[1] Chaklasi is well known in the region for its agriculture—namely, tobacco and potatoes—and its factories that produce condensed milk and plastic footwear.[2] It is connected by roads to all the major centers for trade and commerce in the region and has attracted the attention of national banks, which now operate branches in Chaklasi.

Nearly a century had passed since Ranchod declared the end of the British raj and proclaimed himself king in this village. My initial attempts to locate any direct descendants proved difficult because of the spatial organization of Chaklasi. In fact, this was a point repeated by British officials in their correspondence, especially in reference to the application of the Criminal Tribes Act. Peasants had had to walk several miles to reach the village center for roll call; now several centers existed in the village. But more important, hardly anyone in Chaklasi had even heard of Ranchod Vira. After a series of inquires, I finally located Chaturbhai Fulabhai Waghela and Manibhai Fulabhai Waghela, both septuagenarians, who stated that they could possibly help me because they had cursory knowledge about the case. The two brothers resided on the outskirts of Chaklasi with their respective families, most of whom were peasant farmers. The Waghelas claimed that they had heard stories from their parents about Ranchod, but they simply did not know any details of the movement. Nor did they know anyone else in Chaklasi who might have information about it. I showed Ranchod's letter to them, hoping to gain some further insight, but again both stated they had never heard of this *patra* and had no ideas about the significance of the letter.

Yet when Chaturbhai and Fulabhai spoke of Ranchod's movement, they described it as an *andolan,* or revolution. They said their parents had stated that Ranchod was brave in fighting against the British, but that is all they knew. There were no folk stories or songs about Ranchod or the movement, nor was the religious holiday on which the peasants fought with the colonial police marked with any celebrations. I was perplexed, to say the least, that a movement they identified as a revolution had simply lost its significance. Again, Chaturbhai and Fulabhai did not have an explanation. Perhaps my focus on the event encouraged them to elevate the status of Ranchod's movement, or perhaps this topic simply was not openly discussed with outsiders like myself. In any case, the brothers referred me to a local politician born and raised in Chaklasi who now resided in neighboring Nadiad. They also referred me to Chaklasi's genealogist, who resided in Baroda.[3] They explained that he would have written records dating back to the nineteenth century telling of extraordinary events that had taken place in Chaklasi.

I followed up on Chaturbhai and Fulabhai's suggestions but with no results. The genealogist, with whom I repeatedly tried to speak, was continually traveling to villages in the region and could not be contacted. I met other genealogists who had records for other villages in Kheda district, but they told me they had no information about Ranchod Vira's case. I interviewed the local politician on several occasions, only to be informed that events from the nineteenth century were no longer part of popular memory in the village; he explained that I was searching for something no longer relevant in today's world. Individuals associated with the Gujarat Kshatriya Sabha, an organization that claimed to have brought political awareness to all of Gujarat's Kshatriyas, including the former Dharalas of Chaklasi, simply rejected the idea that a peasant could have declared himself king in 1898. They, too, said that the events I was attempting to write about concerning the peasants of Chaklasi were not a relevant part of history at the end of the twentieth century. In any case, Ranchod and his supporters were not political, because they achieved an understanding of politics only after they had accepted the ideology of the Gujarat Kshatriya Sabha in the postcolonial era.[4]

I began to wonder if these were the only answers to my questions. The fact that the most rigorous application of the CTA in Kheda district took place in Chaklasi was no accident, as officials considered all Dharalas in 1898 to have sympathies with Ranchod's ideas. The legacy of such criminalization continued for the next few decades, as the Government of India did not eradicate the CTA until 1952.[5] Remembrance of Ranchod might evoke the revolutionary ideals of a Dharala leader who had ascended to the status of a king; alternatively, it might signal the beginnings of a period when Dharalas were classified and treated like criminals by colonial officials and elites. In fact, I had asked villagers about the impact of the Criminal Tribes Act in Chaklasi. Although most claimed they knew nothing about this legislation, almost all were willing to talk about the difficulties of *hajri*, the roll call associated with it. The name of the act itself appeared to be foreign, which it was, but the practice of standing in line—of wasting time and being humiliated by local elites—and the lack of employment opportunities, could not be forgotten. This is how the CTA was remembered.

I kept returning to Chaklasi with some regularity, hoping to find something new. As Chaturbhai and Fulabhai had predicted, I was unable to locate anyone who could provide insights into the popular memory of the peasant king. However, on one of these trips, as I casually spoke to an auto-rickshaw driver who was curious why I was visiting the village, I told him the story of Ranchod and about the difficulty I was having. Although he said he had never heard the fantastic tale, he claimed he knew where I might find some information. He took me to a house where a group of about a dozen Patidar men—all in their sixties and seventies—were holding a meeting. As I explained the details of the case to the men and circulated Ranchod's letter, Chotabhai Marghabhai Patel and Purshottamdas Patel told me they had heard of this story but did not know any details. The name of the Patidar headman Kashibhai was discussed, but this turned up no additional leads. The others felt the letter was nonsensical and had no idea of where to look for further information. However, Chotabhai and Purshottamdas had heard that a local Patidar from Chaklasi, who apparently had witnessed the battle in 1898, had written poetry and ballads about the event. Unfortunately, they were unable to remember the name of the author and the contents of these materials. They claimed that the poetry and ballads were never published and were probably lost.

I was never able to establish whether Ranchod's story had achieved the status of a hidden history, or whether his story no longer resonated in popular memory in Chaklasi. Moreover, it took me eight years to discover that an important piece of information about the case was incorrectly noted in the colonial record. I had used this bit of information to construct my narrative, and more important, had kept citing it when asking about Ranchod Vira. In 2004, I discovered the mistake and in the process learned that Ranchod's presence was very much a reality for many peasants.

53 · DADURAM'S LEGACIES

It is difficult to map the details of the peasant movement after Daduram's death. Peasants did not maintain copious records, and colonial officials shifted their attention to pressing matters that were viewed as greater threats to law and order—namely, the upsurge of nationalism and other mass movements.[1] However, I was dissatisfied with the explanation given in official reports that Daduram's movement had ended with his death. I was aware that the government had imposed legal measures in 1911 that prevented Dharalas from holding large meetings and restricted their mobility. Colonial power may have stopped the formal movement from growing into something larger, but I was also aware that the oral transmission of ideas propagated by Daduram simply could not be controlled.[2] I was not sure if Daduram's ideas had survived through the late twentieth century, but official sources provided a small clue that caught my attention: Daduram was the composer of many popular *bhajans*.[3] He had extensively used the informal institution of the *bhajan mandli* among fellow Dharalas as a way to transmit his religious and political messages throughout central Gujarat.[4] The success of the *bhajan mandlis* among the thousands of peasant supporters meant that some of Daduram's compositions might still be in circulation today.[5] After all, similar oral transmissions of religious hymns and folk stories had been reproduced for centuries in India and much of the rest of the world.[6]

My interest in pursuing Daduram's story was influenced by what I had read about the intellectual ideas of peasants.[7] Daduram stood out as a historical figure who influenced public opinion on questions of social relations and everyday life. He had established critiques of local peasant society and the colonial order while articulating messages with political and religious meaning. I was particularly interested in pursuing the claim that the ideas propagated by peasants were integral to the making of public life in India.[8] Peasants had been subject to domination of all varieties, but their thoughts, sentiments, politics, and discourses could find reception among elites in the countryside and cities. Daduram's story shows that ideas circulated from "low to high and high to low" in western India.[9] Although, I was aware of the paucity of evidence and the problems of relying upon colonial sources to write about ideas from "below," I wanted to explore the possibility of examining a peasant's public life.

I traveled to Dakore, which is situated between the urban centers of Ahmedabad and Baroda. I wanted to return to the center of the movement and the site of Daduram's compositions with the hope of meeting the descendants of his original Dharala followers. After I had made some initial queries, it became clear that Daduram's legacies continued to persist, nearly a century after his death. Everyone I spoke to in Dakore was familiar with Daduram's life and identified him with the honorific title of *maharaj*—the "great king," or "leader." Two temples dedicated to Daduram were constructed at some point in the twentieth century, and he is now worshipped as an avatar (earthly form) of the Hindu deity Vishnu.[10] The institution of the *bhajan mandli* devoted to Daduram's compositions continues to flourish in Dakore and has spread to other parts of Gujarat as well. When I visited Dakore, Daduram's movement was being led by a priest named Atmaram, the third successor after Tapsiram and Dalsukhram.

I first met Atmaram on my visit to Dakore in the spring of 1996. I introduced myself as a teacher interested in learning about Daduram, his *bhajans,* and his followers for the purpose of writing a book. Atmaram was pleased but asked few questions. There was little discussion about my own background; however, my presence at the temple and my inquiries about Daduram resulted in comments by Atmaram and others that Daduram's message had traveled beyond the small towns and villages in Gujarat and was now circulating in big cities like Bombay and Delhi. Atmaram narrated several short stories about Daduram's magical powers and quickly ended the meeting. I was unable to elicit any further information and asked Atmaram if I could return to the temple at some point if I had any further questions; he replied in the affirmative. Over the next few months, I frequently traveled to Dakore and spoke to many of Daduram's disciples in neighboring towns and villages. I noticed that all conversations about Daduram's life principally emphasized his ability to challenge the power of two very specific individuals, Sayaji Rao Gaekwar III—the maharaja of Baroda State (also known as the Gaekwar)—and the Shankaracharya.

I was not surprised to hear about the inclusion of narratives regarding the Gaekwar.[11] The colonial sources I had consulted talked about Daduram's public denunciations of the Gaekwar at large gatherings, and about his desire not to enter Baroda State, but nothing else was mentioned in the official record.[12] But today's disciples claim that the Gaekwar was threatened by Daduram's popularity and had him imprisoned in Baroda. They state that the Gaekwar personally went to the prison to talk to Daduram, and that the encounter proved to be a humbling experience for the Gaekwar. Daduram used his magical powers to create fifty-two images of himself as a way to demonstrate that he was more powerful than the leader of Baroda.[13] The Gaekwar acknowledged his mistake and fell to the ground and asked for Daduram's forgiveness.

The reference to the Shankaracharya was less clear, possibly referring to the south Indian Brahmin who produced prolific commentaries on texts like the Upanishads and the Brahma Sutras, and who was credited with founding the doctrine known as *advaita* around the ninth or tenth century.[14] However, as the later disciples of this figure also took on the title of Shankaracharya and were given seats of authority *(gadi)* in four different locations in India, it is difficult to know which Shankaracharya was named in the oral narrative. It is worth noting that Dakore was the site of a public dispute concerning Shankaracharya in 1918.[15] During the 1900s, Madhav Tirth was the Shankaracharya who controlled the seat in Dwarka—a religious pilgrimage site within the Gaekwar of Baroda's territory. However, Madhav Tirth had come to disagree with many of the Gaekwar's reforms and had shifted the *gadi* from Dwarka to Dakore. Upon Madhav's death in 1916, a disciple named Rajeshwarashram assumed the role of the new Shankaracharya. Because of the conflicts with Madhav, the Gaekwar refused to accept this decision and placed a priest of his choosing, named Shantianand, on the *gadi*.

To complicate matters further, the nationalists working in Dakore recognized Bharati Krishna as the new Shankaracharya. Bharati spent a good deal of time campaigning for the nationalist movement and challenging colonial power in Dakore during the early 1920s. While Daduram's disciples do not discuss these early conflicts of succession, they appear to emphasize their own contestation of power with the figure who had refused to accept Daduram as a legitimate priest. Nonetheless, it is important to consider the context in which the ideas that challenge the Shankaracharya may have emerged.

The structure of the narrative about Daduram's encounter with the priest shared important features with the story about Gaekwar. According to the disciples, the Shankaracharya arrived in Dakore and began a dialogue with Daduram. Apparently, the Shankaracharya was unhappy about Daduram's decision to wear a sacred thread, a symbol typically associated with the elite status of "twice born" Hindus. Daduram rejected the Brahmin's interpretation, but continued to debate the issue for many hours. The Shankaracharya decided to resolve the conflict by testing Daduram's powers. Like the Gaekwar, the Shankaracharya was humbled by Daduram's magical skills, and he accepted Daduram's right to wear the sacred thread.

According to the disciples, Daduram is remembered not only as a peasant leader in Dakore but also as a figure more powerful than the strongest king in western India during the early twentieth century, and one of the most influential priests of elite Hinduism in the last millennium. He had met resistance by two elites and, through dialogue and magic, had successfully demonstrated his legitimacy as a political and religious figure. It has been suggested too that both narratives undermine the ritual hierarchy of kingship and the caste system that had historically marginalized people like the Dharalas and their small kings and *bhagats*. In the early decades of the twentieth century, many caste reform movements throughout India rejected the symbols of Hindu elites such as the sacred thread. In contrast, others adopted them as a political strategy for social advancement while simultaneously challenging and undermining elite interpretations of Hindu rituals.[16]

Although the oral narratives provided clues about the ideological nature of Daduram's movement, the specific focus on the Gaekwar and the Shankaracharya remained unclear. Furthermore, in my numerous conversations with the disciples, I found no mention of British colonialism within the narratives about Daduram. Consequently, I frequently asked questions about Daduram's life based on what I had read in the colonial sources. On more than one occasion, I was asked how I had come to know so much about Daduram. I stated that there were many colonial files in the archives in Bombay that talked about the peasant leader, specifically his activities from 1906 to 1909. Several individuals inquired about this information and were suspicious that the government may have misrepresented or misunderstood Daduram in their official records.

It did not help matters that I kept using the terms *Dharala* and *Baraiya* whenever I discussed Daduram's original followers. These had been acceptable terms used by members of the caste throughout the nineteenth century and the early decades of the twentieth century, but now, as the disciples informed me, they no longer identified themselves by these names but belonged to a "high caste" known as Kshatriyas. I realized during these conversations that exploring oral sources was made more difficult by the transformation in identity politics in the twentieth century in this locality.

My reading of colonial sources had pointed to the fact that Daduram was against any notion of a Kshatriya identity for his supporters, but now the fourth-generation followers of the movement had openly accepted this caste identity. Many low-caste communities in Gujarat, and throughout India more generally, had claimed Kshatriya status by reconstructing a past claiming that they were the descendants of the original Kshatriyas, and others adopted the customs, traditions, and ideologies of high-caste groups.[17] The historical process of claiming a Kshatriya identity varied from region to region in India, but, most important, these transformations typically accompanied an assertion of political demands.[18] Despite knowing this historical trend, I could not understand at first why Daduram's disciples would have accepted an identity that had been opposed by their leader in his lifetime.

On my last day in Dakore—nearly four months after I had first met Atmaram—I was invited to a *bhajan mandli* in which nearly one hundred disciples were to gather. I was told that the *mandli* would be composed exclusively of *bhajans* and stories by or about Daduram. Many of the individuals whom I had met over the past several months were present at the *mandli,* and a few said they were pleased I would be able to listen to stories about Daduram not mentioned in colonial sources. These individuals felt it was important for me to have information about Daduram from his followers, especially as I was interested in writing a book. A disciple started the meeting by narrating a story about Daduram's victory over the British government.[19] In all my conversations with Daduram's followers, this was the first time anyone had made reference to colonialism or nationalism. More significant, Daduram was described as "Bapu" and the individual who was responsible for forcing the British out of India: "The British government has told a lot about Daduram Bapu. When the British government was ruling over India, Daduram Bapu organized all of India's Kshatriyas. He spoke and gave them knowledge and information. The Kshatriyas came together and completed the work by forcing the British government to leave India. And, the British government left India."[20]

Bapu literally means "father" and is regularly used in the local vernacular, but within the context of the nationalist movement in India the term was a specific reference to Mohandas K. Gandhi—the Mahatma.[21] Although Gandhi's name was not mentioned during the meeting, several individuals later stated that Daduram was as powerful as Gandhi, and others suggested that Daduram was Gandhi. While Daduram is remembered as the central figure in India's nationalist movement, today's disciples also claim that Kshatriyas were primarily responsible for the victory over British colonialism. I had expected the disciples to sing devotional songs and recite narratives about Daduram, but I did not anticipate the explicit discussion of nationalism at the *bhajan mandli*. By beginning the *bhajan mandli* with this narrative, the disciples may have wanted to reinforce the idea that India was created because of Daduram and his Kshatriya followers.

Ironically, it was Gandhi who had condemned Dharalas in the early decades of the twentieth century for lacking a conceptual understanding of politics. In fact, Gandhi established a critique of Dharalas' desire for a new identity as Kshatriyas by stating, "No purpose is served by changing a name. Status is not gained by assuming a name but only acting in a manner benefiting Kshatriyas."[22] Gandhi may have been unaware of Daduram, or he chose to ignore the historical possibilities of a peasant movement from "below." However, Daduram's disciples were certainly aware of Gandhi's presence in their town. Gandhi had frequently traveled to Dakore, located only a few hours outside of his Ahmedabad ashram, to hold meetings, because the town had become a major nationalist center in Kheda district following the first "no-revenue campaign."[23]

On October 27, 1920, Gandhi delivered a speech at a public meeting in Dakore where he specifically addressed his concerns with Dharalas: "Someone told me that there would be many *Dharalas* in this gathering and that I might address a few words to them. What should I tell them? This at least I must tell them, that, if they have any idea of religion, they should know that it does not tell them to rob others. Rather than live by robbery, it would be better to commit suicide. Rather than rob others that one may eat, it is better to starve to death. Rather than rob for clothes, it is better to go naked."[24] Gandhi's overall purpose was to encourage Dharalas and others in Dakore who remained skeptical of the nationalist politics to join forces with the volunteers of the Non-cooperation Movement. It is unclear how Daduram's disciples or other Dharalas interpreted Gandhi's speech, or if his pleas had any direct impact on Dharalas' support for nationalism. Yet at some point Daduram's disciples not only began to engage with Gandhi's ideas but also appeared to incorporate them into their discourses.

For today's disciples, Daduram had achieved greatness not only as a local leader, but as a nationalist figure. The problem is further complicated when examining government documents of the period stating that Daduram opposed specific nationalists who claimed to be fighting for India's freedom. Officials had reported that Daduram's ideas had influenced a small number of educated Dharalas to start their own caste movement in 1909.[25] By the 1920s these individuals had brought a large number of peasants into their organization—the Baraiya Conference Movement—and had also formally joined forces with nationalists belonging to the Indian National Congress.[26] Unfortunately, the specific details of which ideas and strategies had circulated up from Daduram to the leadership of the Baraiya Conference Movement remain unknown, but it certainly raises questions about how influences from "below" contributed to the making of elite politics.

The oral narratives next turned to the themes of Daduram's occupation and poverty but were contextualized within the development of India as an agricultural nation. Daduram was described as having lived in a *jopdri* (a small hut), and great emphasis was placed on his ability to till the soil and cultivate a rough millet called *bajri*.[27] The following narrative illustrates these themes: "It has been told that [Daduram] worked in the fields and cultivated crops. A great soul like Daduram was born in the homeland of India. Agriculture is the main occupation of Indian people! For the sake of unity, for the agricultural fields, for spirituality, Daduram has told us many things that reside within our soul. It is for this reason that everyone is working today."[28] Apparently, inscribed within this narrative is an acknowledgment of the dignity of Daduram's labor in making the Indian nation, and by extension, the narrative is a celebration of peasants who have worked in the fields throughout the twentieth century.

The assessment of the narrative is correct, as the vast majority of India's population even today are agriculturalists. But the argument emphasizes Daduram's ability to speak about the nexus between spirituality and working in the fields and creating a unified India. The two narratives show that Daduram is remembered as a figure who provided wisdom to his supporters through an oral culture. However, the narratives also illustrate the ways Daduram's disciples have reconceptualized their own past, and they reflect the two central themes of Indian nationalism: anticolonial politics and postcolonial developments. Daduram and the Kshatriya community are remembered as "good nationalists" who were responsible for "forcing" the British out of India and for the productive work involved in unifying and building the nation.

The focus of the *bhajan mandli* shifted to other concerns over the next couple of hours. The disciples sang many devotional songs, and they engaged in a brief discussion of Daduram's life, outlining his religious experiences: he was the son of Ramanand, he became a disciple of Gorakhnath, and he had a divine encounter with Datta and Ram Lakhan. Daduram was also described as an incarnation of Dadu Dayal, and the narratives about Daduram's meetings with the Gaekwar and the Shankaracharya were repeated. There was a brief discussion about Daduram's death in 1909, and the names of the next two leaders of the movement were also given—Tapsiram and Dalsukhram. But there was no discussion about the lives and contributions of these two figures. Today's disciples situate Daduram within a tradition that directly links their guru with the highest of Hindu deities through a preceptor lineage: a practice common in many Vaishnavite traditions in northern and western India.[29] Daduram is interpreted as being directly connected to the deity Ram Lakhan (or Ramchandra) through a spiritual and intellectual genealogy that includes Ramanand, Gorakhnath, Datta, and Dadu Dayal. He is linked with gurus of the highest order and with the historical founders of some of the most inspirational religious movements for uplifting the poor and marginal castes in India.[30] However, the disciples did not explain the significance of the figures associated with Daduram or how Daduram understood their messages.

Nevertheless, the oral narratives about Daduram indicate that today's disciples belong to a Vaishnavite devotional sect known as Ramanandis.[31] The sect was inspired by the teachings of Ramanand, a historical figure of the thirteenth or fourteenth century who is said to have promoted egalitarian devotional ideals in which women, low castes, and "untouchables" could participate in Hindu rituals and practices. It challenged the hierarchy of the caste system and the elite status of Brahmanical ideology and advocated respect for low-status individuals and groups. Ramanandis are devotees of the Hindu god Ramchandra and often add *Ram* to their names to express their spiritual allegiance, as in the names Daduram, Tapsiram, Dalsukhram, and Atmaram. But more important, today's disciples adhere to one of the key organizational principles among Ramanandis in defining a spiritual genealogy that directly links their guru Daduram to Ramanand and Ramchandra.[32] The reason for including the figure Datta within the genealogy is unclear: the name may be a shortened version of Dattatrey, a priest considered to be an avatar of Vishnu, or Ramdatta, a name synonymous with Ramanand. Dadu Dayal was an influential follower of Ramanand in the sixteenth century whose teachings later inspired the development of a separate sect known as the Dadu Panth.[33] Gorakhnath is a historical figure of the fifteenth century whose teachings influenced a devotional sect associated with the Shaivite tradition.[34]

The incorporation of these two overlapping traditions indicates a complementary development of ideas about Hinduism in the region that did not view Gorakhnathis and Ramanandis as antagonistic. However, in the Ramanandi tradition, there is an extensive critique of the Dasnami sect founded by the Shankaracharya, possibly the figure Daduram's followers mention in their oral narratives. In fact, it has been suggested that the Dasnamis propagated the Shankaracharya's elite Hindu ideals that not only were antagonistic to Ramanandis but also served as the "religious and social antithesis" to the fundamental values promoted by Ramanand.[35] In consonance with the historical traditions among Ramanandis, Daduram's disciples continue to subscribe to egalitarian ideals within Hinduism. They have developed a complex discourse with values similar to those of other Ramanandis, and they contest any individual or sect that appears to celebrate caste elitism.

A SPIRITUAL GENEALOGY OF DADURAM'S SECT

Ram Lakhan
(Ramchandra)
↓
Datta
↓
Gorakhnath
↓
Ramanand
↓
Daduram
↓
Tapsiram
↓
Dalsukhram
↓
Atmaram

At the conclusion of the *bhajan mandli*, Atmaram provided a brief commentary about Daduram as a nationalist and as an extremely powerful and influential figure. He also informed me that he possessed several handwritten texts about Daduram. I reflected on the fact that Atmaram had never mentioned these texts before, and had shared this information only on my last day in Dakore. He stated that the words contained in these texts were sacred, had special meaning, and could be read only by the leaders of the movement. However, he pointed out that there was one text I could read, as it was open for public viewing, "Gyan Vilas

Vinayla Moti." I imagined that I finally would be able to examine how Daduram's life had been documented by his followers in the nearly two hundred handwritten pages of the text. It appeared to be recently produced, but it did not identify the author or authors or indicate when it was put together. From a quick appraisal, I noted that the text consisted mainly of *bhajans* and short narratives about Daduram. Atmaram's decision to hand me the text came in the evening, a couple of hours before my departure from Dakore and the end of my research in Gujarat. In a small twist of fate, the town's electricity went out shortly after I began examining the writings. A few minutes before I had to get on my bus, the electricity returned but left me not enough time to read the text. I was granted permission to photocopy a few introductory pages.

Nonetheless, the day had proven to be extremely important. The *bhajan mandli* had introduced me to a new set of concerns about Daduram that otherwise would have remained obscured, especially about how he is remembered by his followers today. Upon reviewing the five pages I had from "Gyan Vilas Vinayla Moti," I realized that much of the information stated in the oral narratives at the *bhajan mandli* had been reproduced in the pages of text. In addition, there was a chronology within the text that included details about Daduram and his disciples.[36] It also provides basic information about Daduram's successors, the construction of the temple, and the year when the text may have been completed. The last entry for the chronology is given as 1985, the year the temple in Dakore opened. There is no mention of Atmaram within the early pages of the text, but I recalled that Atmaram had stated the text was composed before his arrival in Dakore. While it was established that Daduram himself was unable to read or write, it is not clear if the other leaders of the movement received any formal education. If they too were nonliterate, then what were the origins of the texts? At what point were the oral traditions of this group first codified in written form? Unfortunately, I was unable to ascertain the answers to these questions.

It is remarkable that during the twentieth century the movement started by Daduram was able to incorporate the most influential traditions fighting against caste hierarchies and propagating egalitarian ideals within Hinduism. In addition, the movement chose to be directly linked to the politics of Gandhi, possibly because of his own polemics on caste and equality. Yet what remains unclear is where Daduram located the origins of his ideas during his own lifetime: would he have accepted Ramanand, Dadu Dayal, and Gorakhnath as part of his own intellectual and spiritual influences? There may be no satisfactory answer.

Daduram's story illustrates the difficulty of writing about the ideas of a nonliterate peasant. In the best of circumstances, the primary source materials—written and oral, official and nonofficial—are either fragmentary or simply missing. Yet the small clues about Daduram provide insights into the everyday world of a peasant living in colonial India, and equally they illustrate how he is remembered as part of a long history of popular Hinduism and as a central figure in a short history of nationalism. Daduram's story is significant for illustrating how peasant discourses contributed to the making of public life in early-twentieth-century India. His gatherings and *bhajan mandlis* played an important role in the transmission of ideas, where even nonliterate peasants discussed and debated issues of the dominance of local elites, the policies of the colonial government, and the polemics of nationalist figures. Daduram's ideas influenced other peasant communities to start movements of their own, and they had an effect on the development of the Baraiya Conference Movement. Colonial officials had noted Daduram's contributions—"above" and "below"—but after 1909 spoke only of the movement's demise, especially with the rigorous application of the Criminal Tribes Act.

Daduram's disciples continue to sing *bhajans,* serve food, and smoke ganja. However, they do not talk about the CTA, the construction of a criminal identity, or Daduram's struggles for labor rights. There is no mention of Tilak, the Mahua Act, or the Baraiya Conference Movement. And there is no discussion of Daduram's opposition to a Kshatriya classification. Today's Dharalas belong to a caste that identifies itself as the direct descendants of warriors, princes, and kings. In the newly formed nation of India, the kings and princes who governed their autonomous princely states were forced to give up their positions, marking a major transformation in kingship. Similarly, the Government of India banned smaller kings, landlords, and chiefs from maintaining their roles of authority in the countryside.[37] Those who governed the nation were not willing to share the functions of statecraft with others in India. *Bhagats* like Ranchod who had dual roles of authority as political and religious figures lost much of their power with the creation of the nation, because they were forced to abandon specific claims to governance. However, despite the legal abolition of small and large kings, the government could not prevent its citizens from adopting alternative forms of kingship, such as the ideas, customs, and practices associated with becoming a Kshatriya.

Today Daduram is remembered as part of a long history of popular

Hinduism that directly situates him within a tradition of Vaishnava reformers who fought for equality and social reform for the poor and marginalized sections of society. The movement has gone through ideological shifts over the twentieth century, but it is difficult to locate the moments of departure, when followers turned from the earlier concerns raised by Daduram to the contemporary issues that affect their world. However, the discourses of nationalism have also entered into the oral and written narratives of Daduram's past. He is remembered as the central figure in the short history of nationalism, where he is described as the individual responsible for leading the anticolonial struggle against the British raj while contributing his labor to the making of the postcolonial nation.

Why do today's disciples associate the activities of Daduram with Gandhi? Initially, I thought they equated Daduram with Gandhi; it did not occur to me at first that they may have been arguing that Gandhi was an incarnation of Daduram. By accepting the former case, one can argue that such an association legitimates a memory of Daduram's activities as part of a nationalist narrative in the making of India. However, the latter formulation provides a radical interpretation of the emergence of nationalism in Gujarat, which states that Gandhi's legitimacy and authority was actually inspired by Daduram. Although the material conditions of most of Daduram's disciples remain fragile, and the promises of the nationalist movement are obscured at best, today's Dharalas have chosen to make, narrate, and write their own history. It is a history that identifies the community as Kshatriyas; it is a history that links the entire community to the most influential Hindu reformers of the last four or five centuries; and it is a history that says their guru was the most powerful anticolonial leader in the twentieth century.

54 · RETURNING TO KHEDA

In 2004, I returned to Kheda district for the first time since my initial stay there in 1996. Nearly eight years had passed, a period much longer than I had initially planned to be away. I had a specific purpose in making the trip: I wanted to revisit the individuals who had earlier shared their ideas with me, in order to discuss my interpretations of their histories. My own research had been transformed by my extensive fieldwork in 1996, much more than I could have anticipated. In the process of writing earlier drafts of the book, I found it was often impossible to ignore the forms of local knowledge that had influenced my own thinking about the themes of my study. Yet I was aware that my translations and interpretations were situated within an ideological framework very different from that of the subjects of the research. I wanted to discuss my writings with those who had helped to shape my research, but more important, I wanted their feedback.

Typically, these are not the concerns of historians. In most instances, the practitioners of the discipline simply do not have the opportunity to meet the subjects of their research. In instances where subjects exist, it is not a methodological necessity to pursue a critique of one's writings. In fact, I probably would not have made such an attempt on an earlier trip to India. However, I had come across some field notes from 1996 in which I had written that several individuals wanted to see the British colonial documents that spoke of their leaders, ancestors, and villages, and that they wanted to know what I planned to do with the information they had shared with me.

It did not matter that they could not read English; they wanted to see the files. Translators could easily be found. It was impossible for the descendants of Ranchod, Daduram, the Koli chieftains, and the Dharala swordsmen to gain access to the archives maintained by the state governments of Maharashtra and Gujarat, or to the National Archives in New Delhi. It simply would not happen. Most of the individuals I had met could not afford to travel to the archives, and government officials simply would not allow peasants to consult the documents. Peasants could never know how their pasts were narrated and recorded in "official" documents of the imperial archive (the argument could also be extended to contemporary records as well): this was the privilege of educated members of society who had the correct academic credentials and knowledge of historical methodology.

I decided to return to Kheda with relevant notes and photocopies of archival records in my possession. Individuals could respond to, accept, or simply reject the narratives—the colonial ones and my own. Yet there were problems. It would be impossible to carry all the notes and photocopies from the United States back to rural Gujarat—the pages numbered in the thousands. I had neither the time nor the inclination to make duplicates of all the documents. I was happy to share all the material and information, but would this serve any real purpose? Would the individuals I had spoken to in 1996 be interested in my archive in its totality? More practical concerns emerged: How many copies did I need? Who would receive these documents? How would I organize the papers so they would make sense to anyone else?

In the end, I decided to take only those documents that mentioned either Ranchod Vira or Daduram. These were the documents that had initially introduced me to a world made by these two *bhagats* and their supporters. They were also the documents that had influenced the direction of my inquiries on my trip to Gujarat in 1996. Despite knowing the limitations of such sources and my selections, I decided to take several copies of the relevant materials, including the court case, surveillance reports, and a draft of my book.

55 · KALASINH DURBAR

After a day or so in Nadiad, a town in close proximity to Chaklasi, Anand, and Dakore, I realized there were serious problems with my plans. I learned that several individuals I had planned to meet were dead. This was not a complete surprise: all had been either septuagenarians or octogenarians when I last met them. The task was to locate others—an objective that no longer seemed simple. Before proceeding to several villages, I contacted Kalasinh Durbar, a person who had spoken to me in 1996 about his native village of Chaklasi. Kalasinh now asked me about the progress of my research and the purpose of my trip to Kheda. I explained that I was planning to return to Chaklasi and other locations and wanted to meet the people who had spoken to me during my original fieldwork. I was interested in discussing my writings on Ranchod Vira's movement and wanted to share the official government documents in my possession. As I began discussing the details of the case, beginning with how Ranchod had tilled the land of the village *mukhi* named Kashibhai, Kalasinh stopped me. He pointed to an older gentleman sitting in his room and announced, "This is Patel, and he is a close relative of Kashibhai's. They belong to the same family."

I was unable to conceal my surprise, and before I could continue, Kalasinh wanted to know the names of the individuals I had originally met in Chaklasi. I replied, "Chaturbhai Waghela and Manibhai Waghela." Kalasinh said he had known them personally, but both had passed away a few years before. Mr. Patel nodded his head and confirmed their deaths. I realized that I needed to alter my plans, but my conversation with Kalasinh and Mr. Patel (who identified himself only as "Patel" when I asked him his full name) provided new opportunities that I had not considered since starting my research. I explained why I considered the Ranchod Vira case to be politically significant—as a critique of colonial power and local social relations, and as a vision for a new political community for poor peasants in the villages. It was significant that such movements had preceded the emergence of peasant nationalism only two decades later in the same locality, and that the legitimation crises of the colonial state had important antecedents, before the rise of Indian nationalism. The descendants of today's Kshatriyas in Chaklasi—the Dharalas and the Baraiyas who had supported Ranchod—had conceptualized a different sort of polity, one that was more ethical and just than the government administered by the British. Kalasinh stated that my interpretations were incorrect. Mr. Patel added that there was no movement in Chaklasi. I was surprised, to say the least.

Kalasinh argued that the entire movement was actually started by Kashibhai and the village Patidars. Apparently, Kashibhai had used Ranchod Vira and his supporters to challenge colonial authority in the locality; in fact, this was not a movement led by a village priest and his disciples. Ranchod was not aware of the types of issues I was attributing to him: he simply could not know such things. Kalasinh concluded by saying that the events of 1898 were actually part of the Patidar-led nationalist politics for India's independence. Mr. Patel agreed, but pointed out that the movement took place in Raghupura, a village neighboring Chaklasi. He knew this for a fact: he had grown up in Chaklasi, and Kashibhai's land was in Raghupura. I asked if the family still owned the land, but he said that at some point after India's independence the family had had to give up the land.

I quickly turned to Ranchod's letter, which I had with me, and read the first two lines: "The temple of Ranchodji is coming into existence in the middle of Chaklasi on the east side."[1] The letter clearly mentioned Chaklasi, but what was meant by "the east side"? This was one of the details in Ranchod's letter that I had been unable to decipher in all these years. Was this a reference to Raghupura? All the official records, including the court case, identified Chaklasi as the center of the movement, not Raghupura. In fact, Raghupura was mentioned only as a village where Ranchod had some support. I showed the letter and the court documents to Kalasinh and Mr. Patel, but neither could explain it, except to say that this was a mistake. I asked if either had ever heard of Ranchod's letter or the circulating Kashi *patra;* neither had. However, Kalasinh suggested that it would be best for me to go to Raghupura and inquire about the letter and Ranchod Vira. Mr. Patel pointed out that the villagers in Raghupura had actually constructed a small shrine to honor Ranchod; he suggested that this would be a good place to begin. Before I could ask why a shrine was created if the Patidars were actually responsible for leading the movement, Mr. Patel had to leave and the conversation came to a close. I had many other questions to ask Mr. Patel, and I thought I would have another opportunity to speak to him. Unfortunately, a second meeting never took place.

Kalasinh asked if he could keep a copy of the court proceedings and Ranchod's letter, as he wanted to know more about the case. I gave him the documents, all the while recognizing that the purpose of the trip to Kheda was changing. This became further evident when Kalasinh said he wanted to visit Raghupura with me. I could not decline his request, even though I recognized that his presence might alter the direction of any conversation I might have with the villagers. His narrative of the Ranchod Vira case as led by Patidar nationalists could directly influence what the villagers of Raghupura would say to me in his presence. After all, Kalasinh had reached a position of great power and authority in the area. He had certainly been helpful in discussing the historical significance of Chaklasi on my trip in 1996, and our first conversation in 2004 had given me leads that appeared to be important. But his decision to accompany me was less than ideal for many reasons. In fact, it had the potential to be disastrous.

56 · **RAGHUPURA**

The day after my meeting with Kalasinh Durbar, the two of us met up again and proceeded to Raghupura from Nadiad with the necessary documents in hand. It was clear that Kalasinh had read parts of the court case overnight and wanted additional information about Ranchod. He was convinced that it was important for him to learn more about the events of 1898. He thanked me for taking the time to write a history of Kshatriyas, especially one that examined the past of his locality and the role of his community.

I asked him whether it mattered that my interpretation of Ranchod's movement was fundamentally different from his own, and he said that it did not. There were few written histories of Kshatriyas of Gujarat, he said, especially those that examined the contributions of ordinary people like Ranchod. I was confused by these admissions, especially as Kalasinh had claimed the day before that Ranchod had been manipulated by Kashibhai and the village Patidars. It was not clear what significance Ranchod could have within this framework. However, I wondered if the details of the court case had actually influenced his thinking about Ranchod and his supporters. I asked Kalasinh what he expected the villagers of Raghupura would tell us: what kinds of memories might be in circulation today? He replied, "They could never know their history." I did not ask him to explain what he meant by this. My confusion grew: it was no longer clear why Kalasinh was accompanying me.

Before reaching the village, we stopped at a print shop because Kalasinh wanted to make multiple copies of Ranchod's letter to distribute in the village. I could not help but note the irony of this. In 1898, Ranchod had two scribes make more than twenty handwritten copies of the letter; the photocopy machine made reproductions in a fraction of the time. More than a hundred years had passed since these letters were last circulated in this locality, and I was not sure what impact they would have now. Perhaps the villagers had never heard of Ranchod's letter or the Kashi *patra*. I wondered if Kalasinh's plan to circulate it in

Raghupura was the best thing to do under the circumstances, or if it was even appropriate. However, if Mr. Patel was correct that the villagers had constructed a small shrine in Ranchod's memory, then perhaps Ranchod's words would have meaning for the villagers beyond my own expectations.

A group of twenty or thirty men gathered in Raghupura upon our arrival. It was clear that all the villagers knew Kalasinh personally or by reputation. We explained the purpose of the visit and immediately proceeded to the shrine. It was impossible to know, but I wondered if the villagers were taking me to the shrine only because Kalasinh was present. I had expected a small temple of the type often found throughout India, but this shrine was organized in a pattern I had never seen before, with its two identical small structures made of five bricks each. Three bricks were placed parallel to one another, two more bricks were placed on top and served as a cover, forming a rectangular structure. An incomplete ring of small stones was placed near these small constructions; the two structures, plus the ring, were under a very large peepul tree.

The villagers claimed that the spirit of Ranchod Vira would frequently emerge in this location to protect the inhabitants of Raghupura. The peepul tree itself was sacred, because they believed the tree had been planted by Ranchod. I asked if anyone knew where Ranchod had supposedly constructed his *mandwa* that served as the center for all the activities. No one knew for sure. However, several feet away from this shrine were the agricultural fields once owned by the *mukhi* Kashibhai and tilled by Ranchod and his family. If this was indeed the location described in court testimony, we were all standing on the site where Ranchod had declared the end of the British raj and proclaimed himself king. I remembered that in his testimony, Ranchod had mentioned a peepul tree when he was asked by Magistrate Becharlal to discuss the death of the police constable: "Is it true that a dead body of a police peon was found from near your mandwa?" Ranchod had replied: "Not from near my mandwa, but from near a peepul tree, which is at a distance of 50–60 hands from my mandwa."[1] Yet in all our conversations, not one villager mentioned that this was also the location where the policeman was killed, or that the shrine had anything to do with his memory.

I asked the villagers if they knew who was responsible for monitoring the shrine, but everyone claimed to have no information. Kalasinh then inquired who worshipped on this site; again, none of the villagers knew. How could this be? It was clear that everyone in the village knew about this shrine. The villagers had happily taken me to it, possibly under the

Figure 2. Shrine for Ranchod Vira, Raghupura.

impression that I too was planning to worship there. However, as it became clear that I was interested in its origins and everyday functions, the villagers could provide me with no further information, whether out of choice or necessity. There was a "hidden history" here that I decided not to investigate.

The memory of Ranchod may have evoked a moment in the past when a Dharala became king and challenged the highest authority of his time—the British raj. However, the consequences of Ranchod's movement had led to what was interpreted by the villagers as harsh punishments for those men convicted by the colonial judicial system. In addition, the implementation of the Criminal Tribes Act in 1911 had created tremendous hardships for the Dharalas in Chaklasi (and presumably Raghupura) through the most rigorous application of the legislation anywhere in the locality. Presumably this was a direct response to the village peasants' popular support of Ranchod. Patidar nationalists further exacerbated the situation by forcibly extracting labor from local Dharalas.

It was no surprise that today's descendants of the Dharalas were deeply suspicious of and antagonistic to elites and the government. In fact, later on, several village elders spoke of hardships and the impact of the CTA. Within this context, it was not surprising that the villagers were hesitant to build a formal structure that could be identified as a shrine dedicated to Ranchod Vira. The informal nature of the shrine, without markers identifying it as celebrating Ranchod, could exist without posing a threat. In any case, the large peepul tree could serve as a place of worship even if the bricks and rocks were removed. The fact that a shrine was dedicated to Ranchod's memory was in itself important. After a century, some if not all of the residents of Raghupura and its neighboring villages continued to remember Ranchod as a leader. In fact, for the villagers, Ranchod still had a presence in the village.

57 · LOCAL KNOWLEDGE

My visit to Raghupura gave me much insight into the legacies of Ranchod, despite the fact that I could not find answers to all my questions. In any case, I had never expected them. I asked the group of villagers who had joined us if any of Ranchod's descendants resided in the village. They responded to this question just as they had to many of the others I had asked: no one seemed to know, or at least no one was willing to provide the information. But when I inquired if anyone in the village had family members who had participated in Ranchod's movement in 1898, two elderly men—Moti Bhula and Garbad Jena—were identified as having local knowledge that might help me.

Moti claimed that his father had fought alongside Ranchod; Garbad said his father and uncle had supported Ranchod against the British. And both pointed out that their relatives had been injured during the battle on the night of January 12: Garbad's father and uncle had been shot in the neck by the police constables; Moti's father had suffered the same injury. Apparently all three men survived the severe trauma. I asked if they knew how many of Ranchod's supporters were wounded in the battle. Neither could provide a specific number, but both claimed that there had been many victims of British bullets. I showed them a copy of the court testimony and explained that British officials had neglected to include their relatives among those injured in the battle, and that the official record listed a total of only five peasants killed. "This is to be expected," replied Garbad. "After all, the British could not tell the truth that they injured and killed so many of Ranchod's supporters." He continued, "There would be an outrage if everyone knew about this, so the British lied in their documents."

I was particularly struck by the discussion of the three men who were shot in the neck by police but who survived their wounds. It is plausible—though impossible to know for sure—that such injuries had taken place during the battle and were not recorded by police officials, as argued by Garbad and Moti. However, as I listened to the descriptions of the injuries, I was reminded of the discussions in the court testimony that highlighted similar themes. During the trial, Surta Ragha was asked by First Class Magistrate Bahmanji Modi to describe the details of his son's death during the armed conflict:

> *Modi:* Do you know how your son Sama was killed?
>
> *Surta:* He was wounded with bullets in two places on the chest.
>
> *Modi:* What did you do when your son fell?
>
> *Surta:* His wife and I brought him into the *mandwa* and asked the *Bhagat* [Ranchod] to heal him. He burned incense and threw ashes over the wounds. . . .
>
> *Modi:* What did you do afterwards?
>
> *Surta:* On the evening following he died, and we burned his body.[1]

Meru Mitha, an accused person in the case, made the following statement about the injured in the conflict: "Sunna Surta was shot in the breast, and the bullet came out behind. . . . Gema Mitha, my brother, was struck in the chest with a bullet and was taken to the mandup. Baji Batta was wounded in the leg. Lalla Ranchhod got a bullet in the right leg. Rala Jalu was wounded in the right arm. I do not know who else was wounded. Ranchod burned incense near the wounded and said he would cure them. They did not get well, and Gunna died that night. The people dispersed about 8 or 9 P.M., leaving in the mandup the wounded and Ranchod Bhagat [and eleven others]."[2]

From these descriptions, it appears that Ranchod had assumed the role of primary healer for his supporters. Yet his powers were limited, and he was unable to save the lives of some, if not all, of the wounded Dharalas, especially when considering Meru's assertion that "they did not get well." Unfortunately, it is unclear if Meru was claiming that all the injured did not get well, or only Gunna and Sama. I did not discuss these court testimonies with Moti and Garbad, who were already convinced that all government documents had erased the contributions of their family members and community. I wondered how they would have responded to the statements saying that Ranchod could not save those who had suffered bullet wounds. I expect they would have argued that this was a further indication that the government was interested in either hiding the truth about Ranchod's powers or producing lies about their revered leader. After all, their relatives had survived the bullet wounds to the neck.

It was understandable that Garbad questioned the narratives in the official documents produced by the colonial government. Moti was equally adamant that the information was incorrect. He claimed that Ranchod's movement was so large that the British were afraid: "Other-wise, why would they send armed police to our village?" I asked how many people supported Ranchod in the locality; both stated that every-one did. "Everyone, including the Patidars?" I asked. "No, all the Ksha-triyas," said Garbad. I turned to the question of Ranchod's relationship with Kashibhai and asked if they knew why the movement had begun in the first place. Garbad said that all he knew was that Ranchod worked on Kashibhai's land; there must have been some animosity, and Ranchod wanted to improve the condition of Kshatriyas.

Kalasinh, who had remained quiet thus far, interjected that, according to his information, it was Kashibhai who was responsible for the move-ment, not Ranchod. My original worry that Kalasinh would enter the conversation proved to be correct. What I had not anticipated was that villagers like Garbad and Moti would simply reject his narrative. "No, no, no, that is all wrong," stated Moti. Garbad continued: "Ranchod did not lead the movement because of Kashibhai. He actually challenged Kashibhai and the British." They further emphasized that the movement was Ranchod's idea, and that it had nothing to do with Patidars. I did not inquire if they thought Ranchod was part of the nationalist move-ment, and neither of them mentioned this in our discussion. It was be-coming clear that the villagers in Raghupura continued to remember Ranchod as a leader who had used his power to challenge local elites and colonial power. More significant, individuals like Garbad and Moti would not let their memories of the past be transformed because out-siders or caste elites provided interpretations that differed from their own.

They refused to accept a narrative about the village's most significant political movement that effaced Ranchod and replaced him with Kashi-bhai. Further, both were unwilling to define all local politics within the framework of nationalism, especially a nationalism led by dominant Pati-dars. At the same time, the two were unable to answer my questions re-garding how they understood Ranchod's own politics and discourses. I asked Garbad and Moti if they had any information regarding a letter circulated by Ranchod to twenty-one villages in Kheda district. Kalasinh proceeded to distribute copies of Ranchod's letter to the villagers and read its contents aloud. Both Moti and Garbad claimed that they had not heard of this letter before, but they were not surprised that Ranchod was responsible for its production.

I asked if either had heard of a letter called the Kashi *patra*, but again

they had no information. However, Garbad explained that the twenty-
one villages all had large Kshatriya populations and maintained a network even today, especially for the purposes of arranging marriages. He
did not know when the informal network was conceived, but it predated
the late nineteenth century. If this was the case, then Ranchod built upon
well-established social (and political) relationships developed in the nineteenth century. Similar *gols*, or marriage circles, were known to have
emerged in Kheda district in the nineteenth century, but primarily among
Patidars who wanted to strengthen their social status and protect their
fiscal interests by collaborating with other Patidars in neighboring villages through arranging marital ties.[3]

I returned to the topic of the shrine's origins, but Garbad and Moti
claimed they had no information. They had welcomed an extensive conversation about Ranchod's movement but would not discuss the shrine
or its links to contemporary *bhagat* practices. I asked about the figure
who was identified as Ranchod's teacher, Bama Kuberdar of Sarsa. The
name appeared in the court testimony in at least two places. For example, when Surta Ragha was asked if he was a disciple of Bhagat Ranchod,
he replied, "Ranchod and I had been the followers of the Bama Kuberdar
of Sarsa, who had tied the necklace on us."[4] I thought this line of inquiry
might provide some context to Ranchod's ideological development, or at
least to how the villagers might remember such an important figure in
Ranchod's life. Garbad claimed that he had not heard of Bama Kuberdar,
but he knew of a contemporary leader of a religious movement in Sarsa
who had a similar name and was known as the Kuberacharaya. "The
Kuberacharaya has a big following; he even goes to America every year,"
stated Garbad. I asked if Garbad was claiming that Kuberacharaya and
Bama Kuberdar were somehow related. He replied, "I don't know."
Garbad further stated that today's villagers do not follow Kuberacharaya
or visit the Sarsa temple. I noted that neither Garbad nor Moti rejected
the claim that Ranchod was a disciple of Bama Kuberdar. Since I had
mentioned that this information was given in the official court testimony,
I had expected them to say that this was another government lie. Was
there a hidden history about this Bama Kuberdar or Kuberacharaya that
was not being articulated? Again, there was no way to know at this time.

I decided to turn to a different set of concerns not directly related to
Ranchod. "How far is the village of Chalali?" I asked. "Not far at all. It
is only a few kilometers from here," said Moti. "Have you heard of
Daduram?" Garbad said everyone in the village knew about Daduram.
So I asked if there were any followers of Daduram in Raghupura. Moti

said that many fellow Kshatriyas in the area supported Daduram, but there were no disciples in the village. It appeared that all my queries about Daduram's presence in Raghupura and his possible relationship to Ranchod had no answers. I would later discover a different story altogether.

58 · HIDDEN HISTORIES

Garbad Jena wanted to continue discussing Ranchod Vira's movement, rather than talk about Daduram. When I decided to mention the ten individuals arrested by the police after the battle of January 12, Garbad interrupted me to say that he was not finished with his criticism of the court testimony. "No, it is wrong to say that only ten people were arrested," he announced. "There were many more." "How many?" I asked. "Certainly more than ten, I don't know the exact number." "Why do you think the British only listed ten?" "Again, you forget that they lied in their records; they didn't want everyone to know about Ranchod and the large number of supporters." He continued: "Look, the police arrested many people but they did not write everyone's name down; they couldn't. Many were sent to jail and others died. By saying only ten people were responsible, they wanted to make sure that no one would know exactly how big the movement actually was."

Upon reading the list of ten, Moti Bhula pointed to a younger villager and stated, "He is the grandson of Banna Khoda"—one of the men arrested by the police.[1] I asked the man his name and if he could help me. "I don't know very much," he told me; "no one has talked to me about these things. Anyway, both Moti and Garbad have more information." He said nothing else, and I did not question him further. Garbad was eager to continue talking about the arrested villagers: "Do you know what happened to all the men?" he asked me. I said that the British recorded that Ranchod died in the Ahmedabad prison in 1899, and that others stayed in prisons in different parts of India for around ten years. Garbad told me that this was only partially correct. For the first time, he did not claim that the information was wrong; instead, he wanted to discuss the great prison escape of one of the arrested men. Garbad stated that some of the men from the village had received the punishment of *kala pani*—literally, "black water" and a local idiom for being transported to the penal settlement at Port Blair in the Andaman Islands in the Bay of Bengal. He continued: "Did you know that one of the men escaped from the prison? I don't know how he did it exactly, but he escaped from the prison in Singapore or Rangoon."

The court documents state that a few of the men received a sentence of "transportation," usually shorthand for being placed in Port Blair; I had never come across a notation that any of Ranchod's supporters had been sent off to Singapore or Rangoon.[2] I asked, "Who was this villager? What happened to him?" "I don't remember his name, but I remember that he came back to the village after many years and told us about the escape and difficulty in traveling back to Raghupura. I can't remember if he was in Singapore or Rangoon." I further inquired about this man: "How did the villagers respond to him upon his return?" "He was welcomed by everyone in the village; after all, he was a member of our community. The British never found out that he had returned to the village; even the headman did not know anything. He stayed here safely without any problems."

How is this narrative to be read? It is certainly plausible that Garbad confused the Andamans with Singapore or Rangoon (or perhaps even the Prince of Wales Island still resonated in popular memory from the early nineteenth century). He had never left the locality, but was aware that these far-off places were separated by "black water." He also knew that both places were part of British-controlled territory, a part of its empire, although he never used this language in his descriptions. And etched into his memory was the lone supporter of Ranchod who had returned. (According to colonial records, several men returned to their respective villages after serving their prison sentences.)[3] This individual was no ordinary man: he had defied the odds and escaped from a British prison and endured great difficulties in coming back. Garbad believed the man had been protected by everyone, possibly including Ranchod.

In many ways the man represented an ideal: He had initially taken up Ranchod's message that a better life could be made for the villagers and had challenged colonial power. Although he had had to remain "underground" upon his return, he lived the remaining years of his life independent of village elites, such as the *mukhi*, and colonial authorities. And he evoked the solidarity of the Kshatriyas, who had protected a member of the community who had suffered hardships for the purpose of improving the lives of all the villagers. His story was also an indication that it was possible for individuals to live outside the authority and jurisdiction of the colonial government, an objective that Ranchod himself had articulated in 1898.

I wondered if Garbad's memories of this individual were linked only to Ranchod's movement, or if they could be placed within a longer history of Dharala and Koli movements against the colonial government dating back to the early nineteenth century. I began thinking of the reports of jail breaks by Koli gangs to liberate important leaders, and the chieftains who had lived independently in villages outside the jurisdiction of the East India Company till the 1830s or 1840s. These historical pasts may have still resonated for today's Kshatriyas—that is, there were pasts in which earlier generations had seemingly greater freedom within spaces outside the control of the British and local elites. This is not to say that the early chieftains and peasants had not been subjugated by other forms of power, but rather that, at one point, they were independent of groups historically remembered as coercive, authoritarian, and dominant.

There may also have been a more contemporary, postcolonial context to Garbad's narrative. The promises of the nationalist movement and the creation of a nation-state did not transform the lives of Garbad and others in the way that had been articulated by Ranchod and his original supporters. The Patidar nationalists who had wielded the Criminal Tribes Act ensured this would not happen. Garbad's memory of the former prisoner evoked a past when there were autonomous spaces within the village, where individuals could escape the authority of the government. The transition from colonial subject to Indian citizen from 1947 onward had only increased the presence of government in villages. This point was made more evident when I was told that the state had recently created a new official post for the specific purpose of monitoring villages around Chaklasi and Raghupura. I suspect that this new form of governmental control had something to do with the fact that this area now served as one of the main agricultural tracts producing potatoes for McDonald's in India.

59 · ERASING THE PAST

I continued with the topic of Ranchod's movement by asking Moti and Garbad where the movement had begun. I explained that, according to the official records, Chaklasi was the center of all activity, but that several individuals I had spoken to said this was incorrect. Moti said, "No, no, there was nothing in Chaklasi; everything took place in Raghupura. Your information is wrong." Garbad agreed. I asked if Raghupura had ever been a part of Chaklasi, or if it was possible that the British simply saw Raghupura as part of "greater Chaklasi."[1] "It is certainly possible," replied Moti. "It seems anything is possible when looking at the British documents."

Moti wanted to know more about how Ranchod's movement was recorded in the court documents. He asked me to look up how many people were supposed to have joined with Ranchod on the day of the violent attack. I explained that one official had reported that five hundred individuals had participated; others had said the number was slightly higher. Moti was not pleased with the numbers: "That is wrong; there were many more." He did not ask me any other questions about the documents, and I imagine he would have responded similarly to the findings in the final judgment of the case.

To Moti and Garbad, it appeared that the government had effaced a part of their past, details about their families, their village, and their leader Ranchod. Colonial officials could not even correctly identify Raghupura as the center for all political activity, even though they had measured, mapped, surveyed, and taxed the village throughout the nineteenth century. Chaklasi had replaced Raghupura in the official narratives of the event, and in the process, the villagers of Raghupura—the primary supporters of Ranchod—had been replaced with the peasants of Chaklasi. Moreover, the British had minimized the number of Ranchod's supporters and had simply chosen not to record the many Kshatriyas injured, killed, and arrested on that fateful day in 1898. More specifically, the names of Moti's and Garbad's family members were not even mentioned in the official documents of the case. Our dialogue confirmed what Moti and Garbad had probably long known about how colonial power functioned in constructing narratives about Kshatriyas. This was certainly not the only place where the past was rewritten for official purposes: the Criminal Tribes Act, for example, had sought to replace the complex history of Dharalas with simply a criminal past. On the other hand, it was clear that the villagers of Raghupura had produced and were circulating narratives about Ranchod and his supporters independent of those given in the court testimony or official records.

60 · NARSIRAM

Returning to Dakore to speak to the priest Atmaram was central to my fieldwork. First, however, I stopped in a village called Hamidpura, a few miles outside Dakore. Several individuals in Raghupura had suggested that I contact someone at one of Daduram's temples in the area to get information about Daduram, and Hamidpura was one of the temple locations mentioned. I expected this visit to be a short one, because my primary objective was to talk to Atmaram in Dakore and get his feedback. But once again, my plans were rerouted in a direction I did not anticipate.

I met Narsiram, the main priest of the temple, and explained the purpose of my trip. I also told him I was planning to meet Atmaram in Dakore. "You have come too late," he told me. "Atmaram no longer exists in this world." Apparently Atmaram had passed away in 1997, a few months after I had first met him. Narsiram also informed me that he and I had met once in Dakore about ten years earlier, at a *bhajan mandli*. I simply could not remember this meeting. Since I was carrying photographs of the *mandli* with me, I looked through them, but could not find Narsiram. I showed him these photos, and after a few seconds, he pointed to one of the photos and said, "I am in this one." His appearance had changed dramatically since the *mandli* in 1996: he now had very long hair and a full beard.

Narsiram selected another photograph to discuss with me: an image of the main narrator at the *bhajan mandli*. "This is Dayaram," he said, "and he has taken over Atmaram's *gadi* in Dakore. Actually, I was supposed to succeed Atmaram, but Dayaram stole the *gadi*." According to Narsiram, Daduram's movement had split into several factions over the controversy about the succession. Many of Atmaram's followers now refused to visit the Dakore temple, and they accepted Narsiram as the true successor. As we spoke, another individual entered the temple and sat next to us. "Yes," he said to me, "Narsiram is correct." The man identified himself only as Narsi Bhagat, and over the next few days he

Figure 3. Narsiram at the Daduram Mandir,
Hamidpura, 2004.

would provide numerous insights into how Daduram is remembered and commentaries about my own work.

As our conversation in the temple continued, I discussed the details of Daduram's life given in the colonial documents. I offered the reports to Narsiram, but he was not interested in them. Instead, he wanted to continue talking about how he had been robbed of Atmaram's *gadi*. I imagine he wanted to ensure that I would not forget to mention his dissatisfaction with Dayaram in my own writings. Eventually, I was able to discuss with Narsiram my interpretations of Daduram's life. He had little to say in response. I realized that it had been a mistake to announce that I was headed to the Dakore temple after my visit to Hamidpura; this appeared to preoccupy Narsiram.

Narsiram kept looking at the photographs and reflecting on the images of the past when Atmaram was alive and Narsiram was in line to succeed him as leader of Daduram's movement. He finally turned to me and asked if I would like to see a photograph of Daduram. He claimed to possess the only known photo of Daduram. Apparently the numerous paintings of Daduram I had seen were derived from this one image. Narsiram took me into the central worship room of the temple, where he

Figure 4. Photograph of Daduram kept in the
Daduram Mandir, Hamidpura.

kept the photograph and numerous paintings of Daduram and other
individuals associated with the movement. He handed me a small,
framed black-and-white photograph in which Daduram is sitting on a
wooden chair holding an open book in his hand; a painting of a two-
story, modern colonial building hangs in the background. Daduram is
wearing a turban, a dhoti, and a colored shawl with an embroidered bor-
der. A musical instrument and a stack of three or four additional books
are placed directly beside him.

Narsiram did not know when or where the photograph was taken or
its original purpose. He would not allow me to take the photo out of the
frame, as he was afraid it might get damaged. As a consequence, I was

unable to see if any information was printed on the back of the photograph. He did, however, permit me to take a digital photograph of the original to keep with me. It is difficult to know how many copies of the photograph were produced and distributed among Daduram's disciples. Narsiram was unaware of the extent of its circulation and how it came to be placed in the Hamidpura temple.

It occurred to me that, in my emphasis on the convergence between written and oral traditions, I had not considered the role of the visual in the making of history. The photograph and paintings were not simply alternative ways of remembering Daduram: rather, they created one of the primary modes of narrating the peasant leader's past. These images were not simply illustrations of Daduram but suggested that peasants participated in forging new religious and political identities by means of this medium. The written and oral traditions had converged at a time when new visual technologies were also becoming available and affordable throughout the countryside. Peasants, or at least their leaders, could choose how they wanted to be represented visually; this was no longer only in the hands of colonial ethnographers and officials who had primarily used photography for surveillance or illustrating the "primitive" or "backward" aspects of rural society.[1] Apparently any individual with sufficient funds could commission images that would allow future generations to remember the past.

61 · **SEEING DADURAM**

Professional photographers were known to travel in the countryside visiting fairs and bazaars with their cameras, props, and backdrops. A place like Dakore certainly would have attracted such individuals.[1] However, my initial concern was whether this was in fact an image of Daduram. I never asked Narsiram about this point, and it seemed irrelevant: the image is worshipped by today's disciples and accepted as the only known photograph of their spiritual leader. Rather than questioning the authenticity of the photograph, I wanted to examine how disciples such as Narsiram might understand the narratives about Daduram inscribed within the image. Equally, I was interested in how the visual representation became central to remembering the past.

But how widespread was this form among peasants at the turn of the twentieth century or even in later decades? The answer is unclear, and it is doubtful that photography ever had the impact of the printing press and written texts during Daduram's lifetime. Further, whereas the small-scale expansion of village schools in the 1890s had provided opportunities for Dharala boys to learn to read and write, peasant access to photography was certainly more limited. The difficulty in dating the photograph added to the ambiguity in discussing Daduram's role in creating the visual image. But because, for Narsiram, the photograph is an original representation of Daduram that allows disciples in Hamidpura to remember their leader—dating the photograph back to at least 1909—Narsiram is able to construct a past about Daduram.

How should this image be read? Daduram is depicted as a learned man with several books and a musical instrument. The titles of these texts are obscured, but the image suggests that he was actively engaged with the written tradition. Yet there is more. If the musical instrument symbolizes an aspect of Daduram's orality, especially in singing *bhajans*, then the photograph can be read as depicting a convergence of written and oral traditions. The background provides a context to this particular historical moment that is linked to colonialism and its emergent architectural style. But it is impossible to know if Daduram or his supporters selected the placement of the books, the musical instrument, and the background of the building for the photograph, or if these were the only props available to the photographer at the time. The turban may have been an innocuous part of Daduram's attire. Turbans were frequently included in formal images of religious leaders in western India. On the other hand, the turban was also a local symbol of prestige and privilege for Patidars in Kheda district, especially among the village headmen. Patidars were noted for refusing to allow other men to wear turbans in their presence and were known to beat and humiliate Dharalas caught wearing turbans.[2] Daduram's turban may have symbolized a further inversion of social relations and a break in the patron-client bonds he was demanding from Patidars.

But what was the objective in creating this photograph? It is a clear demonstration of Daduram's engagement with books at a time when surveillance reports suggested he was illiterate. This photograph could have been a direct response to the magistrate, but this seems unlikely. More plausible is the idea that Daduram or his disciples wanted an image capturing a historical moment when the power of the written word could be possessed by a Dharala, a peasant, or even a nonliterate person. Whether Daduram was able to read and write is irrelevant, because he is demonstrating that holding and possessing books, especially religious texts, is no longer the monopoly of elites. Daduram would certainly not have been the first to propose such a theme—Ranchod's possession of written texts also attests to this claim—but among Dharalas he appears to have preceded others in illustrating the point through a visual representation. Of course, Daduram's decision to enter a photo studio for the purpose of creating a portrait that he could own or circulate also marked an important juncture: there were new possibilities for narrating the past in a visual form.

I started looking at the paintings of Daduram in the worship room and noticed that all the images—large and small—included a book and a musical instrument. As with the photograph, it was not possible to know the titles of the books in the images. However, as I came out of the worship room, I noted writings on all the walls of the temple and on the ceiling. In addition, a painting of Daduram was placed on a bed within the main temple area, along with a book and musical instrument. I asked Narsiram about the book in Daduram's hand in the photograph, and he replied, "It is the Gita." By this he meant the Bhagavad Gita, or the "Song of the Beloved One," believed to have been composed around 150 BC.[3] He

Figure 5. Painting of Daduram in the
Daduram Mandir, Hamidpura.

did not know the titles of the other books, but explained that the writings
on the wall were also taken from the Gita. In all likelihood, the incorporation of the Gita by the disciples of Daduram is a twentieth-century
occurrence. (After all, Daduram began his movement in the first decade of
the 1900s.)

But within the region, the Gita probably had a much older association
with the Dakore temple and the worship of Krishna—the main figure in
the text. The popularity of the Gita can also be directly associated with
the emergence of nationalism and the engagements of individuals like
Gandhi, who considered the book to be his "spiritual dictionary" and
translated it into Gujarati so that larger numbers of individuals could
engage with its ideas.[4] Gandhi regularly made reference to the Gita in his
speeches as a way to spread the text's message throughout the country-

side. Narsiram did not mention any links to Gandhi and probably would not have dated incorporation of the Gita into Daduram's movement to the last century. For him, it had much older associations.

The only description of Daduram found in the official record was provided by the district magistrate of Kheda on May 23, 1908: "He is himself a Koli, and illiterate, but a man of character, with a good face, and of irreproachable, but not ascetic[,] life."[5] The first thing that occurred to me was that the photograph directly challenged the magistrate's description of Daduram's illiteracy. While the image does not prove that Daduram was actually able to read or write, it puts his engagement with a written tradition in the forefront for any individual viewing the photograph. In fact, it does something more: it requires the observer to ask: "Which book is Daduram holding (or reading)?" "How many books are in the photograph?" "What are the titles of the other books?" "Are the books connected in any way?" It is not easy to claim that Daduram was illiterate when looking at this image, without previous knowledge of the magistrate's report from 1908. (Some of today's contemporary disciples might speak of Daduram's inability to read and write during his lifetime, but this was not mentioned in my presence.) For Narsiram, Daduram is holding the Gita, a religious text that today's disciples in Hamidpura read daily.

Narsiram took me to another worship room in the temple, where I found several more paintings of Daduram and photographs of various disciples. He handed me an album with photographs of Atmaram and other religious men, saying he wanted me to see images of the ceremony in which Atmaram declared Narsiram the formal successor to the movement. (Apparently, these photos were taken shortly before Atmaram's death, in 1997.) I had expected the copies of the colonial documents and my own writings to lead to a dialogue with Narsiram; I had not realized that the handful of photographs from my 1996 fieldtrip would lead to such an extensive discussion between us. Our exchange of photographs permitted each of us to narrate a particular past, albeit with very different purposes. One could say that, at the start of the twenty-first century, photographs were one of the primary ways for Narsiram to construct a past about Atmaram, Dayaram, himself, and the direction of the movement over the past decade. Equally, the black-and-white image of Daduram provided the context for a longer narrative that directly linked Narsiram to Daduram in a way not possible for even Dayaram, specifically because this was supposedly the only known photograph of Daduram.

But there was more. Next to a large painting of Daduram on the wall of the worship room hung a large sword. I asked Narsiram why this weapon was placed right next to Daduram's image, and he told me, "The sword was a gift to Daduram from the Gaekwar of Baroda." Although Narsiram had not directly answered my question, he apparently assumed I would understand the significance of a gift from the maharaja of such an important princely state. Narsiram simply stated that the Gaekwar wanted to acknowledge Daduram's greatness by offering a royal sword. Hindu kings were known to grant gifts to religious men. These were generally land grants for the purpose of building temples, but in principle a sword could also be presented, perhaps to be used to protect pilgrims and temples. To receive a weapon from a king served as a reminder of the collaboration between kings and religious men against the policies of the British raj, which had outlawed the possession of weapons by Dharalas.

Narsiram informed me that Daduram was the last recipient of a royal sword. According to this narrative, Daduram was the last swordsman, the last Dharala. With the coming of India's independence in 1947 and the creation of the nation-state, the royal authority of princely states came to an end. Pilgrims and temples no longer needed the protection of swordsmen. In postcolonial India, such a task was the responsibility of the police and military. This marked an important change: when kings ceased to be kings, and Dharalas ceased to be Dharalas.

62 · DAYARAM

I met Dayaram at the Daduram Mandir (temple) in Dakore. His appearance, too, had changed. I introduced myself and handed over the photographs from my first visit. Initially, Dayaram did not remember me, but after viewing the photographs he was reminded of the *bhajan mandli* and my interactions with Atmaram. I explained that, during my last visit to the temple, Atmaram had asked to see the British documents that mentioned Daduram. I also told him that I had finished writing a book about Kheda's Kshatriyas during the nineteenth and twentieth century based on colonial documents and the oral and written materials I had gathered. I further explained the themes of the project, hoping he would respond to my interpretations.

I handed Dayaram the five pages I had from "Gyan Vilas Vinayla Moti"—the text Atmaram had permitted me to consult in 1996—with the hope that I would be allowed to see the handwritten book. Dayaram reviewed the pages and stated that, after Atmaram's death, the book could no longer be read by anyone except himself. Apparently, the book had acquired special status as a product of Atmaram's *gadi;* it was now part of the collection of sacred texts accessible only to the leader of the temple and movement. I accepted his explanation: I had no other choice. There was no way of knowing which books were included in this collection, or when it was actually started. If I accepted the narrative in the black-and-white photograph kept in the Hamidpura temple, then Dharalas and Baraiyas had already begun to possess and read texts during Daduram's own lifetime—Ranchod Vira had demonstrated this point even earlier, in 1898. I was also willing to accept that Dayaram may have had other reasons for not letting me see the text. In times past, elites had refused to permit Dharalas and other subordinate groups to read, hear, and possess sacred texts. Today, Dayaram was in control of the book collection kept in the temple, and I was seeking his permission to read "Gyan Vilas": this was certainly an inversion of social relations, which Daduram had demanded—although probably not the inversion he had imagined.

Figure 6. Dayaram at the Daduram Mandir, Dakore, 2004.

Dayaram asked me to read one of the British reports on Daduram. This did not come as a complete surprise: Dayaram was keen to learn about what British officials understood about Bapu, the term Dayaram used when referring to Daduram. In 1996, Dayaram had provided me with the narrative explaining that Daduram was responsible for forcing the British to leave India. It was clear that he was aware my own writings were based on these reports, given that I had already explained this to him. Dayaram had turned the tables, and it was my turn to provide a narrative of Daduram's past based on the surveillance reports. I remembered that after the *bhajan mandli* in 1996 Dayaram and I had had a short conversation about his background. He had explained that he had studied engineering at a local college; he was married and had children. But, he told me, he had renounced the world and his family and now was going to spend the rest of his life in Bapu's service.

I asked Dayaram whether I should read the documents to him in English, as I already knew he was fluent in the language. "No, I want you to translate the writings," he replied. By this point some twenty or thirty disciples had arrived in the temple, and Dayaram wanted everyone to hear the British account of Daduram's life. Before starting, I explained to

Dayaram and the others that, throughout the document, the British officials had identified Daduram's followers as Dharalas and sometimes as
Kolis. During my earlier trip to the temple, I had been reminded by several
of the disciples that these terms were no longer used. I wanted to be clear
that these were identifications used during the nineteenth century by colonial officials and some individuals within the community. I explained that
I was aware that Daduram's disciples identified themselves as Kshatriyas
today, but for the purposes of discussing the document I was going to use
the original terminology. Dayaram stated this was fine.

After completing the translation of a detailed five-page surveillance report from the district magistrate in 1908, I handed the document over to
Dayaram. I was concerned about his immediate response: many descriptions in the report directly contradict the oral narratives about Daduram.
Initially, he remained silent, and then he claimed that most of what I had
read was correct. This was the extent of Dayaram's discussion of the document. I had hoped that he or the others present at the temple would provide a critique, but this did not happen. In 1996, Atmaram had asked for
the documents, and I wondered if he would have responded differently to
the reports. I will never know the answer to this question. Unlike Garbad
Jena and Moti Bhula in Raghupura, Dayaram did not directly challenge
the contents of the district magistrate's report. He did not identify the
aspects of the report that he considered to be incorrect. I had expected
some intervention, especially regarding the magistrate's characterization
of Daduram as "ignorant" or "illiterate," or regarding Daduram's interactions with local elites and his desire to avoid the Gaekwar's territory.

However, I did not consider Dayaram's silence to be acceptance of the
surveillance report or even of my own ideas about Daduram. Perhaps he
wanted to think about the report further, or he never intended to have a
discussion. In any case, upon Dayaram's request, I left the papers with
him.

I do not know what Dayaram eventually did with the British reports.
The main purpose of bringing them to the temple in the first place was to
fulfill a promise I had made to Atmaram, who had wanted to see the
reports about Daduram even though he did not know English. I did not
view this as a contradiction. Atmaram had his own reasons for wanting
to possess the documents. He had permitted me to photocopy a few
pages from "Gyan Vilas," and I had agreed to return, but I was too late.

My conversation with Dayaram had shifted to the visual representations of Daduram in the temple. Unlike the Hamidpura temple (which
was significantly smaller), the Dakore temple only had a few images of

Figure 7. Painting of Daduram in the
Daduram Mandir, Dakore.

Daduram on display. One of the central paintings in the temple depicted
Daduram sitting on a tiger skin with a book and musical instrument. The
book and musical instrument reminded me of those found in other
images of Daduram in Hamidpura. This was the only painting I had seen
in which Daduram was wearing a turban, as he had in the black-and-
white photograph in Narsiram's possession. However, in the central worship area of the temple were three life-size idols of Daduram and his first
two disciples, Tapsiram and Dalsukhram. I remembered these idols from
my earlier trip, but now the figures were elaborately painted, clothed,
and decorated, and they served as the primary deities of the temple.

I asked Dayaram if he had any photographs of Daduram that I might

Figure 8. Idol of Daduram in the
Daduram Mandir, Dakore.

see. He presented me with one image that appears to have been assembled from a photocopy of one image superimposed over another photograph. Daduram is shown sitting in the mountains on a tiger skin, with a book and musical instrument. The image is laminated and bears a small advertisement on the bottom right-hand corner that reads: "Arvind Photographer." This image appears to have been commissioned and produced on a large scale for circulation among today's disciples. I was unable to ascertain how many copies were actually created by Arvind Photographer, but it occurred to me that this was not the only time visual representations of Daduram were circulated—the photograph may have been the first. However, Dayaram was very hesitant for me to include this specific image in the book. He complained that Arvind Photographer had misworded the caption under Daduram's image. He did not want anyone to see the caption and minimize Daduram's importance as a result.

Dayaram told me that he appreciated my interest in Daduram, even though my purpose was for writing a book. He said he understood that I had returned to Dakore to finish my research about Daduram. I assumed that he had learned about research methods while training as an engineer. "It is important that others in the United States and England should know the powers of Daduram," he claimed. Dayaram asked if I could send a copy of my published book to him when I had finished, and I agreed to do so.

As I was leaving the temple, I noticed a large plaque with a brief description of the temple's origins. It began by stating that the temple was started by Daduram in 1907. It identified Tapsiram and Dalsukhram as the next two leaders of the temple's *gadi,* but no dates were given for their respective periods of service. The temple was completed by Atmaram in 1997, but Dayaram's name does not appear on the plaque. I noted that this genealogy was consistent with the one presented in "Gyan Vilas" and the oral narratives at the *bhajan mandli.* I did not think about it further, until I spoke again to Narsi Bhagat, the individual I had met in Hamidpura in the company of Narsiram. Narsi claimed that a Patidar-Kshatriya conflict was at the root of how Daduram's disciples have constructed genealogies. Narsi believed Dayaram had effaced an important part of the past.

63 · NARSI BHAGAT

After our initial meeting in Hamidpura, Narsi Bhagat and I arranged to get together at his place in Dakore. He stated that he had much to explain, but first he wanted to make clear that he opposed Dayaram and considered him an illegitimate heir to Atmaram's *gadi:* "Dayaram stole the *gadi.* He doesn't have proper knowledge." Narsi was echoing the claim made by Narsiram in Hamidpura. I asked Narsi what he meant by proper knowledge, to which he replied, "Dayaram doesn't know the real power of the *gadi* because he wasn't supposed to be Atmaram's heir. Only Narsiram knows, and he won't tell Dayaram." He added, "Even I know more than Dayaram. After our conversation today, tell me if you learned more about Daduram from me or Dayaram; I know you went to the temple and spoke to him." Narsi lived down the street from the Daduram temple in Dakore and may have observed me going to the temple, or he may have heard about my visit from Narsiram. I asked him if he ever visited the temple. "No," he told me, "I refuse to see Dayaram, so I go to Hamidpura." When I asked if he was a disciple of Narsiram's, he replied, "No, it is the next-closest temple to my house. I was actually trained by a different guru, named Bholaram."

Narsi explained that Bholaram was a disciple of Sitaram, the third heir to Daduram's *gadi* after Tapsiram. He stated that the present genealogy kept in the Dakore temple neglected to mention Sitaram anywhere in the records: "They say that Dalsukhram followed Tapsiram, but that is wrong! It was Sitaram." Before continuing any further, Narsi asked me to write down the genealogy of Daduram's disciples to ensure that I would understand the problem of succession.

Narsi told me that, around the time Daduram died and Tapsiram took over the *gadi,* a large number of Patidars, including Sitaram, began accepting Daduram as their guru. "This is something that is not discussed by Dayaram today," Narsi claimed. "Tapsiram had selected Sitaram despite the long-standing conflict between Patidars and Kshatriyas." But when I asked Narsi to explain what he meant by "the long-standing con-

Figure 9. Narsi Bhagat in Dakore, 2004.

flict," he simply said it was well known that Patidars and Kshatriyas did not get along.

According to Narsi, Sitaram was the only Patidar to hold the *gadi;* the others were all Kshatriyas, including Sitaram's own disciples—Dalsukhram and Bholaram. Narsi assumed that Dayaram was responsible for removing Sitaram's name from the genealogy. "There is only one explanation for this," argued Narsi: "it is because Sitaram was a Patidar." Yet Narsi was pleased that Daduram's message had influenced Patidars, possibly marking an inversion of social relations in the locality. But there was also a spiritual reason for mentioning the omission: Sitaram was his guru's guru. Bholaram was directly associated with Sitaram; once Sitaram had been eliminated from the genealogy, so was Bholaram's legitimacy as Daduram's third-generation disciple (and this argument could be extended to Narsi as a fourth-generation disciple). In contrast, Dalsukhram had possession of the temple's *gadi,* and when a genealogy was constructed and formally codified within the temple, Dalsukhram was identified as Tapsiram's disciple. I suspect this is the concern Narsi had with Dayaram as well. Now that Dayaram had taken the *gadi* from

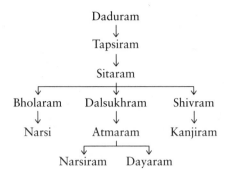

Figure 10. A genealogy of Daduram's sect
according to Narsi Bhagat.

Narsiram in Hamidpura, a new genealogy would eventually be constructed in which the names of many disciples simply would not appear.
For Narsi, this was one way the past was silenced.

Narsi had more to say about the problem of succession, and we traveled several kilometers outside of Dakore to an abandoned temple-like
structure that he wanted me to see. Narsi claimed that the building was
initially constructed to commemorate Daduram's death. As we walked
inside the building, he took me to three sets of marble carvings of two
feet: the first had an inscription that read "Shri Daduram Maharaj ni
Jai"; the second, "Shri Tapsiram Daduram Maharaj ni Jai"; and the third
remained incomplete, with no inscription. Narsi claimed that this was
further evidence of the conflict that continued to rage among Daduram's
disciples. The third inscription, he said, should read, "Shri Sitaram
Tapsiram Daduram Maharaj ni Jai," following the proper line of succession. But when Dalsukhram's disciples wanted to add his name to the
carvings, apparently Sitaram's students objected. Rather than engaging in
further conflict, Narsi explained, the disciples abandoned the entire
building and the inscription was never placed. Narsi posits that it is now
necessary to either include Sitaram's name or simply leave it blank, in its
present condition. Anyone who chooses to visit the site will be aware of
the problem in succession, but, he worries, one of Dayaram's disciples
will one day complete an inscription or continue to add carvings without
mentioning Sitaram. Narsi would resolve the problem himself if he had
the money to do so. "Yes, Kshatriyas and Patidars do not get along," he
said, "but this doesn't mean that Kshatriyas can afford to forget how a
Patidar became a disciple of a Kshatriya."

As we continued to talk, it became clear that Narsi wanted to ensure that I would mention the names of individuals who were not often remembered. He began by explaining that people often forget that Daduram and Dadu Dayal were the same people, and that it was very important to remember this. His point reminded me of the *bhajan mandli* in 1996, when several disciples had claimed that Daduram was an incarnation of Dadu Dayal. Narsi continued with a further discussion of the conflict between Patidars and Kshatriyas by explaining the little-known origins of the first Kuberacharaya of Sarsa. While I had discussed the reference to the Kuberdar of Sarsa in Raghupura in relation to Ranchod Vira and his supporters, I was surprised by Narsi's inclusion of this figure in our conversation. He explained that the Kuberacharaya in Sarsa today was a Patidar, but the original figure was in fact a Kshatriya who had gained his knowledge from Daduram. He could not identify when Patidars had taken over the position of the Kuberacharaya. I asked Narsi if he knew anything about the figure of the Kuberdar. He replied that the Kuberacharaya and Kuberdar were the same individuals. In Raghupura, Garbad and Moti had pointed out that no one in the village visited the Sarsa temple today, but they had not rejected the claim that Kuberdar was Ranchod's teacher. Could all this be explained by the fact that a Patidar was heading the temple? Of course, it was impossible to know whether the Kuberdar mentioned in court testimony was somehow related to the Kuberacharaya, but it raised the question of whether Ranchod Vira was somehow connected to Daduram through the elusive Kuberdar.[1]

He next turned to a discussion of the Gaekwar, Sayaji Rao, claiming that he was also one of Daduram's disciples. He repeated the narrative about Daduram's encounter with the Gaekwar that I had been told many times by others in 1996, but added that Sayaji Rao had constructed a temple for Daduram and presented him with numerous gifts, like a horse and silver. But unlike Narsiram in Hamidpura, Narsi made no mention of a sword. I asked Narsi how he knew all this, and he said, "My Bapu told me these things." In fact, he claimed that Bholaram had read a letter kept in a village near Indore, in central India, which documented everything about Daduram. Narsi could not remember the name of the village, but he said it would not be difficult to find. "When you get to Indore, just ask anyone about the temple, and someone will guide you to the village." (This was a more difficult task than Narsi implied: a few million people currently live in Indore, and hundreds of villages surround the city.)

Narsi used the term *Bapu* throughout the conversation to discuss Daduram, Sitaram, Bholaram, and Atmaram. Although he had not yet mentioned Gandhi, his use of the term prompted me to ask him about Daduram's relationship with the Mahatma. I explained that on my previous trip several disciples in the temple had stated that Daduram was Gandhi. I wanted to find out what Narsi knew about this. Narsi stated that Daduram was not Gandhi. But, he said, "Gandhi received his knowledge from Bapu." According to Narsi, Gandhi had consulted Daduram and became his disciple. Gandhi learned how to challenge the British only after speaking to Daduram. In fact, Daduram was first called Bapu; Gandhi acquired the title once he had accepted Daduram as his guru.

Narsi had little else to say about Gandhi, but the conversation about the British colonizers led him to voice strong objections: "The British came from another *desh*, or country; they had no knowledge. Their *sarkar* [government] was all about slavery. That is why they called us Dharalas and Baraiyas. These are hurtful words." I had earlier asked Narsi about the origin of *Dharala* and *Baraiya*, but he had said he would later explain why the British included these terms in their documents. This was apparently his explanation. He was visibly upset by the terms and preferred *Kshatriya* to describe Daduram's followers. He did not believe the British reports saying that Daduram had objected to this term for his followers.

Narsi was the first person I had spoken to during my fieldwork who had described colonialism as a form of slavery. But more important, it seemed particularly relevant that he associated colonial classifications of caste and community not only with a lack of understanding but also with an institution of oppression. I kept expecting him to expand on his critique of colonialism by discussing the application of the Criminal Tribes Act or the roll call associated with it, but he provided no further details, except to reiterate that Daduram had supplied Gandhi with the knowledge necessary to rid India of the British. I did not mention that Gandhi had regularly used the term *Dharala* in his speeches, or that he was opposed to Dharalas' claims to a Kshatriya identity. I thought of a report written by the district superintendent of police in 1944, which claimed that the term *Dharala* was associated with raids and crimes: "Now they are trying [to change] the name of their tribe and resent being called Dharala. They now call themselves Gohel, Parmar, Padhiar, Solanki, Chavda, Khant, Pagi, Baraiya, etc. . . . They however remain *pucca* [complete] criminals in spite of their new labels."[2]

Perhaps Narsi was well aware of this association, and my questions had evoked a bad memory of a not too distant past. The change in identity had signaled the end of the colonial government, which had officially criminalized Dharalas, as well as a new beginning in which Kshatriyas could construct a past not defined by criminality. The assertion that Daduram was a Kshatriya and was closely allied with Gandhi was certainly a start.

64 · HISTORY WITHOUT ENDS

I met a priest named Meru on a visit to the Hamidpura temple. He was aware that I would soon be departing for the United States, and he asked when I would return. I told him I was not sure of my plans, and that it might be a year or two before I could come again. Meru said that short visits were insufficient, and that if I really wanted to learn about the past, I needed to make a long-term commitment. He did not contest any particular interpretation I had provided about Daduram, nor did he suggest that I ought to reconsider what I had written. It did not matter that I had spent years searching for archival sources in the United Kingdom and India, or that I had spent an extended period of time speaking with numerous disciples in towns and villages in the locality. He suggested that I further consider local knowledge about Daduram before completing my writings. He offered no explanation for his advice.

Meru, of course, was not the first to point out that I should consider local knowledge when writing about the past. Earlier in my fieldwork, others had wanted to ensure that I understood the limitations of my own work because it relied upon government sources. The descendants of Dharalas were fully aware of the dangers of turning to official discourses. What colonial officials recorded in their records was suspect. Meru probably understood how information was codified within official texts and then replicated for the writing of narratives, including historical ones. By claiming that I could not fully interpret the past without local knowledge, he was disrupting my own writing process, highlighting the difference between what I claimed I knew about the past and what remained unknown. Perhaps Meru was suggesting that my arguments would forever remain incomplete and fragmented. Of course, my objective in writing about the past was different from that of Daduram's disciples or of Ranchod's supporters. These processes could never be the same. Nonetheless, the pasts that I had researched had moments of convergence with the pasts of my informants. However, Meru's purpose was not to discourage me. Instead he said, *"The conversation must continue!"*

I agreed that I should return. In fact, I had said this at the end of nearly all my interviews. Those whom I interviewed told me that the process of writing about the past should not end with the publication of a book based on the knowledge shared with me, that I should have further dialogues. While this book must come to a close, some narratives of the past continue to be told and retold. (Others, no doubt, are irretrievably lost.)[1] They generally do not appear in history books, and they may take the form of the oral, the visual, or the written text. They are fashioned to take account of contemporary concerns. In them some ideas are recognized as exigent and necessary in understanding the past. I have used different narrative forms in each part of this book in the spirit of retelling these multiple pasts. Yet it was evident from the conversations that there is no one way to retrieve and understand the past.

Many individuals perceived that my returning with the published book at some point in the future would result in a new round of conversations about the past. Yet there are problems to consider for the future, especially regarding the question of language. I write in English, a language that remains inaccessible to most people in rural Gujarat. However, many individuals have also pointed out that their inability to read English does not prevent them from disagreeing with my ideas and methods. I was reminded that I certainly did not have the last word on any issue. As Ranchod Vira and so many others like him demonstrated, individuals often choose to collect, confiscate, produce, and circulate texts they cannot read, all the while reserving the right to destroy the written word if they wish to do so.

I was aware that there were multiple ways in which my book could be interpreted or even destroyed. These were consequences to be expected from the individuals who had shared their life stories with me. However, the destruction of historical texts took on a new meaning for me after I spoke with Lallubhai Ramsinhbhai Parmar. I first met Lallubhai in the village of Majhatan, located a couple of hours outside of the city of Vadodara. For several years I had searched for the *Baraiya Hittechu and Kshatriya Vijaya*, the publication of the Baraiya Conference Movement—the organization founded by a group of educated Baraiyas inspired by Daduram's movement. Finally, as I was unable to locate these publications through official institutions and libraries, I decided to seek out the descendants of one of the BCM's founders, Garbadbhai Motabhai Parmar. An intelligence report from the early twentieth century stated that he had resided in the village of Majhatan.

Without knowing if there were any living relatives in the village who

226 / PART THREE

might have some leads, I decided to travel there. My queries about Parmar, also known as the village's first *masterji*, or teacher, quickly turned up a grandson—Lallubhai.[2] Lallubhai was a semiliterate peasant farmer who, with his wife and children, cultivated tobacco. He claimed to have been educated up to the age of eight or nine, in direct contrast to his father and grandfather. (The father was also a village teacher.)

After explaining the purpose of my trip, I asked Lallubhai if he had heard of his grandfather's publications. He indicated that he had kept a stack of the journals for many years, but at some point he used the paper for starting fires for cooking. He was unable to provide any details about the contents of the journals, even though he claimed to have read them. However, he did suggest that his grandfather's primary objective was to get rid of the negative associations attached to Dharalas and Baraiyas. Lallubhai took me to several neighboring villages to find others who might have additional information, but nothing more emerged. He was disappointed that he could not help me. However, Lallubhai made a profound statement that has stayed with me ever since. He explained he was aware that the publications symbolized his grandfather's success as a local leader, but it was more important to eat than to save the writings.

Lallubhai asked for my address in case he was able to find his grandfather's publications, but I did not expect to hear from him. Many individuals had taken my address during the years I was doing fieldwork, but no one had actually sent a letter. A few months after meeting Lallubhai, I received a short letter stating that he had located copies of the journal and a few relevant books, and that I should return to Majhatan to see the writings. I immediately wrote back to tell him that I was unsure of when I would be able to travel to Gujarat. Much time has passed now, and I have not heard back from Lallubhai. While he may have saved the writings for me, I expect that he and his family have found alternative uses for the paper by now.

For most historians, the destruction of sources is an unfortunate occurrence—a part of the past may be irretrievable. Perhaps Lallubhai would agree with this, and it may explain why he continued to search for his grandfather's writings. However, as this book nears its conclusion, it is clear that the historical narratives in it have not ended. Even Lallubhai, Meru, and the others whom I met were, in their own respective ways, aware of this.

CONCLUSION

The narratives that make up this book help to explain that the idea of the nation is part of an unresolved conflict within India. I have turned to a place famously associated with M. K. Gandhi and his Patidar supporters, where nationalism was said to have developed, for the purpose of illustrating that there was no agreement on the direction of nationalism, let alone any other form of politics. Perhaps more important, the minor acts discussed exemplify the ambivalence toward nationalism and the direct resistance of peasants who typically do not enter the pages of history. Both the nation and nationalism meant different things to different people at different times. While Dharalas may have contested nationalism and colonialism and offered political alternatives, the fact of the matter is that they became citizens of the Indian nation, along with Patidars, on August 15, 1947. Not surprisingly, the conflicts did not simply end in postcolonial India.

The book began with a discussion of a hidden history of coercion, exploitation, and abuse. I say *hidden* not because the violence was unknown. In fact, it was hidden precisely because it *was* known—to elites, to nationalists, to Gandhi—with the idea that, once India became free from its colonial past, memories of such violence, even though perpetrated by nationalists, would be forgotten and would disappear from the record. Or perhaps it was believed that the idea of becoming "Indian" would supercede all conflict within the nation. The documents of the imperial archive, however sporadic, minor, and fragmented, provide clues that allow us to reconsider the past in ways probably not imagined by the officials who penned reports and letters. David Hardiman has argued that, because Patidars participated in the nationalist movement, they became the "most respected" and "best-known" agrarian community throughout India.[1] The Patidars may have achieved such a reputation nationally, but the story at the local level was quite different, because Dharalas and others were well aware that the celebrated Patidars continued to dominate agrarian society even while demanding freedom for the nation.

One of my central concerns has been to illustrate how peasants conceptualized political community *before* the emergence of nationalism. Many Dharalas engaged in discourses and practices sanctioned by local custom that established critiques of colonial power, but these also offered alternative ways of imagining a political future. My purpose has been to show that the region became a center for anticolonial nationalism *after* Dharalas had already participated in political struggles in the countryside. Politics were not derived from only one community, caste, or class within agrarian society: the political culture in the countryside was dynamic. Of course, the discussion of Dharala peasants presented here reflects only part of the story about the nature of politics. There are many methodological limits to constructing narratives about the everyday lives of peasants, but even so, clues exist that provide a glimpse into the past, indicating a world that peasants made despite the persistence of colonialism in India.

An examination of the peasant movements of Ranchod, Daduram, and their respective supporters suggests that Dharalas adopted a wide range of methods and strategies as political actors, including, but not limited to, taking up arms as a way to contest power. Ranchod and his supporters were not peasant rebels; rather, they were engaged in a battle for political legitimacy. It was only when officials of the colonial state refused to establish reciprocal relations with the peasant king that a violent conflict ensued. I emphasize this point for a specific purpose. If we are to accept Ranajit Guha's claim that peasant kings were a characteristic of revolts throughout the nineteenth century, then the entire idea of rebellion in colonial India must be reconsidered to take into account the relevance of kingship in the lives of peasants. Peasants turned toward the idea of kingship because they considered it to be more ethical than the forms of governance associated with colonialism present in India at the time. Peasants like Ranchod and Daduram did not fail because their movements could not fulfill a set of expectations, such as national liberation or revolution. Rather, their movements reveal that the ideas of anticolonialism and ethical governance were central to the concerns of peasants.

Peasant kings and their supporters did not cede statecraft to the colonial state. Instead, they wanted to establish alternative modes of governance sanctioned by local custom. In addition, peasant kings, like all rajas and maharajas in India, functioned as religious or spiritual leaders within a society that legitimated their claims, as kings, to their peasant supporters. I highlight these points as a way to reconsider the binary division of colonial society into the material domain and spiritual domain as proposed by Partha Chatterjee. Peasant kings played a vital role in both domains. While the colonial state was able to establish its dominance in the countryside, it could neither prevent peasants from participating in the production and circulation of ideas about statecraft and economy, nor obstruct discourses of peasant religion. Locating peasant politics within both the material and spiritual domains, as defined by Chatterjee, opens new directions for the study of the origins of nationalist culture by highlighting the place of intellectual ideas that helped shape the direction of anticolonial politics within agrarian society.

The Dharala political movements also questioned the power of local elites who consolidated their dominance during the nineteenth century. The demand that patron-client bonds be abolished, that new land rights be established, and that menial service be abandoned were central to Dharala politics. However, any gains made at the turn of the century were quickly undone with the implementation of the Criminal Tribes Act. What replaced the organized mass movements of figures like Ranchod and Daduram were smaller protests, strikes, and underground raids. Patidar landholders began using the CTA as a way to reestablish their control of the political economy where it had been weakened by the political movements of Dharala peasants in the midst of the dual crises of famine and plague. Simultaneously, as the colonial state began to demand full revenue payments from the entire agrarian population, Patidars began their own mobilization, questioning the legitimacy of the colonial state and demanding the end of colonial rule.

"Circularity" and "mutually conditioned historicity" are categories that allow us to think about the exchange of ideas in the countryside. Dharalas were certainly neither the first nor the only part of agrarian society engaged in the production and circulation of political discourses and practices. But they were central to the making of the political culture in the region. Further, there was no consensus among Dharalas, Patidars, and others when it came to imagining a political community. The nature of conflict within agrarian society reflected these differences between Patidars and Dharalas, but at the same time the differences existed because ideas were circulating among villages, communities, and classes. Dharalas and Patidars, in their own respective ways, promoted specific thoughts and sentiments about political community with an awareness of how their everyday lives were intertwined historically. The news of the decline of colonial power in the early twentieth century served as an impetus for Dharalas to further resist the power of the nationalists in the region. Dharalas and the descendants of Koli chieftains formed an alliance and organized raids as a way to reestablish control of areas that had been lost during colonial rule, but also to obstruct Patidars from further controlling the means of production in the countryside through their dominance of the nationalist movement. Dharalas were not willing to surrender the functions of statecraft to the Patidars without a struggle.

I have not accepted the judgments of colonial officials when writing this book. Not all Dharalas were necessarily criminals simply because the colonial state passed legislation that gave them this status. Instead, central to my argument is the idea that Dharalas were political. Further, peasant movements did not end when officials declared their demise. It was with these thoughts that I traveled to the Gujarat countryside in search of legacies of the peasant politics. After more than half a century since independence, the descendants of the Dharalas I met do not remember a time when they were not national. It would be impossible to expect that nationalism did not influence and transform the ways in which individuals and groups thought about their world within the nation. At the same time, the discourses and practices of nationalism had to be narrated and reinforced in everyday life, precisely because of the resistance to the structures of dominance within the nation that continued to persist.

Today's Kshatriyas have not simply adopted or accepted the nationalism propagated by the Patidars or Gandhi, despite the fact that oral narratives are full of references to the participation of Kshatriyas in the struggle for India's independence. Gandhi, who was critical of Dharalas, now figures within oral narratives which maintain that he was inspired by a Kshatriya leader. Kshatriyas have reconsidered not only their identity within postcolonial India but also the ways in which they want to participate in the making of the nation. On the other hand, some individuals remember a time when their kinsmen lived autonomously, outside the authority of the state. These memories serve as a reminder of what existed prior to colonialism and nationalism, when Dharalas carried swords and were integral to trade, commerce, and the protection of temples.

Most individuals no longer want to be identified as Dharalas, or even Baraiyas, as the association of these names with criminality that was established in the age of colonialism continues to exist. Instead, identifying oneself as a Kshatriya is much preferred. More important, Kshatriyas are recognized across India and provide a religious and political association with one of the largest caste groupings in the nation. The claim of being a Kshatriya must also be considered alongside the fact that the

Government of India officially abolished princely states and the formal positions of kings and princes in the creation of the independent nation. In the countryside, new policies were implemented that forced the end of institutions associated with small kings, landlords, and traditional chiefs on the ground that they would interfere with the development of the agrarian economy. Kingship was forever transformed in postcolonial India. As the nation-state forced the end of kingship at all levels in society, the ideas about legitimacy, authority, and identity were nevertheless reconstituted by those individuals and groups who had long considered kingship an ethical form of governance. It should be remembered that most peasant kings were also religious men. While the Government of India ensured that such figures ceded the functions of statecraft to the nation, it could not prevent them from occupying their roles as religious leaders and identifying themselves and their supporters as Kshatriyas.

The oral narratives of the religious men attest to these claims. There is little doubt that today they situate themselves within "India." Their narratives are incomplete, incongruent, and minor and full of references to nationalism. Kshatriyas, not Patidars, are at the center of their explanations. But these men are also involved in reconfiguring the narratives of the modes of power related to ritual hierarchy in terms of kingship and caste. They are aware of how local forms of dominance have historically subordinated their supporters, and how the nation has not resolved the material conditions of most Kshatriyas. However, as all the individuals I met were aware of my interest in writing a book about Kshatriyas, the focus of our conversations was not on their explanations of living in poverty, but on articulating an understanding of how they interpreted their place *in* history.

I have sought to disentangle some of the narratives of nationalism and colonialism by rethinking the nature of an agrarian society in western India, while acknowledging that many other histories remain to be written, not only of peasants in Gujarat, but also of other societies marginalized from history. While historians are aware of such arguments, so too are historical actors who recognize the importance of history. I raise this point for a specific purpose. While traveling from one village to another within Kheda district, one becomes aware of when one has entered a village with a substantial Patidar population, because a statue or monument dedicated to a Patidar nationalist hero or to Gandhi will most certainly be present. This is a constant reminder of how the nationalist movement is remembered in postcolonial India. Patidar men and women arrested in the anticolonial struggle continue to receive government pensions as recognition for their contributions to the making of an independent nation. These same individuals receive numerous other benefits in everyday life. However, no such reminders or benefits exist for those Dharalas who opposed colonialism but also disagreed with the direction of the nationalist movement.

Those who govern the nation have ensured that history must be revised to include larger sections of the population and, in the process, nationalize those who may remain on the margins of the nation. But this has not happened for the descendants of Dharalas in Kheda. Instead, today's Kshatriyas have had to reconsider their place within the nation on their own terms and claim that Kshatriyas also contributed to the making of the nation.

The descendants of the Dharalas have learned all too well that they must create their own history. They cannot depend on the nation. These individuals know this is a difficult task to accomplish, especially as they have been told to forget the past for the cause of the nation. It is for this reason that so many individuals want to narrate the past, to tell about resistance to power and dominance of all forms. To remember is to ensure that nothing is lost for history.

ABBREVIATIONS

Admin.	Administration
Asst.	Assistant
BP	Bombay Presidency
BRO	Baroda Records Office
Coll.	Collector
Comm.	Commissioner
comp.	Compilation
CWMG	*Collected Works of Mahatma Gandhi*
CWSVP	*Collected Works of Sardar Vallabhbhai Patel*
DM	District Magistrate
DSP	District Superintendent of Police
Ex.	Exhibit
fn.	Footnote
FP	Financial Proceedings
GBPK	*Gazetteer of the Bombay Presidency,* vol. 3, *Kaira and Panch Mahals* (Bombay, 1879)
GD	General Department
GDP	General Department (Plague)
Gov.	Governor
Gov't	Government
GSA	Gujarat State Archives, Vadodara
HD	Home Department
HP	Bombay Home Proceedings
HPO	Huzur Political Office
IESHR	*Indian Economic and Social History Review*
IGP	Inspector General Police
Imper. vs. R.	"Criminal Sessions Case No. 61 of 1898, *Imperatrix vs. Ranchod Vira and Others*"

IPP	India Police Proceedings
JAS	*Journal of Asian Studies*
JBBRAS	*Journal of the Bombay Branch of the Royal Asiatic Society*
JD	Judicial Department
JP	Bombay Judicial Proceedings
JPS	*Journal of Peasant Studies*
L/PJ	Political and Judicial Department
MAS	*Modern Asian Studies*
Memo.	Memorandum
MSA	Maharashtra State Archives (Bombay)
ND	Northern Division
nd	No date of publication given
np	No place of publication given
no.	Number
OIOC	Oriental and India Office Collections, British Library (London)
OP	Official Publications Room, Cambridge University Library
PD	Political Department
PRBP	*Police Report of the Bombay Presidency, Including Sind and Railways*
RD	Revenue Department
RDF	Revenue Department (Famine)
RDPI	*Report of the Director of Public Instruction in the Bombay Presidency*
Rept.	Report
RFP	Bombay Revenue (Famine) Proceedings
RLP	Bombay Revenue (Land) Proceedings
RNN	*Reports on Native Newspapers for the Bombay Presidency*
SAPI	Secret Abstracts of Police Intelligence, Bombay Presidency
SC	Selected Compilation
Sec.	Secretary
SRBG (NS)	Selections from the Records of the Bombay Government (New Series)
SRBG (OS)	Selections from the Records of the Bombay Government (Old Series)
vol.	Volume

NOTES

INTRODUCTION

1. Cambridge University Library, OP.1198.364.02(1), *Report on the Working of the Criminal Tribes Act in the Bombay Presidency (including Sind) for the year 1918* (Bombay, 1919), Rept. from J. C. Ker, DM, Kaira, to Comm., ND, May 20, 1919. Throughout this book, I have used the contemporary spelling *Kheda* instead of the British *Kaira*, except in direct citations or in references to official correspondence where the latter spelling is maintained.

2. The Criminal Tribes Act was initially implemented in 1871; it was revised in 1897, 1911, 1924, and 1947. For analyses of the act, see Andrew J. Major, "State and Criminal Tribes in Colonial Punjab: Surveillance, Control, and Reclamation of the 'Dangerous Classes,'" *MAS* 33, 1 (1999): 657–88; Sanjay Nigam, "Disciplining and Policing the 'Criminals by Birth,'" pt. 1, "The Making of a Colonial Stereotype—the Criminal Tribes and Castes of North India," *IESHR* 27, 2 (1990): 131–64; Sanjay Nigam, "Disciplining and Policing the 'Criminals by Birth,'" pt. 2, "The Development of a Disciplinary System, 1871–1900," *IESHR* 27, 3 (1990): 257–87; Anand Yang, "Dangerous Castes and Tribes: The Criminal Tribes Act and the Magahiya Doms of Northeast India," in *Crime and Criminality in British India*, ed. Anand Yang (Tucson, 1985); M. Radhakrishna, "The Criminal Tribes Act in the Madras Presidency: Implications for the Itinerant Trading Communities," *IESHR* 26, 3 (1989): 269–95; M. Radhakrishna, "Surveillance and Settlements under the Criminal Tribes Act in Madras," *IESHR* 29, 2 (1992): 178–98; Sandria B. Freitag, "Crime in the Social Order of Colonial North India," *MAS* 25, 2 (1991): 227–261; Radhika Singha, *A Despotism of Law: Crime and Justice in Early Colonial India* (Delhi, 1998); David Arnold, *Police Power and Colonial Rule: Madras 1859–1947* (Delhi, 1986); B. S. Bhargava, *The Criminal Tribes: A Socio-Economic Study of the Principal Criminal Tribes and Castes in Northern India* (Lucknow, 1949); F. Booth-Tucker, *Criminocurology. A Review of the Work of the Salvation Army among Criminal Tribes in India* (Simla, 1915); M. Kennedy, *Notes on Criminal Classes in the Bombay Presidency* (Bombay, 1908).

3. The literature on this subject is extensive, especially as every book that discusses M. K. Gandhi's role in nationalist politics in India highlights Kheda district as the location of one of his first *satyagrahas* in India and the Patidars as being among his primary supporters. See Judith Brown, *Gandhi's Rise to Power, Indian Politics, 1915–1922* (Cambridge, 1972); Crispin N. Bates, "The Nature of Social Change in Rural Gujarat: The Kheda District, 1818–1918," *MAS* 15, 4 (1981):

771–821; Neil Charlesworth, *Peasants and Imperial Rule: Agriculture and Agrarian Society in the Bombay Presidency, 1850–1935* (Cambridge, 1985); David Hardiman, "Peasant Agitations in Kheda District, Gujarat, 1917–34" (PhD diss., Sussex University, 1975); David Hardiman, "The Crisis of the Lesser Patidars: Peasant Agitations in Kheda District, Gujarat, 1917–34, in *Congress and the Raj: Facets of the Indian Struggle, 1917–1947,* ed. D. A. Low (Delhi, 1977), 47–75; David Hardiman, "The Quit India Movement in Gujarat," in *The Indian Nation in 1942,* ed. Gyanendra Pandey (Calcutta, 1980), 77–121; David Hardiman, *Peasant Nationalists of Gujarat: Kheda District, 1917–1934* (Delhi, 1981); David Hardiman, "The Indian 'Faction': A Political Theory Examined," in *Subaltern Studies I,* ed. Ranajit Guha (Delhi, 1982), 198–232; Eric Stokes, "The Return of the Peasant to South Asian History," in *The Peasant and the Raj* (New Delhi, 1980); David Hardiman, ed., *Peasant Resistance in India, 1858– 1914* (Delhi, 1993).

4. For further discussion of agrarian society in Kheda District, see D. F. Pocock, *Kanbi and Patidar. A Study of the Patidar Community of Gujarat* (Oxford, 1972); Ghanshyam Shah, *Caste Association and Political Process in Gujarat: A Study of Gujarat Kshatriya Sabha* (Bombay, 1975); A. M. Shah and R. G. Shroff, "The Vahivanca Barots of Gujarat: A Caste of Genealogists and Mythographers," in *Traditional India: Structure and Change,* ed. Milton Singer (Philadelphia, 1959), 40–70; Alice Whitcomb Clark, "Central Gujarat in the Nineteenth Century: The Integration of an Agrarian Economy" (PhD diss., University of Wisconsin-Madison, 1979); Nico Den Tuinder, "Population and Society in Kheda District (India), 1819–1921: A Study of the Economic Context of Demographic Developments" (PhD diss., University of Amsterdam, 1992); Jaspal Kaur Dhot, "Economy and Society of Northern Gujarat, with Special Reference to Kheda District, ca. 1750–1850" (PhD diss., Maharaja Sayajirao University, Baroda, 1986); Marcia J. Frost, "Population Growth and Agrarian Change in British Gujarat, Kaira District, 1802–1858" (PhD diss., University of Pennsylvania, 1995); Vinay Gidwani, "Fluid Dynamics: An Essay on Canal Irrigation and Processes of Agrarian Change in Matar Taluka (Gujarat), India" (PhD diss., University of California, Berkeley, 1996); Vinay Gidwani, "Labored Landscapes: Agro-Ecological Change in Central Gujarat, India," in *Agrarian Environments: Resources, Representations, and Rule in India,* ed. Arun Agarwal and K. Sivaramakrishnan (Durham, 2000), 216–47; Vinay Gidwani, "The Unbearable Modernity of 'Development'? Canal Irrigation and Development Planning in Western India," *Progress in Planning* 58, 1 (2002): 1–80; Vinay Gidwani, "New Theory or New Dogma? A Tale of Social Capital and Economic Development from Gujarat, India," *Journal of Asian and African Studies* 37, 2 (2002): 83– 112; Marcia Frost, "Coping with Scarcity: Wild Foods and Common Lands: Kheda District (Gujarat, India), 1824–5," *IESHR* 37, 3 (2000): 295–330; Shri Prakash, "The Evolution of Agrarian Economy in Gujarat, 1830–1930" (PhD diss., University of Cambridge, 1984).

5. M. K. Gandhi, "Speech at Virsad," February 12, 1925, *CWMG,* vol. 30, (Ahmedabad, 2000), 255. Gandhi's reference to "lower communities" in his speeches and writings in Kheda district included Dharalas as well as others he identified as Antajayas and Kaliparaj.

6. I have found Michel-Rolph Trouillot, *Silencing the P(* *Production of History* (Boston, 1995) extremely useful in tl issue.

7. Partha Chatterjee, *The Nation and Its Fragments* (Princet(

8. Benedict Anderson, *Imagined Communities: Reflections o)* *Spread of Nationalism,* rev. ed (London, 1991), 7.

9. Chatterjee, *Nation and Its Fragments,* 5–6.

10. Ibid., 5.

11. Ibid., 13.

12. See Partha Chatterjee, *Nationalist Thought in a Colonial World: A Derivative Discourse?* (London, 1986).

13. Chatterjee, *Nation and Its Fragments,* 11. For a further critique of Chatterjee's argument, see Gyan Prakash, *Another Reason: Science and the Imagination of Modern India* (Princeton, 1999); Manu Goswami, *Producing India: From Colonial Economy to National Space* (Chicago, 2004), 23–27.

14. Chatterjee, *Nation and Its Fragments,* 6.

15. Ibid.

16. Similar patterns were noted in other parts of India as well. See, for example, Gyanendra Pandey, *The Ascendancy of the Congress in Uttar Pradesh, 1926–34. A Study in Imperfect Mobilization* (Delhi, 1978); Majid Siddiqi, *Agrarian Unrest in North India: The United Provinces, 1918–22* (Delhi, 1978).

17. Maharashtra State Archives (Bombay); Office of the Deputy Inspector General of Police (Bombay); Gujarat State Archives (Vadodara); Kheda District Collectorate Records Room (Kheda); Kheda District Superintendent of Police Headquarters (Kheda); Anand Rural Police Thana; Nadiad Town Police Station; Kheda Police Thana; Roman Catholic Mission Archives (Anand).

18. I have taken this idea from Antonio Gramsci's discussion of the methodological criteria for writing histories of subaltern classes in *Selections from the Prison Notebooks of Antonio Gramsci,* ed. Quintin Hoare and Geoffrey Nowell Smith (London, 1996), 55.

19. I was initially thinking of Carlo Ginzburg's use of court testimony to write about the now famous miller Menocchio in *The Cheese and the Worms: The Cosmos of a Sixteenth-Century Miller* (New York, 1987). Also see Shahid Amin, *Event, Metaphor, Memory: Chauri Chaura, 1922–1992* (Berkeley, 1995), 1.

20. This idea was discussed in James C. Scott's keynote lecture, "Why Civilizations Can't Climb Walls: The Creation of Non-State Spaces," at the Eighth Annual History Graduate Student History and Theory Conference, University of California, Irvine, January 15, 2005.

21. Again, I have taken this idea from Gramsci's discussion in *Selections from the Prison Notebooks,* 54–55.

22. Carlo Ginzburg, *Clues, Myths, and the Historical Method* (Baltimore, 1992), 164.

23. Ibid., 164; Ginzburg, *Cheese and the Worms,* xiii.

24. Ginzburg, *Clues, Myths,* 159, 164.

25. Carlo Ginzburg, *History, Rhetoric and Proof. The Menahem Stern Jerusalem Lectures* (Hanover, 1999), 25; Ginzburg, *Clues, Myths,* 158; Ginzburg, *Cheese and the Worms,* xiv, xv, xvii. Ranajit Guha also uses the metaphor

of the "distorting mirror" to discuss the reading of archival sources in *Elementary Aspects of Peasant Insurgency in Colonial India* (Delhi, 1982), 333. Eric Stokes, in his writings on peasant studies in India, similarly mentions the "distorted" and "distorting" nature of primary source material and the existence of a "double mirror" within the historiography. See *Peasant and the Raj*, 266, 267, 270.

26. Ginzburg, *Cheese and the Worms*, xvii; Ginzburg, *Clues, Myths*, 158.

27. Ginzburg, *Cheese and the Worms*, xiv.

28. Chatterjee makes a similar claim in *Nation and Its Fragments*, 13. Also see Gyanendra Pandey, "In Defense of the Fragment: Writing about Hindu-Muslim Riots in India Today," *Representations* 37 (1992): 27–55.

29. For an analysis of contemporary debates on methodology in South Asian history, see Vinayak Chaturvedi, ed., *Mapping Subaltern Studies and the Postcolonial* (London, 2000). Also see Hardiman, *Peasant Resistance*; Stokes, *Peasant and the Raj*; Guha, *Elementary Aspects*.

30. MSA, JD, 1899, vol. 78, comp. 457, "Criminal Sessions Case No. 61 of 1898, *Imperatrix vs. Ranchod Vira and Others*" (hereafter cited as Imper. vs. R.).

31. I have found the following writings useful in thinking about the theme of ethical governance: C. A. Bayly, *Origins of Nationality in South Asia: Patriotism and Ethical Government in the Making of Modern India* (Delhi, 1998); Partha Chatterjee, "Agrarian Relations and Communalism in Bengal, 1926–1935," in *Subaltern Studies I*, ed. Ranajit Guha (Delhi, 1982), 9–38; Partha Chatterjee, *The Politics of the Governed: Reflections on Popular Politics in Most of the World* (New York, 2004).

32. Guha, *Elementary Aspects*, 16. Also see Saurabh Dube, *Untouchable Pasts: Religion, Identity, and Power among a Central Indian Community, 1780–1950* (Albany, 1998); Saurabh Dube, *Stitches on Time: Colonial Textures and Postcolonial Tangles* (Durham, 2004); Ajay Skaria, *Hybrid Histories: Forests, Frontiers, and Wildness in Western India* (Delhi, 1999); Nandini Sundar, *Subalterns and Sovereigns: An Anthropological History of Bastar, 1854–1996* (Delhi, 1997); Malavika Kasturi, *Embattled Identities: Rajput Lineages and the Colonial State in Nineteenth-Century North India* (Delhi, 2002); Shail Mayaram, "Kings versus Bandits: Anti-colonialism in a Bandit Narrative," *Journal of the Royal Asiatic Society* 13, 3 (2003): 315–38.

33. SAPI, vol. XXII, no. 18 of 1909, May 8, 1909, 371–73, "Note on Koli Movements in the Kaira and Adjacent Districts during 1906–1909."

34. Vinayak Chaturvedi, "Of Peasants and Publics in Colonial India: Daduram's Story," *Social History* 30, 3 (2005): 296–320.

35. I have borrowed these relevant ideas from Ginzburg, *Clues, Myths*.

36. The Criminal Tribes Act (III of 1911).

37. OIOC, JP, 1914, P/9606, Rept. from J. Ghosal, DM, Kaira, February 2, 1914.

38. See Bayly, *Origins of Nationality*.

39. Hardiman, *Peasant Nationalists*, 250.

40. Ibid., 250–51.

41. See Stokes, "Return of the Peasant"; Bates, "Nature of Social Change."

42. Hardiman, "Crisis of Lesser Patidars," 51.

43. See Vinayak Chaturvedi, "Eine kritische Theorie der Subalternität: Über-legungen zur Verwendung des Klassenbegriffs in der indischen Geschichtsschrei-bung," *WerkstattGeschichte* 41 (2006): 5–23.

44. Hardiman, *Peasant Nationalists.*

45. Ibid., 254.

46. Ibid., 255.

47. This idea is borrowed from Partha Chatterjee, *A Princely Imposter? The Strange and Universal History of the Kumar of Bhawal* (Princeton, 2002), xii, although my interpretation of Ginzburg's writings differs from Chatterjee's on this point. Also see Amin, *Event, Metaphor, Memory*, 1.

48. Ginzburg, *History, Rhetoric, and Proof*, 24.

49. Carlo Ginzburg, *The Judge and the Historian: Marginal Notes on a Late-Twentieth-Century Miscarriage of Justice*, trans. Anthony Shugaar (London, 1999), 17.

50. Ginzburg, *Clues, Myths*, 164.

51. Ginzburg, *Judge and the Historian*, 118.

52. Ginzburg, *History, Rhetoric, and Proof*, 24.

53. Walter Benjamin, "Theses on the Philosophy of History," in *Illumina-tions: Essays and Reflections*, ed. Hannah Arendt (New York, 1969), 257. Also cited by Ginzburg, *History, Rhetoric, and Proof*, 24.

54. MSA, JD, 1899, vol. 78, comp. 457, Exhibit no. 46, "The Examination of Accused No. 1, Ranchod Vira, before the Committing Magistrate."

55. SAPI, vol. XXII, no. 18 of 1909, May 8, 1909, 371–74.

56. See Ginzburg, *Cheese and the Worms*, xi–xii.

57. See Guha, *Elementary Aspects*. Also, I thank Robert Brenner for first introducing me to the ideas within the tradition of political Marxism. I have greatly benefited from his writings: "Agrarian Class Structure and Economic Development in Pre-industrial Europe," *Past and Present* 70 (1976): 30–75; Robert Brenner, "The Origins of Capitalist Development: A Critique of Neo-Smithian Marxism," *New Left Review* 104 (1977): 25–92; Robert Brenner, "Dobb on the Transition from Feudalism to Capitalism," *Cambridge Journal of Economics* 2, 2 (1978): 121–40; Robert Brenner, "The Social Basis of Economic Development," in *Analytical Marxism*, ed. John Roemer (Cambridge, 1986), 23–53. Also, T. H. Aston and C. H. E. Philpin, *The Brenner Debate: Agrarian Class Structure and Economic Development in Pre-industrial Europe* (Cam-bridge, 1985). For further engagements with the Brenner Debate in Indian histo-riography, see Partha Chatterjee, "More on Modes of Power and the Peasantry," in *Subaltern Studies II*, ed. Ranajit Guha (Delhi, 1983), 311–50; Vivek Chibber, "Breaching the Nadu: Lordship and Economic Development in Pre-colonial South India," *JPS* 26, 1 (1998): 1–42; Vasant Kaiwar, "Social-Property Relations and the Economic Dynamic: The Case of Peasant Agriculture in Western India, ca. Mid-nineteenth to Mid-twentieth Centuries" (PhD diss., UCLA, 1989); Vas-ant Kaiwar, "Property Structures, Demography, and the Crisis of the Agrarian Economy of Colonial Bombay Presidency," *JPS* 19, 2 (1992): 255–300; Vasant Kaiwar, "The Colonial State, Capital, and the Peasantry in Bombay Presidency," *MAS* 28, 1 (1994): 793–832.

58. Guha, *Elementary Aspects*, 6.

59. Ibid., 9.

60. Ibid., 10.

61. Ibid.

62. Ibid., 11.

63. Ranajit Guha, "On Some Aspects of the Historiography of Colonial India," in *Subaltern Studies I*, ed. Ranajit Guha (Delhi, 1982), 6.

64. See James C. Scott, *Weapons of the Weak: Everyday Forms of Peasant Resistance* (New Haven, 1985).

65. On this point, I find Pierre Bourdieu's discussion particularly helpful in *Outline of a Theory of Practice*, trans. Richard Nice (Cambridge, 1977).

66. For a further discussion of *bhagat* practices, see Ajay Skaria, "Women, Witchcraft, and Gratuitous Violence in Colonial Western India," *Past and Present* 155 (1997); Ajay Skaria, "Writing, Orality, and Power in the Dangs, Western India, 1800s–1920s," in *Subaltern Studies IX*, ed. Dipesh Chakrabarty and Shahid Amin (Delhi, 1996), 13–58; Harjot Oberoi, *The Construction of Religious Boundaries: Culture, Identity, and Diversity in the Sikh Tradition* (Delhi, 1997); Sarat Chandra Roy, *Oraon Religion and Customs* (Ranchi, 1928). For a comparative perspective on this theme, see Amos Megged, "Magic, Popular Medicine, and Gender in Seventeenth-Century Mexico: The Case of Isabel de Montoya," *Social History* 19, 2 (1994): 189–208; Ann Anagnost, "Politics and Magic in Contemporary China," *Modern China* 13, 1 (1987): 40–61. I thank Ken Pomeranz for the last reference.

67. Benedict Anderson has recently pointed out that, throughout the nineteenth century, nearly all the states outside of the Americas were led by monarchies of one form or another. *Under Three Flags: Anarchism and the Anti-Colonial Imaginary* (London, 2005), 3.

68. See Bayly, *Origins of Nationality*.

69. Scott, *Weapons of the Weak*, 332.

70. Ginzburg, *Cheese and the Worms*, xii.

71. Chatterjee, *Nation and Its Fragments*, 13.

72. For a discussion of oral transmission of ideas and rumors, see Guha, *Elementary Aspects*, chapter 6; Shahid Amin, "Gandhi as Mahatma, Gorakhpur District, Eastern UP, 1921–22," in *Subaltern Studies III*, ed. Ranajit Guha (Delhi, 1984), 1–57; C. A. Bayly, *Empire and Information: Intelligence Gathering and Social Communication in India, 1780–1870* (Cambridge, 1996). For a comparative perspective on this theme, see Paul A. Cohen, *History in Three Keys. The Boxers as Event, Experience, and Myth* (New York, 1997); Robert Darnton, "An Early Information Society: News and Media in Eighteenth Century Paris," *American Historical Review* 105, 1 (2000): 1–35; Robert Darnton, *The Literary Underground of the Old Regime* (Cambridge, 1982); Simon Walker, "Rumor, Sedition, and Popular Protest in the Reign of Henry IV," *Past and Present* 166 (February 2000): 31–65; Chris Wickham, "Gossip and Resistance among the Medieval Peasantry," *Past and Present* 160 (August 1998): 3–24.

73. Here, I was specifically thinking of Benjamin's formulation "Not man or men but the struggling, oppressed class itself is the depository of historical knowledge." *Illuminations*, 260.

74. See Paul Rabinow, *Reflections on Fieldwork in Morocco* (Berkeley, 1977).

75. I have found Amin's *Event, Metaphor, Memory* extremely helpful on this point.

76. Benjamin continues his argument with perhaps a more crucial point regarding the importance of history, which I have found extremely relevant: "To be sure, only a redeemed mankind receives the fullness of its past." *Illuminations*, 254–55. Also cited in Ginzburg, *Cheese and the Worms*, xxvi.

1. RANCHOD

1. Seven or eight *bighas* corresponds to 4.11–4.70 acres of land. For a discussion of land measures used in revenue surveys, see *GBPK*, 65–67.

2. There are many documents in the MSA and OIOC that discuss Ranchod Vira's movement. The most comprehensive source, which includes a wide range of materials, is MSA, JD, 1899, vol. 78, comp. 457. Additional sources include MSA, RD, 1898, vol. 103, comp. 328; MSA, RD, 1899, vol. 24, comp. 1128; OIOC, "Remarkable Events during 1898," *Times of India Calendar and Directory for 1899* (Bombay, 1899), 457; OIOC, L/PJ/6/469, no. 86, Telegram from Viceroy, January 14, 1898; OIOC, L/PJ/6/469, no. 90, Telegram from Governor of Bombay, January 16, 1898; OIOC, JP, 1898, P/5549, Memo. from Comm., ND, May 11, 1898; OIOC, RLP, 1898, P/5544, Memo. from Comm., ND, April 20, 1898; Petition from Kashibhai Ranchhodbhai, Chaklasi, September 17, 1898; OIOC, RLP, 1898, P/5544, Letter from Comm., ND, May 23, 1898; Petition from Chunilal Motilal Desai, Chaklasi, August 3, 1898; Petition from Chunilal Motilal Desai, Chaklasi, September 7, 1898.

Also see SAPI, vol. XI, no. 3 of 1898, January 25, 1898, 16; SAPI, vol. XI, no. 5 of 1898, February 8, 1898, 34; SAPI, vol. XI, no. 6 of 1898, February 15, 1898, 34; SAPI, vol. XI, no. 7 of 1898, February 22, 1898, 55; SAPI, vol. XI, no. 8 of 1898, March 1, 1898, 61, 65; SAPI, vol. XI, no. 10 of 1898, March 15, 1898, 76; SAPI, vol. XI, no. 11 of 1898, March 22, 1898, 84; F. S. P. Lely, *Suggestions for the Better Governing of India, with Special Reference to the Bombay Presidency* (London, 1906), 29. See also the following newspaper reports in *RNN: Bombay Samachar*, January 15, 1898; *Native Opinion*, January 22, 1898; *Mahratta*, January 29, 1898; "Serious Riot in Guzerat," *Times of India*, January 14, 1898; "The Recent Riot in Guzerat," *Times of India*, January 17, 1898.

3. Imper. vs. R., Ex. no. 6, "Deposition of Witness no. 2," Jagannath Sagun, July 5, 1898. (A full reference is given for all "Exhibits" cited the first time from *Imperatrix vs. Ranchod Vira and Others*. Additional citations for the same exhibit from the case appear in the following form: Imper. vs. R., Deposition, Jagannath Sagun). The names of all the individuals who testified in court are given in English and not in Gujarati or any other Indian language. Court translators and typists did not maintain any consistency in the spelling of names. For example, there are three different spellings for Ranchod: Ranchod, Ranchhod, and Ranchore. Similarly Jagannath's surname is spelled as Sagan and Sagun. Teja Bava also appears as Teja Bawa and Teja Bama. I have adopted the spelling of the names as they appear for the first time in the court documents in the "List

of Evidence and Exhibits." However, in direct citations of the court testimony, I have kept the spellings given in the documents.

4. MSA, JD, 1898, vol. 103, comp. 328, Rept. from G. Carmichael, DM, to Comm., ND, January 21, 1898 (hereafter cited as Carmichael Report).

5. Ibid.

6. Imper. vs. R., Ex. no. 2, "List of Property," July 5, 1898; and Deposition, Jagannath Sagun.

7. For a discussion of related themes, see Ajay Skaria, "Writing, Orality, and Power in the Dangs, Western India, 1800s–1920s," in *Subaltern Studies IX,* ed. Dipesh Chakrabarty and Shahid Amin (Delhi, 1996), 13–58; William Cummings, "Rethinking the Imbrication of Orality and Literacy: Historical Discourse in Early Modern Makassar," *JAS* 62, 2 (2003): 531–51; Mathew Innes, "Memory, Orality, and Literacy in an Early Medieval Society," *Past and Present* 158 (1998): 3–36; Jack Goody, *The Interface between the Written and the Oral* (Cambridge, 1987); Jack Goody and Ian Watt, "The Consequences of Literacy," in *Literacy in Traditional Societies,* ed. Jack Goody (Cambridge, 1968); Walter Ong, *Orality and Literacy: The Technologising of the World* (London, 1982).

8. See Guha, *Elementary Aspects,* 51–54; Skaria, "Writing, Orality," 14.

9. Bayly, *Empire and Information,* 39–44; Guha, *Elementary Aspects,* 51–54; David Hardiman, "The Bhils and Shahukars of Eastern Gujarat," in *Subaltern Studies V,* ed. Ranajit Guha (Delhi, 1987), 1–54.

10. For a related discussion on Hindu kingship, see Sanjay Subrahmanyam, *Penumbral Visions: Making Polities in Early Modern South India* (Delhi, 2001); Sanjay Subrahmanyam and David Shulman, "The Men Who Would Be King? The Politics of Expansion in Early Seventeenth Century Northern Tamilnadu," *MAS* 24, 2 (1990): 225–48; Nicholas Dirks, *The Hollow Crown: Ethnohistory of an Indian Kingdom* (Cambridge, 1987); Nicholas Dirks, "From Little King to Landlord: Colonial Discourse and Colonial Rule," in *Colonialism and Culture,* ed. Nicholas Dirks (Ann Arbor, 1992), 175–208; J. C. Heesterman, *The Inner Conflict of Tradition: Essays in Indian Ritual, Kingship, and Society* (Chicago, 1985); Pamela Price, *Kingship and Political Practice in Colonial India* (Cambridge, 1996); Sumit Guha, "Theatre State or Box Office State? A Note on the Political Economy of Eighteenth Century India," *IESHR* 31, 4 (1994): 519–24; Saurabh Dube, "Idioms of Authority and Engendered Agendas: The Satnami Mahasabha, Chhattisgarh, 1925–1950," *IESHR* 30, 4 (1993): 383–412; Norbert Peabody, *Hindu Kingship and Polity in Precolonial India* (Cambridge, 2003); Ronald Inden, *Imagining India* (Bloomington, 2000); Daud Ali, *Culture and Politics in the Courts of Medieval India* (Cambridge, 2002).

11. Chaturvedi, "Daduram's Story," 209.

12. SAPI, vol. XI, no. 4 of 1898, February 1, 1898, 26.

2. THE *BHAGAT* AND THE MIRACLE

1. Imper. vs. R., Ex. no. 45, "The Confession of Accused no. 10, Surta Ragha, before the First Class Magistrate at Kaira," March 2, 1898.

2. See Francoise Mallison, "Lorsque Ranachodaraya Quitte Dwarka Pour Dakor, Comment Dvarakanatha Prit La Succession De Dankanatha," in *Devo-*

tion Divine: Bhakti Traditions from the Regions of India, ed. Diana L. Eck and Francoise Mallison (Paris, 1991), 196–207; Francoise Mallison, "Development of Early Krishnaism in Gujarat: Vishnu-Ranchod-Krsna," in *Bhakti in Current Research, 1979–1982: Proceedings of the Second International Conference on Early Devotional Literature in New Indo-Aryan Languages,* ed. Monika Thiel-Horstmann (Berlin, 1983), 245–55; M. R. Majmudar, "Dwarka Image of Ranachhodji and the Temple of Dakore," *Journal of the University of Bombay* 15, 4 (1948): 57–91. I thank Brock Cutler for his assistance in translation.

3. Dirks, *Hollow Crown,* 41.
4. Imper. vs. R., Confession, Surta Ragha.
5. Imper. vs. R., Ex. no. 3, "Deposition of Kashibhai Ranchhodbhai," July 5, 1898.
6. Imper. vs. R., Ex. no. 46, "The Examination of Accused no. 1, Ranchod Vira, before the Committing Magistrate," May 17, 1898.

3. DHARALA/KOLI/SWORDSMAN

1. Imper. vs. R., Examination, Ranchod Vira.
2. *Dhar* literally means edge, as in the edge of a sword, and is even used to describe the edge of a river *(dhara).* In Kheda, Dharalas, like other peasants, were known to use an agricultural implement resembling a billhook which was called a *dharia*—also derived from the same root word.
3. *Gazetteer of the Bombay Presidency,* vol. 9, pt. 1, *Gujarat Population: Hindus* (Bombay, 1901), 243; hereafter *GBPGP.* Also see R. E. Enthoven, *Tribes and Castes of Bombay,* vol. 2 (Bombay, 1922).
4. *GBPGP,* 243.
5. It should be noted that Dharalas were also called Talabda Kolis in the official record. However, for most of the sources I have consulted, officials preferred to use the classification *Dharala.*
6. *GBPGP,* 243, fn. 3.
7. Imper. vs. R., Confession, Surta Ragha.
8. For a discussion of similar processes in other parts of India, see C. A. Bayly, *Indian Society and the Making of the British Empire* (Cambridge, 1987), 138–50.
9. For a full discussion of this theme, see *GBPK,* chapter 8.
10. See Skaria, *Hybrid Histories;* Stewart Gordon, *Marathas, Marauders, and State Formation in the Eighteenth Century* (Delhi, 1994); Sumit Guha, "Forest Polities and Agrarian Empires: The Khandesh Bhils, c. 1700–1850," *IESHR* 33, 2 (1996): 133–54; Chetan Singh, "Conformity and Conflict: Tribes and the Agrarian System of Mughal India," *IESHR* 25, 3 (1988): 319–40; Chetan Singh, "Forests, Pastoralists, and Agrarian Society in Mughal India," in *Nature, Culture, Imperialism: Essays on the Environmental History of South Asia,* ed. D. Arnold and R. Guha (Delhi, 1994), 21–48.
11. MSA, JD, 1809, Diary (Duplicate) 50A, Letter from R. Barnwall, Asst. to Magistrate, to H. W. Diggle, Judge and Magistrate, Kaira, August 10, 1809.
12. MSA, JD, 1809, Diary (Duplicate) 50A, Letter from H. W. Diggle, Judge and Magistrate, Kaira, to F. Warden, Chief Sec., to Govt., nd.

244 / NOTES TO PAGES 31-34

13. Ibid.

14. MSA, JD, 1809, Diary (Duplicate) 50A, Letter from R. Holford, Judge and Magistrate, to M. F. M. Purmar, nd.

15. Ibid.

16. MSA, JD, 1809, Diary (Duplicate) 50A, Letter from H. W. Diggle, Judge and Magistrate, Kaira, to F. Warden, Chief Sec. to Govt., April 16, 1810. For a discussion of the penal settlement on the Prince of Wales Island, see Clare Anderson, "The Politics of Convict Space: Indian Penal Settlements and the Andaman Islands," in *Isolation: Places and Practices of Exclusion,* ed. Carolyn Strange and Alison Bashford (London, 2003), 40–55.

17. MSA, SC, 1824, vol. 2, Rept., A. Crawford, Coll., Ahmedabad, October 9, 1924.

18. Ibid.

19. For a general discussion of these processes, see *GBPK,* 78–105. Further details are given in OIOC, Mss.Eur.F.88, Box 6F, 36, Elphinstone Papers, "Captain Barnwell's Statement and Other Information regarding Kaira, 1821"; MSA, JD, 1809, Diary (Duplicate) 50A; MSA, JD, 1810, Diary (Duplicate), 54A; MSA, JD, 1810, Diary 52.

20. *Source Material for a History of the Freedom Movement in India,* vol. 1, *1818–1885* (Bombay, 1957), 207–31. Original references cited for Kheda district from the Bombay Government Records include: PD, vol. 48 of 1857; PD, vol. 52 of 1857; PD, vol. 59 of 1858; PD, vol. 54 of 1858; PD, vol. 60 of 1858; PD, vol. 61 of 1858; PD, vol. 51 of 1859. Also see R. K. Dharaiya, *Gujarat in 1857* (Ahmedabad, 1970).

4. THE PATIDARS AND THE KANBIS

1. *GBPK,* 2. Also see Lieutenant Colonel Melvill, "Notes on the Agriculture of the Cherotar District of Gujarat," *JBBRAS* 10, 28 (1871–72): 93–119. Official documents throughout the nineteenth century provide extensive discussions of the Charotar's "exceptional" status: specific selections of these sources are cited throughout the text. For example, see some of the earliest reports on the Charotar tract, in SRBG (OS), no. 10, *Reports on the Portions of the Duskroee Purgunna Situated in the Ahmedabad and Kaira Collectorates,* by Captain J. Cruikshank, Revenue Surveyor, Guzerat (Bombay, 1853); SRBG (OS), no. 11, *Reports on the Portions of the Dholka Purgunna Situated in the Ahmedabad and Kaira Collectorates; also, on the Mehemoodabad and Nureead Purgunnas, and on the Oomret and Bhaluj Tuppas, in the Kaira Collectorate; and on the Pitlad Purgunna and Nepar Tuppa in the same Collectorate,* by Captain J. Cruikshank, Revenue Surveyor, Guzerat (Bombay, 1853).

2. *Manual of the Bhagdari and Narwadari Act. no. V of 1862, and Standing Orders* (Bombay, 1914); B. H. Baden-Powell, *The Land-Systems, Being a Manual of the Land-Tenures and the Systems of Land-Revenue Administration Prevalent in the Several Provinces,* vol. 3 (Oxford, 1892), 260; *GBPK,* 105.

There appears to be some discrepancy regarding the nature of the *narwadari* system after the implementation of the direct revenue collection under the *ryotwari* system during the 1860s. According to one interpretation, the *narwadari* system in ninety villages was dismantled after the introduction of direct revenue collection, thereby "convert[ing] the Patidars from being village shareholders into individual owners of plots of land." See Hardiman, *Peasant Nationalists,* 39. Another interpretation suggests that there were only eight *narwadari* villages in the Charotar tract under British rule, while the others were classed as *ryotwari* (with the exception of thirty-seven villages with rent-free status). See Bates, "Social Change in Rural Gujarat," 777. For further discussion on this point, see H. Fukazawa, "Western India," in *The Cambridge Economic History of India,* vol. 2, ed. Dharma Kumar (Cambridge, 1983), 190–93.

In addition to the above evidence given in Baden-Powell's writings on "the modern condition of *[narwadari]* villages," Revenue Department reports state that the *narwadari* tenure was abolished during the 1930–31 Civil Disobedience Movement in specific villages of the Charotar tract: in Sandesar, Gana, and Thamna Talpad, all in Anand *taluka;* in Bhumel, Uttersanda, and Dabhan, all in Nadiad *taluka;* and in Vasna, Porda, Bochasan, Vadadla, Palej, Isnav, Amod, Sunav, Virsad, Vahera, Santokpura, Piplav, Dabhasi, Bodal, Dhundakuwa, Virol, Davol, Rupiapura, Danteli, and Ras, all in Borsad *taluka.*

See MSA, RD, 1930, file 5083/28, part 1, from J. H. Garrett, Comm. ND, to Sec. to Gov't, RD, October 1930; from the Coll., Kaira, nd; from S. Aminuddin, Deputy Sec. to Gov't, nd; from A. Master, Coll., to Comm. ND, June 18, 1930; Reports from A. Master, to Comm. ND, May 11, 1930, June 19, 1930, June 26, 1930; Series of Gujarati Petitions, nd; Memo. from Comm. ND, May 12, 1930, June 24, 1930.

3. SRBG (NS), no.114, *Correspondence Relating to the Introduction of the Revenue Survey Assessment in the Kaira Collectorate of the Province of Guzerat* (Bombay, 1869), from W. G. Pedder, Survey Settlement Officer, to Capt. C. J. Prescott, Superintendent Revenue Survey and Assessment, Guzerat, March 21, 1862, 8; "Appendix: Inquiry into the Management of Certain Village Communities in Guzerat," 27, 38. Also, from A. C. Trevor, Settlement Survey Office, to C. J. Prescott, September 18, 1865, 113.

4. Ibid.

5. The classification *Patidar* specifically referred to the revenue collecting elites among Lewa Kanbis in the nineteenth century. However, prior to colonial rule the term was applied to any individual and his family who had proprietary rights, including Kolis. See SRBG (NS), no. 114, *Revenue Survey Assessment,* Report from W. G. Pedder, Survey Settlement Officer, to Capt. C. J. Prescott, Superintendent Revenue Survey and Assessment, Guzerat, March 21, 1862, 8.

6. In Bates, "Nature of Social Change"; Hardiman, *Peasant Nationalists;* and Pocock, *Patidar and Kanbi,* there are differences in the interpretation of the number of divisions among Lewa Kanbis. Bates, following the classifications established by Pocock, suggests there were three divisions within the Lewa Kanbis that are relevant for the study of the region: "superior Patidars," "lesser Patidars," and ordinary Kanbis. He contrasts this division with Hardiman's typology of two divisions: "superior Patidars" and "lesser Patidars." These divisions are delineated in the colonial record in the early to mid-nineteenth century, but it is apparent that the classifications were becoming more essentialist and blurred in the later colonial period. And by the 1931 census, *all* Lewa Kanbis—"superior,"

"lesser," and "ordinary"—themselves adopted the "official" classification of *Patidar.* The focus here is the nature of agrarian dominance at the intergroup level between different communities of direct producers, rather than the intragroup dynamic, which Bates, Hardiman, and Pocock focus on, for the fact that colonial policies favored the Lewa Kanbis collectively, in contrast to other sections of rural society in Kheda district.

7. *GBPK,* 2. Also John Augustus Voelcker, *Report on the Improvement of Indian Agriculture* (London, [1893]), 11.

8. On a related topic, see A. B. Orlebar, "Notes Accompanying a Collection of Geological Specimens from Guzerat," *JBBRAS* 1, 4 (1842): 191–98.

9. SRBG (OS), no. 11, Cruikshank, *Reports of Dholka Purgunna;* SRBG (NS), no. 16, *Tours for Scientific and Economical Research Made in Guzerat, Kattiawar, and the Conkuns in 1787–1788,* by Dr. Hove (Bombay, 1855); SRBG (NS), no. 39[a] *Reports on the Resources &c. of the Districts of Neriad, Matur, Mondeh, Beejapoor, Dholka, Dhandhooka, and Gogo; the Tuppa of Napar; and the Kusba of Ranpoor; in the Province of Guzerat,* by Lieut. Colonel A. Walker (Bombay, 1893); Alexander Mackay, *Western India: Reports Addressed to the Chambers of Commerce of Manchester, Liverpool, Blackburn, and Glasgow* (London, 1853).

10. For a description of the agricultural tract, see OIOC, V/27/243/5, "Civil Administration of the Different Provinces of Gujarat," Minute by Major-General John Malcolm, October 15, 1830, Paragraph 25. Special thanks to Rajit Mazumder for his assistance with this reference. On the visual aesthetic, see OIOC, Mss.Eur.B3, James Forbes, "Memories of the Campaign on behalf of Raonath Row 1775." Cited in Hardiman, *Peasant Nationalists,* appendix 1, 260.

11. OIOC, V/27/243/5, Minute by Malcolm.

12. See Baden-Powell, *Land Systems,* vol. 3.

13. SRBG (NS), no. 114, *Revenue Survey Assessment,* from A. Rogers, Rev. Comm. ND, to A. A. Borradaile, December 23, 1865, 181.

14. Bayly, *Indian Society,* 130–50.

15. *GBPK,* 78–115.

16. See SRBG (NS), no. 114, *Revenue Survey Assessment.*

17. SRBG (NS), no. 295, *Papers Relating to the Revision Survey Settlement of the Nadiad Taluka of the Kaira Collectorate* (Bombay, 1895).

18. SRBG (NS), no. 114, *Revenue Survey Assessment,* from Captain C. J. Prescott, December 5, 1863, 613.

19. MSA, RD, 1886, vol. 26, Admin. Rept., P. H. Dastur, Deputy Coll., Kaira, July 15, 1886.

20. MSA, RD, 1881, vol. 15, no. 1372, Admin. Rept., J. Campbell, Coll., Kaira, July 11, 1881.

21. MSA, RD, 1885, vol. 22, comp. 1865, Admin. Rept., A. H. Spry, Coll., Kaira, July 24, 1884.

22. MSA, RD, 1884, vol. 22, comp. 1550, Admin. Rept., R. M. Kennedy, Asst. Coll., Kaira, July 18, 1884.

23. MSA, RD, 1898, vol. 26, comp. 1528, part 2, Admin. Rept., F. X. D'Souza, Asst. Coll., Kaira, August 17, 1897.

24. SRBG (NS), no. 295, *Revision Survey of Nadiad,* 11–12. There were a

total of thirty villages classed under the second-highest land rates in Nadiad *taluka*. All these villages were located within a radius of six miles from the towns of Nadiad or Anand.

25. MSA, RD, 1899, vol. 24, comp. 1128, Memo. from F. X. D'Souza, Acting Coll.

26. Carmichael Report.

27. MSA, RD, 1899, vol. 24, comp. 1128, Memo. from F. X. D'Souza, Acting Coll.

5. BECOMING A COLONIAL EMISSARY

1. Imper. vs. R., Deposition, Kashibhai Ranchhodbhai.

2. See Christopher Baker, "Madras Headmen," in *Economy and Society: Essays in Indian Economic and Social History*, ed. K. N. Chaudhuri and Clive J. Dewey (Delhi, 1979) 26–52. Thanks to Chris Isett for his help with this note.

3. Irfan Habib, *The Agrarian System of Mughal India, 1556–1707* (Bombay, 1963), 129–35. Also see Andre Wink, *Land and Sovereignty in India: Agrarian Society and Politics under the Eighteenth Century Maratha Svarajya* (Cambridge, 1986).

4. See Wink, *Land and Sovereignty*.

5. See Baden-Powell, *Land-Systems*, vol. 3.

6. See E. C. Cox, *Police and Crime in India* (London, 1910), 255; A. S. Holland, "Improvement of the Village Police," *Indian Police Association Bulletin* 2 (January 1923).

7. Regulation II of 1814: A Regulation for Establishing the Office of Tullaties, or Village Accountants, and Defining the Duties of the Paid Office, in the British Territories, under the Presidency of Bombay.

8. MSA, SC, 1815–1849, vol. 42, Administrative Report of the Case of Dessoys of Neriad in the Kaira Collectorate (hereafter cited as Rept. of Neriad Dessoys).

9. MSA, SC, 1815–1849, vol. 42, Statement made by Purbhoodas Patel of Sarsa, to the Coll., Kaira, nd, and Rept. of Neriad Dessoys.

10. MSA, SC, 1815–1849, vol. 42, Rept. of Neriad Dessoys.

11. MSA, SC, 1815–1849, vol. 42, Letter from A. Robertson, Coll., Kaira, to Edward Ironside, Judge and Magistrate, Kaira, September 1815 (specific date can not be read on original document).

12. MSA, SC, 1815–1849, vol. 42, Letter from J. Sutherland, Chief Judge, to Evan Napean, President and Judge of the Honorable Court of Superior Tribunal, November 1815 (specific date can not be read in original document).

13. MSA, SC, 1815–1849, vol. 42, "Translation of the Petition of Ajoobhaee Purbhoodas and Ajoobhaee Kishundas."

14. MSA, SC, 1815–1849, vol. 42, Letter from J. Sutherland, Third Judge of Circuit, to John Bax, Register to the Honorable Court of Superior Tribunal, March 9, 1818.

15. Ibid.

16. MSA, SC, 1815–1849, vol. 42, Petition of Raghubhaee Valalabhaee Desaee, to Gov. in Council, nd.

17. MSA, SC, 1815–1849, vol. 42, "Translation of the Neriad Dessoys' Petition."

18. MSA, SC, 1815–1849, vol. 42, Letter from Thomas Williamson, Acting Coll., to L. R. Reid, Acting Sec. to Gov't, September 26, 1826.

19. MSA, SC, 1815–1849, vol. 42, Rept. of Neriad Dessoys, and Letter from J. Sutherland, Second Judge, to L. R. Reid, Acting Sec. to Gov't, October 20, 1826.

20. MSA, SC, 1815–1849, vol. 42, Rept. of Neriad Dessoys, and Letter from Thomas Williamson, Acting Coll., to L. R. Reid, Acting Sec. to Gov't, September 26, 1826.

21. MSA, SC, 1815–1849, vol. 42, Rept. of Neriad Dessoys.

22. *GBPK,* 79.

6. THE *MUKHI* AND THE *FOUZDAR*

1. Imper. vs. R., Ex. no. 24, "Deposition of Baji Bapu," July 6, 1898.

2. H. H. Wilson, *A Glossary of Judicial and Revenue Terms and of Useful Words Occurring in Official Documents Relating to the Administration of the Government of British India: From the Arabic, Persian, Hindustani, Sanskrit, Hindi, Bengali, Uriga, Marathi, Guzarathi, Telugu, Karnata, Tamil, Malayalam, and Other Languages* (London, 1855), 247–48.

3. Singha, *Despotism of Law,* 1. Also see Habib, *Agrarian System;* John Richards, *The Mughal Empire* (Cambridge, 1995); Muzaffar Alam, *The Crisis of Empire in Mughal North India: Awadh and the Punjab, 1707–1748* (Delhi, 1986).

4. See Singha, *Despotism of Law,* chapter 1.

5. *GBPK,* chapter 9.

6. David Hardiman defines a *faujdar* in Kheda district during the colonial period as a police subinspector. See *Peasant Nationalists,* 53, 282. However, the *mukhi* Kashibhai Ranchodbhai did not have an official position as subinspector and the reference to *faujdar* appears to be used colloquially.

7. Imper. vs. R., Deposition, Kashibhai Ranchhodbhai.

7. MONITORING PEASANTS

1. Imper. vs. R., Examination, Ranchod Vira; my emphasis.

2. Imper. vs. R., Deposition, Kashibhai Ranchhodbhai.

3. Imper. vs. R., Ex. no. 21, "Deposition of Kanji Samal," July 6, 1898.

4. Imper. vs. R., Ex. no. 18, "Deposition of Surajram Mahipatram," July 6, 1898.

8. PROPHESY UNFULFILLED

1. Imper. vs. R., Deposition, Kashibhai Ranchhodbhai.

2. Imper. vs. R., Deposition, Kanji Samal.

3. Imper. vs. R., Confession, Surta Ragha.

4. Imper. vs. R., Examination, Ranchod Vira.

5. Imper. vs. R., Ex. no. 42, "The Confession of Accused no. 4, Meru Mitha, before the District Magistrate at Kaira," January 20, 1898.

6. Imper. vs. R., Ex. no. 43, "The Confession of Accused no. 5, Gema Mitha, before the First Class Magistrate at Kaira," January 29, 1898.

7. Ibid.

9. DEFEATING THE PLAGUE, CONTROLLING DHARALAS

1. See Arnold, *Colonizing the Body,* 200–239; Rajnarayan Chandavarkar, *Imperial Power and Popular Politics: Class, Resistance, and the State in India, c. 1850–1950* (Cambridge, 1998), 234–65.

2. For details on the history of the plague in the city of Bombay, see Chandavarkar, *Imperial Power;* Ian J. Catanach, "Plague and Tensions of Empire: India, 1896–1918," in *Imperial Medicine and Indigenous Societies,* ed. David Arnold (Delhi, 1989), 149–71.

3. For illustrative purposes, see the discussion regarding the aftermath of the bubonic plague within England: John Hatcher, "England in the Aftermath of the Black Death," *Past and Present* 144 (August 1994): 3–35.

4. "Plague Precautions in Guzerat," *Times of India,* February 4, 1898.

5. *The Bombay Plague, Being a History of the Progress of Plague in the Bombay Presidency from September 1896 to June 1899,* compiled by Capt. J. K. Condon (Bombay, 1900), 161 (hereafter cited as Condon, *Bombay Plague*); MSA, RD, 1899, vol. 24, comp. 1128, Admin. Rept. from Coll., Kaira, to Comm., ND, August 14, 1898.

6. Condon, *Bombay Plague,* 161.

7. RNN: *Din Mani,* April 4, 1899; *Rast Gaftar,* December 24, 1897; *Satya-vatka,* January 1, 1898; *Gurakhi,* January 8, 1898; *Gujarati,* January 22, 1898; *Deshbhakta,* January 29, 1898, and February 12, 1898; *Ahmedabad Times,* February 12, 1898; *Swadesh Bandhu,* August 9, 1899.

8. MSA, GDP, 1898, vol. 320, comp. 202, "Complaints and Memorials." Also, "The Anand Quarantine Camp," *Times of India,* February 22, 1898; and, RNN: *Raja Patrika,* September 30, 1899; *Pratinidhi,* April 18, 1899; *Mahratta,* November 1, 1896; *Dnyan Prakash,* December 13, 1897, and December 20, 1897; *Indu Prakash,* November 15, 1897.

9. Condon, *Bombay Plague,* 161.

10. SAPI, vol. XI, no. 7 of 1898, February 22, 1898, 55; OIOC, FP, 1898, P/5551, "Expenditure Incurred in the Kaira and Panchmahals Districts," July 5, 1898.

11. *Indian Social Reformer,* vol. 7, no. 43, July 4, 1897; SAPI, vol. XI, no. 4 of 1898, February 1, 1898, 41. For discussion of the popular responses to the plague epidemic, see David Arnold, "Touching the Body: Perspectives on the Indian Plague, 1896–1900," in *Subaltern Studies V,* ed. Ranajit Guha (Delhi, 1987): 55–90; Chandavarkar, *Imperial Power,* 234–65. For a comparative perspective on late-nineteenth-century state policies and popular responses to epidemics, see Mike Davis, *Late Victorian Holocausts: El Niño Famines and the Making of the Third World* (London, 2001). Also see Sheldon Watts, "British Development Policies and Malaria in India, 1897–c. 1929," *Past and Present*

165 (1999): 141–81; R. J. Evans, "Epidemics and Revolutions: Cholera in Nineteenth Century Europe," *Past and Present* 120 (1988): 123–46; Pule Phoofolo, "Epidemics and Revolutions: The Rinderpest Epidemic in Late Nineteenth Century Southern Africa," *Past and Present* 138 (1993): 112–43; Ira Klein, "Imperialism, Ecology, and Disease: Cholera in India, 1850–1950," *IESHR* 31, 4 (1994): 491–518; Mark Harrison, "Quarantine, Pilgrimage, and Colonial Trade: India, 1866–1900," *IESHR* 29, 2 (1992): 117–44.

10. THE DAKORE PILGRIMAGE

1. Imper. vs. R., Deposition, Kashibhai Ranchhodbhai.
2. *GBPK*, 167–68. In popular folklore, it is said that Dakore had already become a site for the worship of Ranchodrai (Krishna) in the mid-twelfth century. Also see Condon, *Bombay Plague*, 167.
3. *GBPK*, 167–68.
4. Bayly, *Rulers, Townsmen, and Bazaars*, 137.
5. MSA, RD, 1874, vol. 5, comp. 1375, Admin. Rept., G. H. D. Wilson, Asst. Coll., Kaira, to G. F. Sheppard, Coll., Kaira, July 6, 1874; MSA, RD, 1881, vol. 15, comp. 1372, Admin. Rept., J. Campbell, Coll., Kaira, to G. F. Sheppard, Comm., ND, July 11, 1881. The large-scale clearing and metaling of roads in Kheda district began in the 1860s. The process involved constructing roads with stones or limestone. Sometimes these roads were then covered with bitumen or tar. For a general discussion of roads in Kheda in the nineteenth century, see *GBPK*, 68–70.
6. *Pilgrim Taxthi Dakoreni Dhoordhshano Haval* (Ahmedabad, 1888). I thank Makhrand Mehta for helping me locate this text and for discussing the details of the poem. The translation of the poem is mine.
7. See H. C. Bhayani and Hasu Yagnik, "Krsna in the Gujarati Folk-Song Tradition," and Alan W. Entwistle, "The Cult of Krishna-Gopal as a Version of Pastoral," in *Devotion Divine: Bhakti Traditions from the Regions of India*, ed. Diana L. Eck and Francoise Mallison (Paris, 1991), 39–48, 73–90.
8. In fact, similar themes were associated with "Tamil temple myths" in southern India and may have been popular throughout other parts of the country for centuries. See David Shulman, *Tamil Temple Myths: Sacrifice and Divine Marriage in the South Indian Saiva Tradition* (Princeton, 1980). I thank Daud Ali for this reference.
9. David L. Haberman, *Journey through the Twelve Forests: An Encounter with Krishna* (New York, 1994), 100–110.
10. Imper. vs. R., Examination, Ranchod Vira.

11. THE KING'S PROCESSION

1. Imper. vs. R., Confession, Gema Mitha.
2. Ibid.
3. Imper. vs. R., Confession, Meru Mitha.
4. Ibid.
5. Imper. vs. R., Deposition, Kashibhai Ranchhodbhai.

6. Imper. vs. R., Confession, Meru Mitha.
7. Imper. vs. R., Deposition, Kashibhai Ranchhodbhai.
8. Ibid.
9. Imper. vs. R., Examination, Ranchod Vira.

12. RANCHOD'S LETTER

1. MSA, JD, 1898, vol. 103, comp. 328, "Seditious Letter." Additional translations given in Imper. vs. R., Ex. no. 10, "Seditious Letter addressed to Kashibhai Ranchhodbhai," and Ex. no. 11, "Seditious Letter." Madgh (or Magha) is
the name of a lunar month in the Hindu calendar. Samwat (or Samvat) is a reference to the Vikram Samwat era adopted in the Hindu calendar. The year 1956
corresponds to 1898.
2. Imper. vs. R., Examination, Ranchod Vira.
3. Imper. vs. R., Confession, Gema Mitha.
4. Imper. vs. R., Ex. no. 12, "List of Villages." The following twenty villages
are listed: Sunj, Kangoda, Vansole, Panhora, Chaklasi, Dakore, Vansole, Jakhla,
Meghna, Sura Samal, Raninu, Chhipdi, Khot, Kasare, Samarkha, Shanali, Sherry,
Anand, Par, Thamna, Dedda. (The order of the villages appears as such in the
original). Vansole is listed twice, and was perhaps considered by local custom to
consist of two autonomous parts, or there were two villages that shared the same
name. There is wide support in the sources for a total of twenty-one villages.
5. Imper. vs. R., Confession, Gema Mitha.
6. Imper. vs. R., Ex. no. 15, "Deposition of Shankar Dola," July 5, 1898.
7. Imper. vs. R., Ex. no. 29, "Deposition of Jhaverbhai Shivabhai," July 6,
1898.
8. Imper. vs. R., Examination, Ranchod Vira.
9. Skaria, "Writing, Orality."
10. Ginzburg, *Cheese and the Worms*, 17.
11. OIOC, V/26/860/5, "Appendix to the Education Commission Report,"
in *Report of the Bombay Provincial Committee*, vol. 1 (Calcutta, 1884), 32; T. R.
Metcalf, *The Aftermath of Revolt: India, 1857–1870* (Delhi, 1990), 127.
12. Indigenous schools were defined as "an assembly of pupils belonging to
more than one family or house, and receiving instruction together from a teacher,
who has set up his own account, or is not solely employed as a family tutor," in
Report on Education in the Bombay Presidency (Bombay, 1882), 69.
13. OIOC, V/26/860/5, "Appendix to the Education Commission Report," 32.
14. Evidence of Rao Sahed Mahipatram Rupram, Principal, Gujarat Training
College, in "Appendix to the Education Commission Report," 444.
15. *Report on Education in the Bombay Presidency* (Bombay, 1882), 60.
16. *RDPI during the Quinquennium from 1907–08 to 1911–12* (Bombay,
1912), 71.
17. Ibid.
18. Ibid., 73.
19. The information about examinations is incomplete and inferred from the
following reports: *RDPI during the Quinquennium from 1907–08 to 1911–12*,
73; and *RDPI during the Quinquennium from 1932–37* (Bombay, 1938), 212.

20. *RDPI for the year 1914–15* (Bombay, 1915), 25. Also see R. P. Paranjpye, *Free and Compulsory Education* (Poona, 1916).

21. MSA, RD, 1897, vol. 19, comp. 1528, part 2, Admin. Rept., F. X. D'Souza, Asst. Coll., Kaira, July 18, 1896.

22. Ibid.

23. Ibid.

24. J. P. Naik, ed., *Review of Education in Bombay State, 1855–1955* (Poona, 1958), 416.

13. THE BOOK COLLECTION

1. Imper. vs. R., Confession, Gema Mitha.

2. Imper. vs. R., "List of Property." My attempts to locate copies of these books in Gujarat, Bombay, and London have been unsuccessful. Unfortunately, no further publication details are included in the official court records of the case. However, an examination of the book titles suggests that most, if not all, were related to some form of religious discourse, especially those on Krishna. Moreover, it is not clear whether Ranchod had purchased these texts or had confiscated them along with the moneylenders' account books and ledgers.

3. Chaitra is the name of a lunar month in the Hindu calendar. Each lunar month is divided into two halves: the Sudi and the Vadi (or Vad). The Sudi is known as the bright half of the month (Sukla Paksha), from the new moon to the full moon. The Vadi is the dark half of the month (Krishna Paksha), from the full moon to the new moon.

4. Imper. vs. R., Ex. no. 31, "A Bond, Dated Bhadarwa Sudi 2nd, Samvat 1947, Alleged to Be Passed by Baji Bava and Teja Bava to Somabhai Bhulabhai." Bhadarwa Sudi is the period from the new moon to the full moon in the lunar month of Bhadarwa. "Samvat 1947," or 1947 of the Vikram Samwat era, corresponds to the year 1890.

14. KASHI *PATRA:* A CIRCULATING LETTER

1. Similar circulating letters were also documented in Southeast Asia. See Scott, *Weapons of the Weak,* 334–35, 362–63.

2. Kashi is the popular vernacular name for the city of Varanasi, or Benares, located in northern India.

3. See, for example, Bayly, *Empire and Information,* 315–64; Eric Stokes, *The Peasant Armed: The Indian Rebellion of 1857,* ed. C. A. Bayly (Oxford, 1986).

4. SAPI, vol. XI, no. 36 of 1898, September 13, 1898, 277–78.

5. SAPI, vol. IX, no. 48 of 1896, December 2, 1896, 391.

6. The earliest copy of a Kashi *patra* in Kheda district was actually documented in June 1897. A copy printed at the Anglo-Persian Press arrived at a temple in Mahuda from Songadh. No other information about this letter is discussed, and it appears to have had no direct bearing on Ranchod Vira and the Chaklasi case in the same year. SAPI, vol. X, no. 26 of 1897, June 21, 1897, 170.

7. Carmichael Report.

8. Ibid.

9. Ibid.

10. This may be an unlikely name, for *jadu* is the Gujarati word for magic and deception.

11. Carmichael Report.

12. SAPI, vol. XI, no. 2 of 1898, January 18, 1898, 25; SAPI, vol. XI, no. 13 of 1898, April 5, 1898, 104.

13. Bayly, *Empire and Information,* 60; P. L. Koffsky, "Postal Systems of India," *Bengal Past and Present* 90 (1971): 47–69; Irfan Habib, "Postal Communications in Mughal India," *Proceedings of the Indian Historical Congress, 46th Session* (Delhi, 1986), 236–52; Michael Fischer, "The East India Company's Suppression of the Native Dak," *IESHR* 31, 3 (1994): 319–26. The mass reproduction of these letters could have been accomplished only with the help of the new technology in the region. The spread of information was a rapid process on the Indian subcontinent—merchant routes provided established networks by which news could travel quickly. The postal service, like the existing merchant networks, acquired an important role in transmitting the chain letters between 1896 and 1898. In fact, postal markings became the primary method of tracing the origins of many of the letters confiscated by the police.

14. Condon, *Bombay Plague,* 163.

15. Ibid.

16. The list of twenty-one villages confiscated by the police corresponds with the villages where the *patras* were distributed.

17. Carmichael Report.

18. Condon, *Bombay Plague,* 160; MSA, GDP, 1897, vol. 84, comp. 139, Letter from Coll., Kaira, to Sec. to Gov't, GD, June 18, 1897; MSA, GDP, 1899, vol. 565, comp. 181, Letter from Coll., Kaira, to Sec. to Gov't, GD, February 10, 1899.

15. THE PRACTICE OF CUTTING TREES

1. For a similar discussion about eastern India, see, for example, K. Sivaramakrishnan, *Modern Forests: Statemaking and Environmental Change in Colonial Eastern India* (Stanford, 1999), 85.

2. Imper. vs. R., Confession, Gema Mitha.

3. *GBPK,* 15, fn. 3.

4. MSA, RD, 1897, vol. 19, comp. 1528, part 2, Admin. Rept. from H. W. I. Bagnell, Acting Coll., Kaira, to F. S. P. Lely, Acting Comm., ND, July 23, 1896.

5. Imper. vs. R., Deposition, Kashibhai Ranchhodbhai.

6. Calculated from the figures given in *GBPK,* 45–46.

7. See Shahid Amin, *Sugarcane and Sugar in Gorakhpur: An Inquiry into Peasant Production for Capitalist Enterprise in Colonial India* (Delhi, 1984).

16. OFFICIAL BATTLE NARRATIVES

1. Imper. vs. R., Deposition, Surajram Mahipatram.

2. Imper. vs. R., Deposition, Kashibhai Ranchhodbhai.

3. Imper. vs. R., Ex. no. 13, "Deposition of Mr. Naranshankar Mani-shankar," July 5, 1898.

4. Imper. vs. R., Deposition, Kashibhai Ranchhodbhai.

5. Imper. vs. R., Deposition, Jagannath Sagun.

6. Imper. vs. R., Ex. no. 16, "Deposition of Hamid Dallu," July 5, 1898.

7. Imper. vs. R., Deposition, Jagannath Sagun.

8. Imper. vs. R., Deposition, Kashibhai Ranchhodbhai.

9. Imper. vs. R., Deposition, Jagannath Sagun.

10. Imper. vs. R., Deposition, Surajram Mahipatram.

11. Imper. vs. R., Ex. no. 25, "Deposition of Jora Meru," July 6, 1898.

12. Imper. vs. R., Ex. no. 26, "Deposition of Bhaiji Amtha," July 6, 1898.

13. Imper. vs. R., Ex. no. 28, "Deposition of Satyanarayan Ajodhyaprasad," July 6, 1898.

14. Imper. vs. R., Deposition, Naranshankar Manishankar.

17. DHARALA BATTLE NARRATIVES

1. Imper. vs. R., Confession, Meru Mitha.

2. Imper. vs. R., Confession, Gema Mitha.

3. Imper. vs. R., Deposition, Kashibhai Ranchhodbhai.

4. Imper. vs. R., Confession, Meru Mitha.

5. Imper. vs. R., Confession, Gema Mitha.

6. Imper. vs. R., Confession, Surta Ragha.

7. Ibid.

8. Imper. vs. R., Ex. no. 47, "The Examination of Accused no. 2, Sallia Baji, before the Committing Magistrate," May 7, 1898.

9. Imper. vs. R., Ex. no. 48, "The Examination of Accused no. 3, Baber Mana, before the Committing Magistrate," May 17, 1898.

10. Imper. vs. R., Confession, Meru Mitha.

11. Imper. vs. R., Ex. no. 51, "The Examination of Accused no. 6, Mathur Nara, before the Committing Magistrate," May 18, 1898.

12. Imper. vs. R., Ex. no. 54, "The Confession of Accused no. 9, Mala Halu, before the Committing Magistrate," May 18, 1898.

13. Imper. vs. R., Confession, Meru Mitha.

14. Imper. vs. R., Confession, Surta Ragha.

15. Imper. vs. R., Confession, Meru Mitha.

18. THE ARRESTS

1. Carmichael Report.

2. Imper. vs. R., Deposition, Jhaverbhai Shivabhai.

3. Imper. vs. R., Ex. no. 30, "Deposition of Jivabhai Mithabhai," July 7, 1898.

4. Carmichael Report.

5. Ibid.

6. Imper. vs. R., Examination, Ranchod Vira.

19. RANCHOD'S TESTIMONY

1. Imper. vs. R., Examination, Ranchod Vira.

20. THE KINGSHIP

1. Imper. vs. R., Deposition, Baji Bapu.

2. Imper. vs. R., Deposition, Naranshankar Manishankar.

3. See Stewart Gordon, *The Marathas, 1600-1818, The New Cambridge History of India,* 2.4 (Cambridge, 1998), 59-90.

4. Dirks, *Hollow Crown,* 40-44.

5. Uthran is mentioned in Imper. vs. R., Ex. no. 72, "Deposition of Nangan Lakhman," July 8, 1898. For further discussion, see Romila Thapar, *Time as a Metaphor of History: Early India* (Delhi, 1996).

6. Uthran is associated with the holiday Makar Sankranti, which occurs on January 14 every year. While witnesses state that the day of the battle (January 12) was Uthran, it is not possible to resolve this apparent discrepancy. I thank David Hardiman for alerting me to this point. The reference to sugarcane in Ranchod's *patra* may be explained in part by the tradition of distributing pieces of sugarcane as gifts on Makar Sankranti. See Margaret Sinclair Stevenson, *The Rites of the Twice-Born* (Delhi, 1971), 273. The reference might also be connected to Surat, an area with widespread sugarcane cultivation and one of the earlier locations of the Kashi *patra.* Also see Jan Breman, *Patronage and Exploitation: Changing Agrarian Relations in South Gujarat, India* (Berkeley, 1974).

7. Imper. vs. R., Ex. no. 69, "Deposition of Mansi, wife of Natha Jija," July 8, 1898.

8. Guha, *Elementary Aspects,* 296; Oscar Lewis, *Village Life in Northern India: Studies in a Delhi Village* (New York, 1965), 229-33; McKim Marriott, "Feasts of Love," in *Krishna: Myths, Rites, and Attitudes,* ed. Milton B. Singer (Honolulu, 1966), 210, 212; William Crooke, *The Popular Religion and Folk-Lore of Northern India* (Delhi, 1968), 320-21.

9. Crooke, *Popular Religion,* 320.

10. Price, *Kingship and Political Practice,* 78.

11. Gordon, *Marathas,* 76-77; H. Fukazawa, "Agrarian Relations and Land Revenue: The Medieval Deccan and Maharashtra," in *The Cambridge Economic History of India,* vol. 1, ed. Tapan Raychaudhuri and Irfan Habib (Cambridge, 1984), 259.

12. Hardiman, "The Bhils and Sahukars," 22-23.

13. David Hardiman, *Feeding the Baniya. Peasants and Usurers in Western India* (Delhi, 1996), especially chapter 6.

14. Bayly, *Rulers, Townsmen, and Bazaars,* 379. Also Hardiman, *Feeding the Baniya,* 172-81; Jack Goody, *The East in the West* (Cambridge, 1996), 49-81. By the end of the nineteenth century, moneylenders were charging Dharala peasants between 12½ and 25 percent interest on loans, in contrast to 6¼ percent for other agricultural communities. Interest rates given in MSA, RD, 1908, vol. 17, comp. 511, pt. 3, Admin. Rept. from Arthur Wood, Coll., Kaira, to Comm., ND,

October 2, 1897; MSA, RD, 1883, vol. 23, comp. 1550, Admin. Rept. from A. H. Spry, Coll., Kaira, to G. F. Sheppard, Comm., ND, July 28, 1883.

21. FRIENDS AND ENEMIES OF THE KING

1. Imper. vs. R., Deposition, Jagannath Sagun.
2. Bayly, *Empire and Information,* 97. Cited from "Notes on Interviews with Sindhia" (Shinde), 1781, David Anderson Papers, Additional Manuscripts 45,419, f. 39, BL. Also see Sanjay Subrahmanyam, "Turbans and Hats: South India between Two Regimes," *Penumbral Visions* (Delhi, 2001), 1–21; Hardiman, "Quit India Movement," 84; Prem Poddar and David Johnson, eds., *A Historical Companion to Postcolonial Thought in English* (New York, 2005), 537–38; Srinivas Aravamudan, "Postcolonial Affiliations: *Ulysses* and *All About H. Hatterr,*" in *Transcultural Joyce,* ed. Karen Lawrence (Cambridge, 1998), 118; Rudrangshu Mukherjee, "Ashin Das Gupta: Some Memories and Reflections," in *Politics and Trade in the Indian Ocean World: Essays in Honour of Ashin Das Gupta,* ed. Rudrangshu Mukherjee and Lakshmi Subramanian (Delhi, 1998), 13; Peabody, *Hindu Kingship,* chapter 3.
3. *Government men* is substituted for *topiwallah* in Imper. vs. R., Ex. no. 16, "Testimony of Head Constable Hamid Dala," July 5, 1898.
4. Arnold, "Perspectives on the Indian Plague," 76.
5. Imper. vs. R., Deposition, Jagannath Sagun.

22. SYMBOLS OF LEGITIMACY

1. See Bernard Cohn, "Political Systems in Eighteenth Century India: The Benaras Region," *Journal of the American Oriental Society* 82 (1962): 312–20.
2. The idea of a "text of legitimation" is borrowed from Romila Thapar, although I have used it in a different context. See Romila Thapar, *Cultural Pasts: Essays in Early Indian History* (Delhi, 2000), 218. According to the Hindu calendar, the era of *satyug* lasts for approximately ten thousand years. For further discussion, see Thapar, *Time as a Metaphor.*
3. Rosalind O'Hanlon, *Caste, Conflict, and Ideology: Mahatma Jotirao Phule and Low Caste Protest in Nineteenth-Century Western India* (Cambridge, 1985), 180.
4. Inden, *Imagining India,* 229–50.
5. See Edwin F. Bryant, trans., *Krishna: The Beautiful Legend of God (Srimad Bhagavata Purana Book X)* (London, 2003).
6. Ibid., 284.
7. Pinch, *Peasants and Monks,* 25.
8. MSA, JD, 1828, vol. 1/149, Rept. to Charles Norris, Sec. to the Gov't. (Full details not given in original.)

23. ORAL CULTURE AND WRITTEN CULTURE

1. Ginzburg, *Cheese and the Worms,* 33.
2. Imper. vs. R., Confession, Gema Mitha.

3. Bayly, *Empire and Information,* 8–9.

4. MSA, JD, 1898, vol. 103, comp. 328, *Svadesh Bandhu and Cambay Gazette,* vol. 13, no. 1, January 5, 1898.

5. MSA, RD, 1898, vol. 103, comp. 328, Letter from Maneklal Khusaldas Desai, Manager of the *Svadesh Bandhu and Cambay Gazette,* to G. Carmichael, DM, Kaira, January 16, 1898.

6. Ibid.

24. THE CRIMINAL CASE

1. Imper. vs. R., Examination, Ranchod Vira.

2. Imper. vs. R., Ex. no. 77, "Judgement," E. H. Leggatt, Joint Sessions Judge, Nadiad, July 9, 1898.

3. MSA, JD, 1899, vol. 78, comp. 457, Vernacular Petition from Ranchod Vira to the Governor in Council, October 26, 1898.

4. MSA, JD, 1899, vol. 78, comp. 457, Rept. from H. R. Hume, Acting DSP, Kaira, to DM, Kaira, December 14, 1898.

5. Ibid.

25. THE AFTERMATH

1. SAPI, vol. XX, no. 2 of 1907, January 12, 1907, 33.

27. AGE OF DARKNESS

1. *Report of the Indian Famine Commission of 1901* (Calcutta, 1901). Also see Davis, *Victorian Holocausts;* David Arnold, *Famine: Social Crisis and Historical Change* (Oxford, 1988).

2. Between 1898 and 1899, in Ahmedabad the levels dropped from 34.89 inches to 4.84, and in Bharuch from 47.51 to 9.61. A comprehensive listing of the annual rainfall figures for Gujarat between 1858 and 1920, is found in M. B. McAlpin, *Subject to Famine* (Princeton, 1983), appendix A.

3. See Bela Bhatia, "Lush Fields and Parched Throats: The Political Economy of Groundwater in Gujarat" (working paper no. 100, World Institute for Development Economics Research, Helsinki, August 1992).

4. See *Report on the Famine in the Bombay Presidency, 1899–1902,* vol. 2 (Bombay, 1903), 34 (hereafter cited as *Famine Report*).

5. Kheda's cattle population from 1872 to 1921 can be broken down as follows:

1872: 391,000	1902: 212,000
1891: 385,000	1906: 285,000
1899: 418,000	1910: 321,000
1900: 184,000	1916: 420,000
1901: 183,000	1921: 379,000

These figures are collated from the *Famine Report; Report on the Census of the Bombay Presidency taken on the 21st February 1872* (Bombay, 1875); and *GBPK.*

6. MSA, RDF, 1900, vol. 163, comp. 59, pt. 1, Letter from the Famine Department, to Coll., Kaira, February 7, 1900.

7. MSA, RDF, 1900, vol. 163, comp. 59, pt. 1, Petition from Patel Narotamdas Venidas, to the Viceroy and Gov. General of India in Council, nd.

8. Condon, *Bombay Plague*, 161.

9. OIOC, RFP, 1900, P/5987, Rept. from the Coll., Kaira, June 19, 1900; *RNN: Praja Bandhu*, September 23, 1899; and, *Ahmedabad Times*, December 16, 1898. Also "Kaira Vartman Defamation Case," *Praja Bandhu*, September 17, 1899; "Cruelty in Extracting Revenue," *Praja Bandhu*, September 24, 1899.

10. OIOC, RFP, 1900, P/5987, Rept. from the Coll., Kaira, May 31, 1900; "Alleged Oppression in Collecting Land Revenue in the Kaira District," *Praja Bandhu*, June 2, 1901; "Effects of the Late Famine," *Praja Bandhu*, March 17, 1901; *RNN, Ahmedabad Times*, December 16, 1898.

11. OIOC, RFP, 1900, P/5987, Rept. from the Coll., Kaira, June 19, 1900.

12. OIOC, RFP, 1900, P/5989, Rept. from the Coll., Kaira, May 19, 1900.

13. *RNN, Svadesh Bandhu*, October 11, 1899.

14. OIOC, RFP, 1900, P/5988, Rept. from the Coll., Kaira, July 31, 1900.

15. MSA, RD, 1905, vol. 21, comp. 177, pt. 2, Admin. Rept., C. Hudson, Coll., Kaira, August 1904 (nd). Also, MSA, RDF, 1899, vol. 48, comp. 186. The following are the names of the famine relief works in Kheda district in 1900 (the number of workers on each project is given in parentheses):

Borsad-Agas Road (100)
Borsad Tank (12,763; increased to 24,586)
Dakore-Alina Road (2,036)
Dakore Grave (1,435)
Dakore Tank (11,385)
Deoki Vansol Tank (12,554)
Gajna Local Fund Tank (284)
Iawa Tank (7,841)
Ladwel Road [I] (195)
Ladwel Road [II] (41)
Ladwel Tank (4,420)
Mahuda Tank (1,652)
Matar Drainage Work (4,757)
Mehmedabad-Mahuda Road (489)
Nadiad Tank (116)
Napa Tank (1,529)
Pali-Metal Breaking (6,093; reduced to 1,150)
Traj Tanks (5,396)
Vansar Tank (804)

Figures collated from OIOC, RFP, 1900, P/5986, Rept. from the Coll., Kaira, March 24, 1900, and April 14, 1900.

16. OIOC, RFP, 1900, P/5989, Rept. from the Coll., Kaira, May 19, 1900.

17. *Famine Report*, vol. 1, 90.

18. OIOC, RFP, 1900, P/6490, Rept. from the Coll., Kaira, March 7, 1902.

19. OIOC, RFP, 1900, P/5986, Rept. from the Coll., Kaira, April 25, 1900.

20. MSA, RD, 1905, vol. 21, comp. 177, pt. 2, Admin. Rept., C. Hudson, Coll., Kaira, August 1904 (nd).

28. DADURAM

1. SAPI, vol. XXI, no. 19 of 1908, May 16, 1908, 293; vol. XXI, no. 21 of 1908, May 30, 1908, 372; vol. XXI, no. 22 of 1908, June 6, 1908, 408–9; vol. XXI, no. 23 of 1908, June 13, 1908, 432; vol. XXI, no. 40 of 1908, October 10, 1908, 957; vol. XXII, no. 18 of 1909, May 8, 1909, 371–74; vol. XXII, no. 39 of 1909, October 2, 1909, 844; MSA, RD, 1910, vol. 11, Admin. Rept., J. Ghosal, Coll., Kaira, to Comm., ND, September 25, 1909; *A Jamabandi Revision Settlement Report of the Bhadran Peta Mahal of the Petlad Taluka of the Baroda Division for AD 1920* (Baroda, 1921), 24; *Annual Administration Report of the Balasinore State for the Year 1912–1913* (Ahmedabad, 1913), 16.

2. For a comparative perspective, see R. Rajasekher, "Famines and Peasant Mobility: Changing Agrarian Structure in the Kurnool District of Andhra, 1870–1900," *IESHR* 28, 2 (1991), 73–96; David Arnold, "Famine in Peasant Consciousness and Peasant Action: Madras, 1876–78," in *Subaltern Studies III*, ed. Ranajit Guha (Delhi, 1984), 62–115. For a list of projects, see OIOC, RFP, 1900, P/5986, Repts. from the Coll., Kaira, March 24, 1900, and April 14, 1900.

3. SAPI, vol. XXII, no. 18 of 1909, May 8, 1909, 371.

4. There is a body of literature on the subject of caste reform that identifies the processes of purification, especially abstinence from alcohol and meat, as "sanskritization." M. N. Srinivas initially developed this concept to describe how a "low Hindu caste, or tribal or other group, change[d] its customs, ritual, ideology, and way of life in the direction of a high, and frequently 'twice-born,' caste." M. N. Srinivas, *Social Change in Modern India* (Bombay, 1972), 6. For recent debates and analysis on caste in India, see Nicholas B. Dirks, *Castes of Mind: Colonialism and the Making of Modern India* (Princeton, 2001); Susan Bayly, *Caste, Society, and Politics in India from the Eighteenth Century to the Modern Age, The New Cambridge History of India*, 4.3 (Cambridge, 2000).

5. David Hardiman, *The Coming of the Devi: Adivasi Assertion in Western India* (Delhi, 1995), 157–62; William Pinch, *Peasants and Monks in British India* (Berkeley, 1996), 82–83.

6. SAPI, vol. XXII, no. 18 of 1909, May 8, 1909, 372.

7. Ibid.

8. The Dev Samaj was another movement promoting similar ideals in Gujarat. See "Report on the Temperance Work of the Dev Samaj for 1905," *Indian Social Reformer*, January 21, 1906.

9. SAPI, vol. XXII, no. 18 of 1909, May 8, 1909, 371–72.

10. Ibid.

29. SURVEILLANCE

1. SAPI, vol. XXII, no. 18 of 1909, May 8, 1909, 371–72.

2. Ibid.

3. Ibid.

4. Ibid.
5. Ibid.
6. Ibid.
7. Ibid.
8. Ibid.

30. THE POLITICS OF FOOD

1. SAPI, vol. XXI, no. 23 of 1908, June 13, 1908, 432.

2. SAPI, vol. XXII, no. 18 of 1909, May 8, 1909, 372; *Annual Administration Report of the Balasinore State for the Year 1912–1913* (Ahmedabad, 1913), 16; *A Jamabandi Revision Settlement Report of the Bhadran Peta Mahal of the Petlad Taluka of the Baroda Division for AD 1920* (Baroda, 1921).

3. For example, the district magistrate commented that other communities, notably the Barbers, organized their own movements after being inspired by the Dharalas. SAPI, vol. XXII, no. 18 of 1909, May 8, 1909, 373.

4. For a discussion of the development of a public sphere in Gujarat, see Douglas E. Haynes, *Rhetoric and Ritual in Colonial India. The Shaping of a Public Culture in Surat City, 1852–1928* (Berkeley, 1991).

5. SAPI, vol. XXI, no. 19 of 1908, May 16, 1908, 293; SAPI, vol. XXI, no. 21 of 1908, May 30, 1908, 372; SAPI, vol. XXI, no. 23 of 1908, June 13, 1908, 432; SAPI, vol. XXI, no. 22 of 1908, June 6, 1908, 408; SAPI, vol. XXII, no. 18 of 1909, May 8, 1909, 371–72.

6. *Gujarati Punch*, May 7, 1908, reported in SAPI, vol. XXI, no. 19 of 1908, May 16, 1908, 293.

7. See Thapar, *Cultural Pasts.*

8. OIOC, RLP, P/6490, Rept. from the Coll., Kaira, March 25, 1902.

9. W. G. Orr, *A Sixteenth Century Indian Mystic* (London, 1947), 153.

10. Winand M. Callewaert, *The Hindi Biography of Dadu Dayal* (Delhi, 1988), 61. [Emphasis mine.] Also see Orr, *Indian Mystic,* 36.

11. See K. N. Upadhyaya, *The Compassionate Mystic* (New Delhi, 1980); Monika Thiel-Hortsmann, *Crossing the Ocean of Existence: Braj Bhasa Religious Poetry from Rajasthan* (Wiesbaden, 1983).

12. See David Hardiman, "From Custom to Crime: The Politics of Drinking in South Gujarat," in *Subaltern Studies IV,* ed. Ranajit Guha (Delhi, 1985), 165–228.

13. MSA, RD, 1879, vol. 20, comp. 972, Admin. Rept., G. H. D. Wilson, Coll., July 4, 1879; MSA, RD 1898, vol. 26, comp. 1528, pt. 2, Admin. Rept., H. W. T. Bagnell, Coll., August 22, 1897. Mahua was also processed into a cooking oil and used as a fertilizer. See Rao Bahadur D. L. Sahasrabuddhe, *Composition of Important Manures in Western India*, Bombay Agricultural Series, Bulletin no. 174 (Bombay, 1933); Hardiman, "From Custom to Crime"; Hardiman, *Coming of the Devi.* According to Hardiman, most, if not all, social movements from "below" prescribing prohibition in this period should be understood as responses to colonial alcohol legislation. I thank David Hardiman for this insight (personal communication).

14. SAPI, vol. XXII, no. 18 of 1909, May 8, 1909, 373.
15. Ibid.
16. SAPI, vol. XXIII, no. 23 of 1908, June 13, 1908, 432.
17. Interview with Khan Bahadur Dadabhai Deenshah, Huzur Deputy Collector and Magistrate, Kaira, *Evidence of Witnesses from Bombay, Sind, Berar, Ajmere, Coorg, Baluchistan, and Burma taken before the Indian Hemp Drugs Commission* (Calcutta, 1894), 46.
18. Interview with Desaibhai Kalidas, the Government Pleader and Public Prosecutor, Kaira, *Evidence of Witnesses from Bombay, Sind, Berar, Ajmere, Coorg, Baluchistan, and Burma taken before the Indian Hemp Drugs Commission* (Calcutta, 1894), 197.
19. Imper. vs. R., Examination, Ranchod Vira.

31. "THE DIGNITY OF LABOR"

1. Collector Arthur Wood suggested that the effect of the demographic crisis was "a general rise in status for the labouring classes," where agricultural workers were getting paid up to eight annas per day with food. See MSA, RD, 1908, vol. 17, comp. 511, pt. 3.
2. MSA, RD, 1910, vol. 11, comp. 511, Admin. Rept., J. Ghosal, Coll., September 25, 1909.
3. Pinch, *Peasants and Monks*, 75.
4. SAPI, vol. XXI, no. 23 of 1908, June 13, 1908, 432; SAPI, vol. XXII, no. 18 of 1909, May 8, 1909, 373.
5. MSA, RD, 1911, vol. 10, comp. 511, pt. 3, Admin. Rept., A. Chuckerbutty, Coll., September 30, 1910.
6. Ibid.
7. SAPI, vol. XXII, no. 18 of 1909, May 8, 1909, 373.

32. THE BARAIYA CONFERENCE MOVEMENT

1. SAPI, vol. XXII, no. 18 of 1909, May 8, 1909, 373.
2. Ibid.
3. Ibid.
4. SAPI, vol. XXI, no. 22 of 1908, June 6, 1908, 409.
5. The activities of the BCM after the first decade of the twentieth century remain uncertain. The publication of its monthly journal ceased in 1909, and the role of its founders no longer interested colonial authorities in light of the upsurge of nationalist and extremist activities in the locality. It appears that the BCM formed an alliance with the Indian National Congress in organizing a Baraiya Conference in 1924 and the Kshatriya Sudharak Mandal in the 1930s. See Shah, *Caste Association*.
6. SAPI, vol. XXII, no. 18 of 1909, May 8, 1909, 372.
7. Ibid.
8. SAPI, vol. XXI, no. 22 of 1908, June 6, 1908, 409.
9. SAPI, vol. XXII, no. 18 of 1909, May 8, 1909, 373.

262 / NOTES TO PAGES 118-120

33. CONTESTING NATIONALISM

1. SAPI, vol. XXII, no. 18 of 1909, May 8, 1909, 373.

2. Richard Cashman, *The Myth of the Lokamanya: Tilak and Mass Politics in Maharashtra* (Berkeley, 1975); Dhananjay Keer, *Lokamanya Tilak, Father of the Indian Freedom Struggle* (Bombay, 1969); Ram Gopal, *Lokamanya Tilak: A Biography* (New York, 1965); T. V. Parvate, *Bal Gangadhar Tilak: A Narrative and Interpretive Review of His Life, Career, and Contemporary Events* (Ahmedabad, 1958); Dattatraya Parashuram Karmarkar, *Bal Gangadhar Tilak: A Study* (Bombay, 1956); Theodore Shay, *The Legacy of the Lokamanya: The Political Philosophy of Bal Gangadhar Tilak* (Bombay, 1956); D. V. Tahmankar, *Lokamanya Tilak: Father of Indian Unrest and Maker of Modern India* (London, 1956); Stanley Wolpert, *Tilak and Gokhale: Revolution and Reform in the Making of Modern India* (Berkeley, 1961).

3. See Paul B. Courtright, "The Ganesh Festival in Maharashtra: Some Observations," in *The Experience of Hinduism,* ed. Eleanor Zelliot and Maxine Berntsen (Albany, 1988), 76–77; Richard Cashman, "The Political Recruitment of God Ganapati," *IESHR* 7 (1970): 347–73.

4. Dirks, *Hollow Crown,* 237.

5. SAPI, vol. XXII, no. 18 of 1909, May 8, 1909, 372.

6. Hardiman, "Lesser Patidars," 56–57.

7. For similar arguments about western India, see O'Hanlon, *Caste, Conflict;* Gail Omvedt, *Cultural Revolt in a Colonial Society: The Non-Brahman Movement in Western India, 1873 to 1930* (Bombay, 1976).

34. PEASANT FREEDOM

1. SAPI, vol. XXII, no. 18 of 1909, May 8, 1909, 372.

2. See Brenner, "Agrarian Class Structure," 10–63.

3. On the related topic of patron-client relations in South Gujarat, see Breman, *Patronage and Exploitation.*

4. OIOC, IPP, 1911, P/8711, Rept. from R. P. Barrow, Comm., ND, October 10, 1910; OIOC, HP, 1923, P/11323, Rept. from F. W. O'Gorman, DSP, Kaira, to DM, Kaira, April 9, 1923.

35. POLICE REORGANIZATION

1. Cox, *Police and Crime in India,* 253–54.

2. *PRBP for the Year 1890* (Bombay, 1891), 46, Abstract of Rept. by the DM, Kaira, nd; *PRBP for the Year 1887* (Bombay, 1888), 24, Abstract of Rept. by L. H. Spence, DSP, Kaira, nd.

3. Cox, *Police and Crime,* 229–52.

4. *PRBP for the Year 1897* (Bombay, 1898), 31, Abstract of Rept. by J. E. Down, Acting IGP, August 17, 1898.

5. *PRBP for the Year 1890* (Bombay, 1891), 45, Abstract of Rept. by L. H. Spence, DSP, Kaira, nd.

6. *PRBP for the Year 1897* (Bombay, 1898), 160, Abstract of Rept. by the Comm., ND, October 3, 1898.

7. *PRBP for the Year 1893* (Bombay, 1894), 48, Abstract of Rept. by the Comm., ND, nd; also see *PRBP for the Year 1890* (Bombay, 1891), 45, Abstract of Rept. by L. H. Spence, DSP, Kaira, nd; *PRBP for the Year 1889* (Bombay, 1890), 47, Abstract of Rept. by the Comm., ND, nd; *PRBP for the Year 1897* (Bombay, 1898), 31, Abstract of Rept. by J. E. Down, Acting IGP, August 17, 1898.

8. *PRBP for the Year 1909* (Bombay, 1910), 5, Abstract of Rept. by the Comm., ND, nd. Also see OIOC, IPP, 1911, P/8711, Rept. by R. P. Barrow, Commissioner, ND, October 10, 1910.

9. On similar themes of food-grabbing during periods of crisis, see David Arnold, "Looting, Grain Riots, and Government Policy in South India, 1918," *Past and Present* 84 (1979): 111–45; David Arnold, "Dacoity and Rural Crime in Madras, 1860–1940," *JPS* 6, 2 (1979): 140–67; Hardiman, "The Bhils and Shahukars," 1–54.

10. OIOC, JP, 1911, P/8833, Rept. from R. P. Barrow, Comm., ND, to Sec. to Gov't, JD, nd.

11. For similar themes, see Ajay Skaria, "Timber Conservancy, Desiccationism, and Scientific Forestry: The Dangs, 1840s–1920s," in *Nature and the Orient. The Environmental History of South and Southeast Asia,* ed. R. Grove, V. Damodaran, and Satpal Sangwan (Delhi, 1998), 596–635; Sivaramakrishnan, *Modern Forests,* 130, 137.

12. OIOC, P/472, Bombay Revenue Forest Consultations, 1873–75, Rept. from Revenue Comm., ND, January 22, 1873. Also see Baden-Powell, "Rights in Trees," in *Land-Systems,* vol. 3, 304–6.

13. OIOC, IPP, 1911, P/8711, Rept. from C. A. Kincaid, Sec. to Gov't, Bombay, January 27, 1911. After the 1911 reorganization scheme, the size of the police force in Kheda district was as follows: 3 inspectors; 22 subinspectors; 40 armed head constables; 81 unarmed head constables; 262 armed constables; 365 unarmed constables.

14. *PRBP for the Year 1911* (Bombay, 1912), 34, Abstract of Rept. by the DM, Kaira, nd.

15. Ibid.

16. *PRBP for the Year 1912* (Bombay, 1913), 33, Abstract of Rept. by the Comm., ND, nd.

17. For similar themes in the Madras Presidency, see Arnold, *Police Power,* 16; *Report of the Commissioners for the Investigation of Alleged Cases of Torture in the Madras Presidency* (Madras, 1855).

36. THE CRIMINAL TRIBES ACT

1. The Criminal Tribes Act, 1911 (III of 1911), gave government the legal authority to declare any group or community a "criminal tribe." Paragraph 3 of the CTA defines the notification of criminal tribes: "If the Local Government has reason to believe that any tribe, gang or class of persons is addicted to the systematic commission of non-bailable offences, it may, by notification in the local

official Gazette, declare that such tribe, gang or class is a criminal tribe for the purposes of this Act" (3).

2. The Criminal Tribes Act, 1871 (XXVII of 1871); Also cited in Yang, "Dangerous Castes and Tribes," 109.

3. OIOC, JP, 1919, P/10542, Rept. from F. G. Pratt, Comm., ND, to Sec. to Gov't, JD, September 30, 1918.

4. The Criminal Tribes Act, 1911, 13.

5. Ibid., 14.

6. OIOC, JP, 1911, P/8835, Rept. from H. G. White, DSP, Kaira, to DM, Kaira, nd.

7. OIOC, JP, 1914, P/9606, Rept. from J. Ghosal, DM, Kaira, to Sec. to Gov't, JD, February 2, 1914.

8. OIOC, JP, 1917, P/10131, Rept. from J. Ghosal, DM, Kaira, to Comm., ND, June 4, 1916; OIOC, HP, 1925, P/11467, Rept. from J. W. Smith, DM, Kaira, to Sec. to Gov't, HD, October 11, 1924.

9. The Criminal Tribes Act, 1911, 4.

10. Singha, *Despotism of Law*, 29.

11. Ginzburg, *Clues, Myths*, 122–23. "Dharalas had argued that the registration process would lead to greater control over their labour-power." See *Report on the Working of the Criminal Tribes Act in the Bombay Presidency (including Sind) for the Year 1918* (Bombay, 1919), 20.

12. For a different, more positive discussion of "leisure" in agrarian society, see M. Atchi Reddy, "Work and Leisure: Daily Working Hours of Agricultural Labourers, Nellore District, 1860–1989," *IESHR* 27, 3 (1990): 257–87.

13. OIOC, JP, 1913, P/9338, G. K. Parekh, Rept. on the CTA in Kheda, November 22, 1912.

14. *Report on the Working of the Criminal Tribes Act in the Bombay Presidency (including Sind) for the Year 1918* (Bombay, 1919), 20. For a discussion on fingerprinting in India, see Ginzburg, *Clues, Myths*, 120–23, 212; Bengal Police, *Criminal Identification by Means of Anthropometry*, 2nd ed., rev. up to 1st January 1895, from E. R. Henry, IG Police; J. C. Curry, *The Indian Police* (London, 1932), 279–83.

15. OIOC, JP, 1913, P/9338, G. K. Parekh, Rept. on the CTA in Kheda, November 22, 1912.

16. OIOC, JP, 1914, P/9606, Rept. from J. Ghosal, DM, Kaira, to Sec. to Gov't, JD, February 2, 1914.

17. Ibid.

18. OIOC, JP, 1914, P/9606, Rept. from E. E. Turner, DSP, Kaira, to DM, Kaira, September 24, 1913.

19. OIOC, HP, 1923, P/11323, Rept. from F. W. O'Gorman, DSP, Kaira, to DM, Kaira, April 9, 1923.

20. *PRBP for the Year 1921* (Bombay, 1922), 5, Abstract of Rept. by Comm., ND, nd.

21. OIOC, JP, 1914, P/9606, Rept. from J. Ghosal, DM, Kaira, to Sec. to Gov't, JD, February 2, 1914.

22. *PRBP for the Year 1917* (Bombay, 1918), 13, Abstract of Rept. by Mr. Bailey, DSP, Kaira, nd.

23. OIOC, JP, 1914, P/9606, Rept. from J. Ghosal, DM, Kaira, to Sec. to Gov't, JD, February 2, 1914.

24. MSA, JD, 1898, vol. 103, comp. 328, Judgement of E. H. Leggatt, Joint Sessions Judge, July 9, 1898.

25. OIOC, JP, 1914, P/9606, Rept. from J. Ghosal, DM, Kaira, to Sec. to Gov't, JD, February 2, 1914.

26. Ibid.

27. OIOC, JP, 1913, P/9338, G. K. Parekh, Rept. on the CTA in Kheda, November 22, 1912.

28. OIOC, JP, 1914, P/9606, Rept. from J. Ghosal, DM, Kaira, to Sec. to Gov't, JD, February 2, 1914.

29. Ibid.

30. Ibid.

37. UNDERGROUND ACTIVITIES

1. OIOC, JP, 1914, P/9606, Rept. from J. Ghosal, DM, Kaira, to Sec. to Gov't, JD, February 2, 1914.

2. For a discussion on the question of agrarian migrations and mobility, see Anand Yang, "Peasants on the Move: A Study of Internal Migration in India," *Journal of Interdisciplinary History* 10 (1979): 38–45; Ravi Ahuja, "Labour Unsettled: Mobility and Protest in the Madras Region, 1750–1800," *IESHR* 35, 4 (1998): 381–404; Douglas E. Haynes and Tirthankar Roy, "Conceiving Mobility: Weavers' Migrations in Pre-colonial and Colonial India," *IESHR* 36, 1 (1999): 35–67; Shri Krishan, "Peasant Mobilization, Political Organization and Modes of Interaction: The Bombay Countryside 1934–41," *IESHR* 32, 4 (1995): 429–46.

3. OIOC, JP, 1914, P/9606, Rept. from J. Ghosal, DM, Kaira, to Sec. to Gov't, JD, February 2, 1914.

4. OIOC, JP, 1915, P/9851, "Report of the Committee Appointed to Consider Proposals Made by O. H. Starte, Assistant Collector on Special Duty, for the Settlement of Criminal Tribes," October 30, 1914.

5. OIOC, JP, 1915, P/9852, Rept. from Lieut. Colonel, L. Impey, Resident at Baroda, to Sec. to Gov't, JD, February 19, 1915.

38. "MY LAND CAMPAIGN"

1. MSA, RD, 1918, file no. 511, pt. 2, from J. Ghosal, Coll., Kaira, to F. G. Pratt, Comm., ND, September 10, 1917.

2. Ibid.

3. Ibid.

4. See Mahesh Rangarajan, "Imperial Agendas and India's Forests: The Early History of Indian Forestry, 1800–1878," *IESHR* 31, 2 (1994): 147–67.

5. MSA, RD, 1918, file no. 511, pt. 2, from J. Ghosal, Coll., Kaira, to F. G. Pratt, Comm., ND, September 10, 1917. As discussed in part 1, the policy of providing incentives to Patidars to invest in opening up new agricultural land began early in the nineteenth century. New loans were provided to select Patidars to cul-

tivate lands in the Mal tract between the 1860s and 1880s. In the first decade of the twentieth century, colonial authorities also provided Patidars with special access to grasslands and allowed settlers to take up land at nominal rates. Although an investigation revealed corrupt practices in distributing land in the locality, the government maintained its close relations with the Patidars. (See MSA, RD, 1913, comp. 511, pt. 3.) Under Ghosal's program the first Patidar settlers arrived in 1914 in villages in the Mal tract. (See MSA, RD, 1915, comp. 511, pt. 3, from J. Ghosal, Coll., Kaira, to Comm., ND, September 10, 1914.)

6. Ibid.
7. Ibid.
8. Ibid.
9. Ibid.

39. THE LABOR STRIKE

1. MSA, RD, 1918, comp. 511, pt. 2, from J. Ghosal, Coll., Kaira, to Comm., ND, September 10, 1917.
2. Ibid.
3. Ibid.
4. Ibid.
5. Ibid.
6. Ibid.
7. Ibid.
8. Ibid.

40. THE KHEDA *SATYAGRAHA*

1. See Charlesworth, *Peasants and Imperial Rule;* R. D. Choksey, *Economic Life in the Bombay Gujarat (1800–1939)* (New York, 1968).

2. See Tirthankar Roy, *The Economic History of India, 1857–1947* (Delhi, 2000).

3. SAPI, vol. XXXI, no. 7 of 1918, February 16, 1918, 135; SAPI, vol. XXXI, no. 12 of 1918, March 23, 1918, 229–30.

4. Hardiman, *Peasant Nationalists,* 93–94.

5. *Bombay Chronicle,* December 24, 1917, and January 18, 1918.

6. MSA, RD, 1918, file no. 511, pt. 1a, from F. G. Pratt, Comm., ND, to Chief Sec. to Gov't, February 6, 1918.

7. M. K. Gandhi, "In Touch with Labour," in *An Autobiography: The Story of My Experiments with Truth* (Boston, 1993), 426; M. K. Gandhi, "Bombay Secret Abstract, 1918," Ahmedabad, February 5, 1918, cited in *Source Material for a History of the Freedom Movement in India,* vol. 3, *Mahatma Gandhi,* pt. 1, *1915–1922* (Bombay, 1965), 79.

8. See Brown, *Gandhi's Rise.*

9. Gandhi, "The Duty of the Ryots of Kaira District," in *Source Material for a History of the Freedom Movement in India,* vol. 3, *Mahatma Gandhi,* pt. 1, *1915–1922* (Bombay, 1965), 81–82.

10. M. K. Gandhi, "The Kheda Satyagraha," *Autobiography,* 435.

11. *Bombay Chronicle,* January 18, 1918.

12. *Satyagraha* is a term derived by combining *satya,* or "truth," and *agraha,* the "process of taking or seizing." It literally means to seize the truth. Gandhi's own extensive writings on truth provide further complexity to the term by equating *satya* with God. As a result, some scholars have also defined the term to mean "soul-force." Gandhi's practice of nonviolent resistance is understood to have incorporated the principles of *satyagraha.*

13. Gandhi, *Autobiography,* 434.

14. Ibid., 437.

15. M. K. Gandhi, "Speech at Nadiad," March 22, 1918, *CWMG,* vol. 14 (Ahmedabad, 1965), 275.

16. *Bombay Chronicle,* April 2, 1918.

17. Gandhi, "End of Kheda Satyagraha," *Autobiography,* 339. In fact, Hardiman points out that only 1 percent of the land revenue was not paid when the four-month-long movement ended in June 1918. See Hardiman, *Peasant Nationalists,* 108.

18. Gandhi, "End of Kheda Satyagraha," *Autobiography,* 440.

19. *Report of the Working of the Criminal Tribes Act in the Bombay Presidency for the Year 1918* (Bombay, 1919), 21.

41. STRIKES AND RAIDS

1. SAPI, vol. XXXI, no. 23 of 1918, June 5, 1918, 521.

2. Ibid.

3. Ibid.

4. OIOC, JP, 1918, P/10324, Letter from V. K. Namjoshi, DM, Kaira, to Comm., ND, nd; OIOC, JP, 1918, P/10324, Rept. from J. Ghosal, DM, Kaira, April 18, 1918; OIOC, JP, 1918, P/10325 (B Proceedings), Telegram from Trikambhai Uttambhai Patel, Khambholej, Kaira, to J. C. Ker, DM, August 20, 1918; Telegram from Jesangbhai Bhaiabhai Patel, Sarsa, Kaira, to J. C. Ker, DM, August 19, 1918; OIOC, JP, 1919, P/10543, from Sec. to Gov't, Bombay, to Sec. to Gov't of India, HD, June 28, 1919; Nadiad Town Police Station, Village Crime Notes, Rept. from Janoobhai B. Desai, Circle Police Inspector, Nadiad, to DM, Kaira, November 16, 1919.

5. DSP Office, Kheda, Confidential Notes on the District, File C1, Rept. from DSP, October 10, 1919.

6. MSA, JD, 1920, file no. 1652, Class A, from A. C. J. Bailey, DSP, Kaira, to IGP, December 3, 1918.

7. Ibid.; OIOC, JP, 1918, P/10325 (B Proceedings), Telegram from Trikambhai Uttambhai Patel, Khambholej, Kaira, to J. C. Ker, DM, August 20, 1918; Telegram from Jesangbhai Bhaiabhai Patel, Sarsa, Kaira, to J. C. Ker, DM, August 19, 1918; Rept. from J. C. Ker, DM, August 27, 1918.

8. MSA, JD, 1920, file no. 1652, Class A, from A. C. J. Bailey, DSP, Kaira, to IGP, December 3, 1918.

9. Ibid.

10. Ibid.

11. Ibid.

12. Skaria, *Hybrid Histories*, 124; Dhot, "Economy and Society," 330–31.
13. Skaria, *Hybrid Histories*, 124.
14. MSA, JD, 1920, file no. 1652, Class A, from A. C. J. Bailey, DSP, Kaira, to IGP, December 3, 1918.
15. MSA, JD, 1920, file no. 1652, Class A, from N. V. Trivedi, Deputy Superintendent of Police, Kaira, to Coll., Kaira, February 19, 1920. The alliance of disenfranchised elites with "bandits" has been discussed by Kasturi, *Embattled Identities*. For similar themes in China, see Cohen, *History in Three Keys*, 17, 19.
16. MSA, JD, 1920, file no. 1652, Class A, from A. C. J. Bailey, DSP, Kaira, to IGP, December 3, 1918.
17. Ibid.
18. Attacks on Christians during periods of revolt are also discussed in Rudrangshu Mukherjee, *Awadh in Revolt: A Study of Popular Resistance* (Delhi, 1984).
19. BRO, HPO, section 124/file 10, from Robert Boyd, to R. S. Maubhai, Dewan Baroda, September 17, 1891.
20. Roman Catholic Mission Archives, Anand, Mission Notes and Files, file 4, from Rev. J. Umbricht, to Coll., Kaira, September 10, 1918.
21. MSA, RD, 1881, vol. 15, no. 1372, Admin. Rept., J. Campbell, Coll., Kaira, July 11, 1881.

42. NATIONALIZING DHARALA RAIDS

1. Hardiman, *Peasant Nationalists*, 129.
2. Between 1918 and 1922, the number of raids reported in Kheda district were as follows: 1918: 45; 1919: 27; 1920: 48; 1921: 70; 1922: 48. Figures given in *Bombay Chronicle*, December 22, 1923, 9.
3. Select raiders in Kheda district, c. 1917–1924, are as follows: Kalya Abha, Ahmedali Amir, Mahiji Anop, Dabhai Baja, Dahya Bhula, Keya Daji, Babar Deva, Chhagan Gaga, Gagla, Chaklasi Gang, Golel Gang, Namdar Garbad, Dola Jaga, Moti Jena, Dabhla Jibhai, Gaga Jija, Jogan, Kala Lala, Magan Nana, Shankar Raiji, Alimiya Sadak.
Collated from the following: *Times of India*, February 21, 1923; BRO, HPO, PD, file 24, sect. 134, from C. N. Seddon, "Dacoity Operations in the Baroda District," June 25, 1923; BRO, HPO, PD, file 134, sect. 24, from C. N. Seddon, to E. H. Kealy, January 24, 1924; BRO, HPO, file 7, sect. 135, Political Office, "Arrangement for Capture of Outlaws between Kaira and Baroda State," from First Resident Asst., Baroda, to Minister, Baroda, December 19, 1919; BRO, HPO, file 7, sect. 135, from Subha's Office, to Dewan, Baroda, June 5, 1923; BRO, HPO, file 7, sect. 135, from DSP, Kaira, to Dewan, June 30, 1924; BRO, HPO, file 7, sect. 135, from M. N. Mehta, Dewan, to W. P. Barton, Resident, Baroda, December 26, 1919; BRO, HPO, file 7, sect. 135, from Comm. Police, Baroda, February 3, 1920; BRO, HPO, file 7, sect. 135, from S. H. Coverton, DM, Kaira, to Comm. ND, January 1, 1922; SAPI, vol. XXXVII, no. 1 of 1924, January 5, 1924, 4, 12; SAPI, vol. XXXVII, no. 4 of 1924, January 24, 1924, 57.
4. SAPI, vol. XXXVII, no. 6 of 1924, February 9, 1924, 85; SAPI, vol. XXXVII, no. 1 of 1924, January 5, 1924, 4; SAPI, vol. XXXVII, no. 1 of 1924,

January 5, 1924, 12; SAPI, vol. XXXVII, no. 4 of 1924, January 26, 1924, 57; SAPI, vol. XXXVII, no. 6 of 1924, February 9, 1924, 85; OIOC, JP, 1920, P/10790, Letter from N. J. Wadia, DM, Kaira, to Sec. to Gov't, JD, Bombay; GSA, HPO, section 165/file14a, Note by Police Commissioner, September 9, 1922. Also see *CWSVP,* vol. 1, *1918–1925: The Kheda Non-Cooperation Movement, Nagpur Flag Agitation and Borsad Satyagraha* (Delhi, 1990).

5. SAPI, vol. XXXVII, no. 1 of 1924, January 5, 1924, 4; SAPI, vol. XXXVII, no. 1 of 1924, January 5, 1924, 12; *CWSVP,* vol. 1, 272.

6. MSA, JD, 1920, file no. 1652, A Class, from A. C. G. Bailey, DSP, Kaira, to Comm., ND, nd.

7. Ibid.

8. Many newspaper articles on the subject were published. The following are selections from the *RNN* for the period 1920–27: *Hindusthan,* February 7, 1920; *Hindusthan,* February 14, 1920; *Hindusthan,* June 17, 1920; *Hindusthan,* August 7, 1920; *Bombay Chronicle,* January 28, 1921; *Gujarat Vartman,* February 2, 1921; *Kaira Vartman,* February 2, 1921; *Hindusthan,* September 20, 1921; *Hindusthan,* October 15, 1921; *Hind Mitra,* October 23, 1921; *Asahakar,* December 2, 1921; *Young India,* December 6, 1921; *Navayug,* December 7, 1921; *Shri Bharat,* May 11, 1922; *Gujarati Punch,* May 21, 1922; *Praja Bandhu,* December 16, 1923; *Bombay Chronicle,* December 19, 1923; *Voice of India,* December 19, 1923; *Kaira Vartman,* December 19, 1923; *Voice of India,* December 21, 1923; *Navayug,* December 21, 1923; *Kaira Vartman,* September 17, 1924; *Kranti,* October 1, 1927.

9. SAPI, vol. XXXIII, no. 43 of 1920, October 23, 1920, 1505 (emphasis mine).

43. A SECOND "NO-REVENUE CAMPAIGN"

1. Hardiman, *Peasant Nationalists,* 152.

2. SAPI, vol. XXXIV, no. 1–2 of 1921, January 26, 1921, 137.

3. Ibid.

4. See *RNN: Praja Bandhu,* February 6, 1921; *Bombay Chronicle,* January 28, 1921; *Gujarat Vartman,* February 2, 1921; *Kaira Vartman,* February 2, 1921; *Navayug,* December 7, 1921.

5. SAPI, vol. XXXIV, 1921, 1738, 1838, originally cited in Hardiman, *Peasant Nationalists,* 154.

6. Hardiman points out that the most powerful support for the movement emerged in six Patidar-dominated villages. The CTA was fully enforced in the following villages: Chikhodra, Od, Khambholaj, and Samarkha.

7. SAPI, vol. XXXIII, no. 52 of 1920, January 26, 1920, 137.

8. See Amin, *Event, Metaphor, Memory.*

44. DEPORTING DHARALAS

1. OIOC, HP, 1923, P/11323, Rept. from Deputy Sec. to Gov't, Bombay, August 31, 1923.

2. OIOC, HP, 1925, P/11467, Rept. from J. W. Smith, DM, Kaira, to Sec. to Gov't, HD, July 7, 1924.

3. OIOC, HP, 1923, P/11323, Rept. from F. W. O'Gorman, DSP, Kaira, to DM, Kaira, April 9, 1923.

4. OIOC, HP, 1925, P/11467, Rept. from J. W. Smith, DM, Kaira, to Sec. to Gov't, HD, July 7, 1924.

5. OIOC, IPP, 1920, P/10839, Rept. from R. Ramchandra Rao Avargal, Sec. to Gov't, Madras, July 27, 1917.

6. Rept. from O. H. B. Starte, "Dharalas of Kaira District," 52, Starte Papers, Centre of South Asian Studies, University of Cambridge.

7. The Criminal Tribes Act, 1911, 6–7.

8. OIOC, HP, 1925, P/11467, Rept. from J. W. Smith, DM, Kaira, to Sec. to Gov't, HD, July 7, 1924; OIOC, L/PARL/2/407, East India (Jails Committee), *Report of the Indian Jails Committee, 1919–20*, vol. 1 (London, 1921), chapter 22: "Criminal Tribes," 317, 322. For an official discussion on the "criminal" propensity of Kaikadis, classified as a "nomadic tribe of robbers and dacoits," and Chhapparbands, see Cox, *Police and Crime in India*, 229–52. Also, for a discussion of all four communities, see R. E. Enthoven, *The Tribes and Castes of Bombay* (Bombay, 1922).

9. OIOC, JP, 1918, P/10324, "Report on Creating a Settlement of Criminal Tribes at Shivrajpur to Be Composed of Kaira Criminal Tribes," December 16, 1917.

10. Ibid.

11. *Report on the Working of the Criminal Tribes Act in the Bombay Presidency for the Year 1918* (Bombay, 1919), 7.

12. OIOC, IPP, 1920, P/10839, Rept. from R. Ramchandra Rao Avargal, Sec. to Gov't, Madras, July 27, 1917; OIOC, L/PARL/2/407, *Report of Jails Committee*, vol. 1, 317; and *Report of Jails Committee*, vol. 4. *Minutes of Evidence Taken in Bihar and Orissa, the Central Provinces, and the Bombay Presidency* (Calcutta, 1922), 1209–10.

13. OIOC, L/PARL/2/407, East India (Jails Committee), *Report of the Indian Jails Committee*, 317. Other occupations taken up by settlement workers included masonry, carpentry, blacksmithing, weaving, and tailoring.

Also see Starte Papers, "Dharalas of Kaira District," 55. A similar point is made for the criminal tribes settlement in Sholapur, in Manjiri Kamat, "Labour and Nationalism in Sholapur: Conflict, Confrontation, and Control in a Deccan City, Western India, 1918–1939" (PhD diss., University of Cambridge, 1997), 296.

14. OIOC, HP, 1925, P/11467, Rept. from J. W. Smith, DM, Kaira, to Sec. to Gov't, HD, July 7, 1924.

15. OIOC, HP, 1923, P/11323, Rept. from Criminal Tribes Settlement Officer, Bijapur, September 2, 1923.

16. OIOC, HP, 1925, P/11467, Rept. from J. W. Smith, DM, Kaira, to Sec. to Gov't, HD, July 7, 1924.

45. THE PUNITIVE POLICE TAX

1. For a discussion of the punitive police tax, see chapter 42, note 8. The denomination of currency in India was the rupee, anna, and pie up until 1957, when the system was formally decimalized. The amount "Rs. 2–7–0" is read as

2 rupees, 7 annas, and 0 pie. Within this currency system, 1 rupee was made up of 16 annas, and 1 anna consisted of 12 pies. In other words, there were 192 pies in 1 rupee. Within the decimal currency in India, 1 rupee is made up of 100 paise.

2. See MSA, RD, 1924, file 5714(a), Rept. from J. W. Smith, Coll., Kaira, nd.

3. See SAPI, vol. XXXVI, no. 50 of 1923, December 15, 1923, 1447; SAPI, vol. XXXVI, no. 51 of 1923, December 22, 1923, 1463–65.

4. Ibid.

5. Hardiman, *Peasant Nationalists*, 169.

6. *Praja Bandhu,* January 13, 1924; *RNN, Kaira Vartman,* February 4, 1920.

7. OIOC, HP, 1925, P/11467, Rept. from J. W. Smith, DM, Kaira, to Sec. to Gov't, HD, July 7, 1924.

8. *PRBP for the Year 1921* (Bombay, 1922), 15, Abstract of Rept. by Comm., ND, nd.

9. *PRBP for the Year 1922* (Bombay, 1923), 13, Abstract of Rept. by F. C. Griffith, Acting IGP, BP, October 10, 1923.

10. OIOC, HP, 1925, Rept. from J. W. Smith, DM, Kaira, to Sec. to Gov't, HD, July 7, 1924.

46. "TO FORGET PAST ENMITIES"

1. The dates and locations of select Dharala conferences sponsored by the Indian National Congress included the following (for some of the meetings, the exact dates and locations are not provided in the official sources):

January 19, 1921, Vadtal
May 1922, place not given
1923, Sojitra
January 13–15, 1924, Anklav, Kathana, Piplav
March 1, 1924, Kathana
March 29, 1924, Vehra
May 31, 1924, place not given
1924, place not given
March 16–17, 1926, Golel
February 13, 1926, Anklav
April 23, 1930, Dakore

Collated from the following sources: SAPI, vol. XXXIII, no. 52 of 1920, January 26, 1920, 137; SAPI, vol. XXXVII, no. 6 of 1924, February 9, 1924, 85; SAPI, vol. XXXVII, no. 11 of 1924, March 15, 1924, 170; SAPI, vol. XXXVII, no. 15 of 1924, April 12, 1924, 250; SAPI, vol. XXXVII, no. 22 of 1924, May 31, 1924, 355; SAPI, vol. XXXIX, no. 8 of 1926, February 27, 1926, 140; SAPI, vol. XXXIX, no. 13 of 1926, April 3, 1926, 215; MSA, HD (Special), file no. 800 (73) (4) for 1932, Daily Rept. from the Acting Coll., Kaira, regarding the Civil Disobedience Movement, 1932; MSA, HD (Special), file no. 800 (74) (4) III for 1941–43, Rept. from DM, Kaira, September 10, 1942; Hardiman, *Peasant Nationalists,* 174, 200; M. K. Gandhi, "Dharalas," January 22, 1925, *CWMG,* vol. 26 (Ahmedabad, 1967), 25; Shah, *Caste Association,* 36.

2. SAPI, vol. XXXVII, no. 5 of 1924, February 2, 1924, 73; SAPI, vol.

XXXVII, no. 6 of 1924, February 9, 1924, 85; SAPI, vol. XXXVII, no. 9 of 1924, March 1, 1924, 139; SAPI, vol. XXXVII, no. 11 of 1924, March 15, 1924, 170; SAPI, vol. XXXVII, no. 15 of 1924, April 12, 1924, 250; SAPI, vol. XXXVII, no. 22 of 1924, May 31, 1924, 355.

3. SAPI, vol. XXXVII, no. 22 of 1924, May 31, 1924, 355.

4. SAPI, vol. XXXVII, no. 6 of 1924, February 9, 1924, 85.

5. Gandhi, "Dharalas," 25. For a later development on this issue, see "Claims to a New Caste Nomenclature," in *Census of India, 1931*, vol. 8, pt. 1: *Bombay Presidency, General Report*, ed. A. H. Dracup and H. T. Sorley (Bombay, 1933), appendix C, 398.

6. SAPI, vol. XXXVII, no. 6 of 1924, January 26, 1924, 88; SAPI, vol. XXXIX, no. 13 of 1926, April 3, 1926, 215.

7. Gandhi, "Dharalas," 39-40.

8. M. K. Gandhi, "Speech at Virsad," February 12, 1925, *CWMG*, vol. 30 (Ahmedabad, 2000), 255.

9. M. K. Gandhi, "To 'Dharalas,' 'Garasias,' and Others," *CWMG*, vol. 21 (Ahmedabad, 1966), 529-30.

47. RAVISHANKAR VYAS

1. SAPI, vol. XXXVII, no. 11 of 1924, March 15, 1924, 170; SAPI, vol. XXXVII, no. 15 of 1924, April 12, 1924, 250.

2. SAPI, vol. XXXVII, no. 5 of 1924, February 2, 1924, 73; SAPI, vol. XXXVII, no. 9 of 1924, March 1, 1924, 139; SAPI, vol. XXXVII, no. 11 of 1924, March 15, 1924, 170; SAPI, vol. XXXVII, no. 15 of 1924, April 12, 1924, 250; SAPI, vol. XXXVII, no. 22 of 1924, May 31, 1924, 355; *Bombay Chronicle*, May 1, 1928, reproduced in *CWSVP*, vol. 2, 165.

3. *Bombay Chronicle*, February 24, 1928, reproduced in *CWSVP*, vol. 2, 91–92; "Stray Bulletin" by Jagatram Dave, March 9, 1928, reproduced in *CWSVP*, vol. 2, 119–20; "News Bulletin 61," March 1928, reproduced in *CWSVP*, vol. 2, 137–38; "News Bulletin 52," March 1928, reproduced in *CWSVP*, vol. 2, 139–41; *Prajabandhu*, April 7–14, 1928, reproduced in *CWSVP*, vol. 2, 148–49; *Bombay Chronicle*, May 9, 1928, reproduced in *CWSVP*, vol. 2, 170–71; *Bombay Chronicle*, May 14, 1928, reproduced in *CWSVP*, vol. 2, 173–74.

4. SAPI, vol. XXXVII, no. 22 of 1924, May 31, 1924, 355.

5. SAPI, vol. XXXVII, no. 15 of 1924, April 12, 1924, 250.

6. SAPI, vol. XXXVII, no. 22 of 1924, May 31, 1924, 355.

7. Hardiman, *Peasant Nationalists*, 176.

8. Ibid., 177.

48. THE LAST "NO-REVENUE CAMPAIGN"

1. *Bombay Chronicle*, March 9, 1930; March 11, 1930.

2. Hardiman, *Peasant Nationalists*, 198.

3. Following the Civil Disobedience Movement, there was a brief increase in *dacoities*, which were quickly stopped with the arrest of nearly forty people. See SAPI, vol. XLIII, no. 38 of 1930, September 20, 1930, 1437.

4. SAPI, vol. XLIII, no. 37 of 1930, September 13, 1930, 1376.

5. *PRBP for the Year 1933* (Bombay, 1934), 38, Abstract of Rept. by DSP, Kaira, nd.

6. *PRBP for the Year 1934* (Bombay, 1935), 39, Abstract of Rept. (source not specified).

7. *PRBP for the Year 1933* (Bombay, 1934), 3, Abstract of Rept. by DSP, Kaira, nd.

8. GSA, HPO, sec. 38/file 53, "Migration of British Subjects into Baroda Territory," January 19, 1932.

9. For a discussion of the abolition of *narwadari* tenure, see chapter 4, note 2.

10. MSA, RD, 1930, file no. 5083/28, pt. 1, from A. Master, to Comm. ND, June 18, 1930.

11. Ibid.

12. M. K. Gandhi, "Letter to K. B. Bhadrapur," Coll., Kaira, June 25, 1931, *CWMG*, vol. 52 (Ahmedabad, 2000), 421–22.

13. *Bombay Chronicle*, October 31, 1930; November 3, 4, 5, 6, 26, 1930; December 10, 11, 15, 23, 26, 27, 1930; January 13, 1931.

14. M. K. Gandhi, "Letter to K. B. Bhadrapur," Coll., Kaira, June 24, 1931, *CWMG*, vol. 52 (Ahmedabad, 2000), 405.

15. M. K. Gandhi, "Letter to R. M. Maxwell," Private Sec. to the Gov. Bombay, July 5, 1931, *CWMG*, vol. 53 (Ahmedabad, 2000), 26.

49. THE COMING OF THE POSTCOLONIAL

1. MSA, RD, 1940, file no. 7159/33-XXXI-B, from E. W. Perry, Sec. to Gov't of Bombay, RD, October 19, 1938; Weekly Confidential Rept. of the DM, Kaira, October 20, 1938; Memo., Deputy Sec. to Gov't, November 17, 1938; Memo., Sec. to Gov't, November 4, 1938; Report from S. B. Vaidya, Coll., Kaira, to Sec. to Gov't, December 8, 1938.

2. See Hardiman, "Quit India Movement."

3. DSP Office, Kheda, Confidential Notes on the District, file C1, Report by DSP, March 25, 1938.

50. BECOMING INDIAN

1. Partha Chatterjee, *The Politics of the Governed: Reflections on Popular Politics in Most of the World* (New York, 2004), 25.

2. Ibid.

3. See Shah, *Caste Association*. Also see Atul Kohli, *Democracy and Discontent: India's Growing Crisis of Governability* (Cambridge, 1991).

4. Ghanshyam Shah, "Caste and Land Reforms in Gujarat," in *Land Reforms in India*, vol. 8, *Performance and Challenges in Gujarat and Maharashtra*, ed. Ghanshyam Shah and D. C. Sah (New Delhi, 2002), 127–43.

5. Ibid., 142.

6. Ibid.

51. SMALL DISCOVERIES

1. I read David Hardiman's "Peasant Agitations," which briefly discusses Ranchod Vira's movement, only after my fieldwork in 1996.

2. See Guha, *Elementary Aspects.*

3. For a brief discussion on the SAPI, see H. M. Joshi, introduction to *Source Material for a History of the Freedom Movement in India,* vol. 3, *Mahatma Gandhi,* pt. 1, *1915–1922* (Bombay, 1965).

4. SAPI, vol. XI, no. 5 of 1898, February 8, 1898, 34.

5. See Hardiman, *Peasant Nationalists,* 49.

6. SAPI, vol. XXII, no. 18 of 1909, May 8, 1909, 371.

7. See Ginzburg, *Clues, Myths.*

8. For a discussion of this theme in the context of colonial Gujarat, see Harry Borradaile, *Gujarat Caste Rules: Published from the Original Answers of the Castes with the Sanction of Her Imperial Majesty's High Court of Judicature of Bombay,* 2 vols. (Bombay, 1884, 1887).

9. SAPI, vol. XXII, no. 18 of 1909, May 8, 1909, 371.

10. Imper. vs. R., Examination, Meru Mitha.

11. Imper. vs. R., Examination, Gema Mitha.

12. Various colonial officials advocated the use of torture for obtaining confessions. See, for example, SRBG (NS), no. 39[a], Rept. from H. W. Diggle, to Lieut. Col. A. Walker, Resident, Baroda, May 10, 1804, appendix; OIOC, V/10/1, "Report on the Administration of Public Affairs in the Bombay Presidency for the Year 1855–56"; *Report of the Commissioners for the Investigation of Alleged Cases of Torture, in the Madras Presidency* (Madras, 1855).

52. CHAKLASI

1. S. B. Rajyagor, ed., *Gujarat State Gazetteers, Kheda District* (Ahmedabad, 1977), 792.

2. Ibid.

3. See Shah and Shroff, "The Vahivanca Barots."

4. See Shah, *Caste Association.*

5. For a relevant discussion on banning the CTA, see "Repeal the Criminal Tribes Act," *Congress Socialist,* vol. 4, no. 8, February 19, 1939.

53. DADURAM'S LEGACIES

1. For a discussion on this theme regarding central Gujarat, see Hardiman, *Peasant Nationalists.*

2. I have further developed this argument in Chaturvedi, "Peasant King."

3. SAPI, vol. XXII, no. 18 of 1909, May 8, 1909.

4. *Bhajan mandlis* are informal groups who sing devotional songs and religious hymns.

5. For a discussion of *bhajan mandlis* organized by Dharalas in Kheda district, see D. F. Pocock, *Mind, Body, and Wealth: A Study of Belief and Practice in an Indian Village* (Oxford, 1973); H. M. Patel, "Adaptation as a Process of

Social Change: A Case Study of the Marriage of Baraiya Caste of Village Juni-Ardi" (masters thesis, Maharaja Sayajirao University, Baroda, 1963).

6. For a comparison to similar themes, see Ruth B. Bottigheimer, "Fairy Tales, Folk Narrative Research, and History," *Social History* 14, 3 (1989): 343–58.

7. Here, I am specifically referring to Ginzburg, *Cheese and the Worms;* Steven Feierman, *Peasant Intellectuals: Anthropology and History in Tanzania* (Madison, 1990); Guha, *Elementary Aspects;* Amin, *Event, Metaphor, Memory;* Hardiman, *Coming of the Devi;* Skaria, *Hybrid Histories.*

8. The conceptualization for this idea comes from Geoff Eley, "Nations, Publics, and Political Cultures: Placing Habermas in the Nineteenth Century," in *Habermas and the Public Sphere,* ed. Craig Calhoun (Cambridge, 1992), 288–339; Geoff Eley, "Edward Thompson, Social History, and Political Culture: The Making of a Working-Class Public, 1780–1850," in *E. P. Thompson: Critical Perspectives,* ed. Harvey J. Kaye and Keith McClelland (Philadelphia, 1990), 12–49.

9. This idea is taken from Ginzburg, *Cheese and the Worms,* xii.

10. The major traditions within Hinduism are based on the worship of Vishnu (Vaishnavism) and Shiva (Shaivism). It is worth noting that Daduram is associated with several of Vishnu's avatars, including Krishna, Ramchandra, and Dattatrey, a theme discussed later in this chapter.

11. See David Hardiman, "Baroda: The Structure of a 'Progressive' State," in *People, Princes, and Paramount Power: Society and Politics in the Indian Princely States,* ed. Robin Jeffrey (Delhi, 1978), 107–35; Edward Thompson, *The Making of Indian Princes* (London, 1978); Ian Copland, *The Princes of India in the Endgame of Empire, 1917–1947* (Cambridge, 1997); Manu Bhagavan, *Sovereign Spheres: Princes, Education, and Empire in Colonial India* (Delhi, 2003).

12. SAPI, vol. XXII, no. 18 of 1909, May 8, 1909.

13. Fifty-two is a recurring number within various Vaishnava discourses, and it is the number of accepted *dwaras* (doors or pathways) to god. I thank William Pinch for the reference (personal correspondence).

14. See Romila Thapar, *A History of India,* vol. 1 (London, 1990); Romila Thapar, *Ancient Indian Social History: Some Interpretations* (Delhi, 1990).

15. I thank David Hardiman for reminding me of these issues. The above discussion is based on Hardiman's own analysis of the Shankaracharya in his *Peasant Nationalists,* 141–42. Also see *Bombay Chronicle,* November 7, 1921.

16. Pinch, *Peasants and Monks,* 76–77.

17. The literature on this theme is extensive. For a discussion of such processes in Gujarat, see Shah, *Caste Association;* Lancy Lobo, *The Thakors of North Gujarat: A Caste in the Village and the Region* (Delhi, 1995). For a general discussion, see Nicholas B. Dirks, *Castes of Mind: Colonialism and the Making of Modern India* (Princeton, 2001); Susan Bayly, *Caste, Society, and Politics in India from the Eighteenth Century to the Modern Age* (Cambridge, 2001).

18. See, for example, Hardiman, *Coming of the Devi;* Sumit Sarkar, *Modern India, 1885–1947* (Madras, 1983), 53–58.

19. I taped the folk stories, oral narratives, and *bhajans* on two audio cassettes numbers 1 and 2, on July 15, 1996, in Dakore. Both tapes are presently in my possession.

20. Ibid., audio cassette number 1 (my translation).

21. For a discussion of how Gandhi became Bapu, the father of India's national family, see Bhikhu Parekh, *Colonialism, Tradition, and Reform: An Analysis of Gandhi's Political Discourse* (New Delhi, 1989), 13, italics in the original.

22. Gandhi, "Dharalas," *CWMG*, vol. 26, 25.

23. See SAPI, vol. XXXVI, no. 9 of 1923, March 3, 1923, 231, 277; M. K. Gandhi, "Speech at Public Meeting, Dakor," October 27, 1920, *CWMG*, vol. 21 (Ahmedabad, 2000), 396–403; M. K. Gandhi, "Speech at Women's Meeting, Dakor," October 27, 1920, *CWMG*, vol. 21 (Ahmedabad, 2000), 404–8; M. K. Gandhi, "To Women," *CWMG*, vol. 22 (Ahmedabad, 2000), 25–26; *Source Material*, vol. 3, pt. 1, 61–62.

24. Gandhi, "Speech at Public Meeting, Dakor," 397, italics in the original.

25. SAPI, vol. XXII, no. 18 of 1909, May 8, 1909.

26. Shah, *Caste Association.*

27. *Bajri* was the largest cultivated crop in Nadiad *taluka,* the subdistrict in which the village of Chalali was located. For poor peasants, it was an easy crop to cultivate as it required minimal investment in the means of production. MSA, RD, 1879, vol. 20, comp. 972, Admin. Rept., G. H. D. Wilson, Coll., Kaira, July 4, 1879; *GBPK*, 47, 155.

28. Audio cassette number 1 (my translation).

29. Pinch, *Peasants and Monks,* 53.

30. Ibid.; Richard Burghart, "The Founding of the Ramanandi Sect," *Ethnohistory* 25, 2 (1978): 121–39; Peter van der Veer, "Taming the Ascetic: Devotionalism in a Hindu Monastic Order," *Man,* n.s., 22, 4 (1987): 680–95; W. G. Orr, *A Sixteenth Century Indian Mystic* (London, 1947); Winand M. Callewaert, *The Hindi Biography of Dadu Dayal* (Delhi, 1988); K. N. Upadhyaya, *The Compassionate Mystic* (New Delhi, 1980); Monika Thiel-Hortsmann, *Crossing the Ocean of Existence: Braj Bhasa Religious Poetry from Rajasthan* (Wiesbaden, 1983).

31. Burghart, "Ramanandi Sect"; van der Veer, "Taming the Ascetic"; Peter van der Veer, *Gods on Earth: The Management of Religious Experience and Identity in a North Indian Pilgrimage Centre* (London, 1988).

32. Pinch, *Peasants and Monks.*

33. Orr, *Indian Mystic;* Callewaert, *Dadu Dayal;* Upadhyaya, *Compassionate Mystic;* Thiel-Hortsmann, *Crossing the Ocean.*

34. Pinch, *Peasants and Monks.*

35. Ibid., 71.

36. From the "Gyan Vilas Vinayla Moti," handwritten manuscript, presently kept in the Daduram Temple in Dakore (I have converted the dates from the Vikram Samwat era here; my translation):

1816   Daduram was born in the village of Chalali, Nadiad *taluka,*
               Kheda district.

1840	Daduram went to Girnar in Junagadh; had *darshan* with Guru Datta, Guru Gorakhnath, and Ramanand.
1901–1902	Daduram arrived in Dakore, started building the temple.
1909	Daduram's death.
	Tapsiram became successor to the *gadi* (seat of authority).
1954	Tapsiram's death.
1954–1955	Dalsukhram became successor to the *gadi*.
1964	Idols of Lord Ram, Daduram, and Tapsiram placed in the temple.
1966	Other idols placed in temple.
1985	Temple opened.

37. K. S. Singh, "Agrarian Dimensions of Tribal Movements," in *Agrarian Struggles in India after Independence*, ed. A. R. Desai (Delhi, 1986), 147.

55. KALASINH DURBAR

1. Imper. vs. R., Ex. no. 10, "Seditious Letter addressed to Kashibhai Ranchhodbhai."

56. RAGHUPURA

1. Imper. vs. R., Examination, Ranchod Vira.

57. LOCAL KNOWLEDGE

1. Imper. vs. R., Confession, Surta Ragha.
2. Imper. vs. R., Confession, Meru Mitha.
3. See Pocock, *Kanbi and Patidar*.
4. Imper. vs. R., Confession, Surta Ragha.

58. HIDDEN HISTORIES

1. Imper. vs. R., Ex. no. 56, "The Examination of Accused no. 11, Bana Koda, before the Committing Magistrate," May 18, 1898.
2. See MSA, JD, 1899, vol. 78, comp. 457, Letter from DM, Kaira, to the Under Sec. to the Gov't, JD, Bombay, October 14, 1898.
3. SAPI, vol. XXII, no. 18 of 1909, May 8, 1909, 371.

59. ERASING THE PAST

1. Ninety-two villages are listed in SRBG (NS), no. 295, *Papers Relating to the Revision Survey Settlement of the Nadiad Taluka of the Kaira Collectorate* (Bombay, 1895), 12. The village of Raghupura, however, does not appear in this source, nor is it listed for the neighboring Anand *taluka* in SRBG (NS), no. 296, *Papers Relating to the Revision Survey Settlement of the Anand Taluka of the Kaira Collectorate* (Bombay, 1895).

60. NARSIRAM

1. See MSA, JD, 1882, vol. 61, comp. 1228, Letter from G. F. M. Grant, DM, Kaira, to G. F. Sheppard, July 5, 1882, for a discussion of using photography to control criminals in Kheda.

61. SEEING DADURAM

1. See Christopher Pinney, *Camera Indica: The Social Life of Indian Photographs* (London, 1997); Christopher Pinney, *Photos of the Gods: The Printed Image and Political Struggle in India* (Delhi, 2004).
2. See Pocock, *Kanbi and Patidar;* Guha, *Elementary Aspects.*
3. Robert N. Minor, ed., *Modern Interpreters of the Bhagavadgita* (Albany, 1986), 3.
4. Ibid., 6.
5. SAPI, vol. XXII, no. 18 of 1909, May 8, 1909, 371.

63. NARSI BHAGAT

1. It is worth noting that the root for both *Kuberacharaya* and *Kuberdar* is *Kuber,* the name for the god of wealth. However, at no point was the issue of Kuber as the god of wealth raised in my conversations with Narsi Bhagat or with Moti and Garbad in Raghupura.
2. DSP, Headquarters, Kheda, Confidential Notes on the District, file C1, Rept. by DSP, March 1, 1944.

64. HISTORY WITHOUT ENDS

1. See Benjamin, *Illuminations,* 255.
2. In Gujarat, children adopt their father's first name as their middle name, thereby making it possible to identify the names of two generations for men. Women drop their father's name and adopt their husband's first name as their middle name after marriage.

CONCLUSION

1. Hardiman, *Peasant Nationalists,* 250.

GLOSSARY

ADALAT	court of law
ANDOLAN	revolution
ANNA	monetary unit, equivalent to one-sixteenth of a rupee
ARTI	set of rituals, an offering to a deity
AVATAR	earthly form of a deity
BABUL	type of tree *(Acacia nilotica indica)*
BADMASH	outlaw, person of bad character
BAHIS	account books
BAJRI	millet
BANIA	merchant or moneylender
BHAGAT	village priest; a devotee
BHAJAN	devotional song
BHAJAN MANDLI	group that sings devotional songs
BIGHA	a measurement of land, approximately 0.59 acre in Gujarat
CHAKRAVARTIN	universal monarch (literally, one who turns the wheel)
CHAUTH	one-fourth
CHORA or CHOWRA	village center
DACOIT	bandit
DACOITY	banditry
DADHS	organized peasant raids
DARSHAN	a viewing of a deity, sacred place, or person
DESAI	chief revenue-farmer in the Mughal administration
DESH	homeland, country
DHAR or DHARA	edge; edge of a sword
DHARIA	agricultural implement, similar to a billhook

DURBAR	court, royal audience, assembly
DWARA	door or doorway
FAUJ	army
FOUZDAR or FAUJDAR	military commander under the Mughal administration
GADI	seat of authority
GAM	village
GANJA	marijuana
GHEE	clarified butter
GIRAS	dues collected from villages
GOL	marriage circle
GOMTI	tank of sacred water
GORADU	light, shallow loam; soil
GURU	teacher
GURU PARAMPARA	preceptor lineage
HAZRI or HAJRI	roll call
HIJRAT	a protest migration
JADU	magic
JAMADAR	chief or leader of a unit of persons, especially in the army
JOPDRI	hut
KALA PANI	literally, black water: a reference to a prison sentence in the Andaman Islands
KALI	dark or black
KALIYUG	age of darkness
KANTHI	wooden bead from the *tulsi* plant
KARKUN	accountant or clerk
KASHI	a name for Varanasi or Benares
KHARIF	monsoon crop
KOTWAL	police chief
MAHARAJ	great king or leader
MAHUA or MHOWRA	tree whose flowers are used for making daru *(Bassia latifolia)*
MALA	necklace
MAMLATDAR	revenue officer in charge of a *taluka*
MANDWA or MANDUP	a canopy; a part of a temple
MASTERJI	teacher
MATADAR	head of a Patidar lineage
MELA	festival, carnival
MUKHI	village headman
NARWADARI	form of land tenure under which revenue payments are paid jointly by shareholders
PANCHAYAT	village council
PARGANA	subdivision of a district
PATRA	letter, almanac, or horoscope
PEEPUL	sacred tree *(Ficus religiosa)*
PUCCA	complete or solid
PUCKERY WALLAH	turban wearer

PUNEM	full moon
RABI	winter crop
RAWANIA	village watchman
RYOTWARI	form of land tenure under which cultivators make payments directly to government
SADHU	holy man, ascetic
SARKAR	government
SATYA	truth
SATYUG	age of truth
SEPOY	soldier
SHIGRAM	carriage or cart
TALATI	village accountant
TALUKA	an administrative subdivision of a district
TOPIWALLAH	hat wearer
TULSI	sacred plant also known as holy basil *(Ocimum sanctum)*
TURAI	trumpet
VETH	labor rent
WANSLE	agricultural implement
YUG or YUGA	age or era

BIBLIOGRAPHY

ARCHIVAL RECORDS

ANAND RURAL POLICE THANA, NADIAD TOWN POLICE STATION, AND KHEDA POLICE THANA
Village Crime Notebooks

CENTRE OF SOUTH ASIAN STUDIES, UNIVERSITY OF CAMBRIDGE
Sorley Papers
Starte Papers

DISTRICT SUPERINTENDENT OF POLICE HEADQUARTERS, KHEDA
Confidential Notes on the District

GUJARAT STATE ARCHIVES, VADODARA
Baroda Records Office Files
Huzur Political Office Files

KHEDA DISTRICT COLLECTORATE RECORDS ROOM, KHEDA
Bundles of Records on the District

MAHARASHTRA STATE ARCHIVES, BOMBAY
General Department (Plague) Records
General Department Records
Home Department (Political) Records
Home Department Records
Home Department (Special) Records
Judicial Department Records
Revenue Department Records
Selected Compilations

OFFICE OF THE DEPUTY INSPECTOR GENERAL OF POLICE, BOMBAY
Secret Abstracts of Police Intelligence, Bombay Presidency

ORIENTAL AND INDIA OFFICE COLLECTIONS,
BRITISH LIBRARY, LONDON
Bombay Education Proceedings
Bombay Financial Proceedings
Bombay Home Proceedings
Bombay Judicial Proceedings
Bombay Public and Judicial Proceedings
Bombay Revenue (Famine) Proceedings
Bombay Revenue (Forest) Proceedings
Bombay Revenue (Land) Proceedings
India Police Proceedings
Manuscripts: Mountstuart Elphinstone Collection, Arthur Walter Pryde Oral
    Collection

ROMAN CATHOLIC MISSION ARCHIVES, ANAND
Mission Notes and Files

PUBLISHED GOVERNMENT RECORDS

A Jamabandi Revision Settlement Report of the Bhadran Peta Mahal of the
    Petlad Taluka of the Baroda Division for AD 1920. Baroda, 1921.
Annual Administration Report of the Balasinore State for the Year 1912–1913.
    Ahmedabad, 1913.
Baroda Banking Inquiry Committee Report, 1929–30. Baroda, 1930.
Bengal Police. Criminal Identification by Means of Anthropometry. 2nd ed. Rev.
    up to 1st January 1895, from E. R. Henry, Inspector General Police.
The Bombay Plague, Being a History of the Progress of Plague in the Bombay
    Presidency from September 1896 to June 1899, compiled by Capt. J. K. Con-
    don. Bombay, 1900.
Census of India, 1881. Vol. 7. Bombay Presidency. Pt. 1. Bombay, 1882.
Census of India, 1891. Vol. 7. Bombay Presidency. Pt. 1. Bombay, 1892.
Census of India, 1901. Vol. 7. Bombay Presidency. Pt. 1. Bombay, 1902.
Census of India, 1911. Vol. 7. Bombay Presidency. Pt. 1. Bombay, 1912.
Census of India, 1921. Vol. 8. Bombay Presidency. Pt. 1. Bombay, 1922.
Census of India, 1931. Vol. 8. Bombay Presidency. Pt. 1. Bombay, 1933.
Gazetteer of the Bombay Presidency. Vol. 3, Kaira and Panch Mahals. Bombay,
    1879.
Gazetteer of the Bombay Presidency. Vol. 9, pt. 1, Gujarat Population: Hindus.
    Bombay, 1901.
Manual of the Bhagdari and Narwadari Act. No. V of 1862, and Standing
    Orders. Bombay, 1914.
Police Report of the Bombay Presidency, Including Sind and Railways, 1857–
    1941. Bombay, 1858–1942.
Rajyagor, S. B., ed. Gujarat State Gazetteers, Kheda District. Ahmedabad, 1977.
Report of the Commissioners for the Investigation of Alleged Cases of Torture in
    the Madras Presidency. Madras, 1855.

Report of the Criminal Tribes Act Enquiry Committee, 1939. Bombay, 1939.

Report of the Director of Public Instruction in the Bombay Presidency, 1899–1921. Bombay, 1900–1922.

Report of the Education Commission. Bombay. Vol. 2. Calcutta, 1884.

Report of the Indian Famine Commission of 1901. Calcutta, 1901.

Report of the Indian Hemp Drugs Commission, 1893–94. 3 vols. Simla, 1894.

Report of the Indian Jails Committee, 1919–1920. 4 vols. London, 1921–1922.

Report of the Indian Police Commission and Resolution of the Government of India. London, 1905.

Report of the Royal Commission on Agriculture in India, 1926–1928. London, 1928.

Report on the Census of the Bombay Presidency Taken on the 21st February 1872. 4 vols. Bombay, 1875.

Report on the Famine in the Bombay Presidency, 1899–1902. 3 vols. Bombay, 1903.

Report on the Working of the Criminal Tribes Act in the Bombay Presidency (Including Sind), 1918–1941. Bombay, 1919–1942.

Reports on the Native Newspapers for the Bombay Presidency.

Source Material for a History of the Freedom Movement in India. Vol. 1, 1818–1885. Bombay, 1957.

Source Material for a History of the Freedom Movement in India. Vol. 3, Mahatma Gandhi. Pt. 1, 1915–1922. Bombay, 1965.

SRBG (NS), no. 16. *Tours for Scientific and Economical Research Made in Guzerat, Kattiawar, and the Conkuns in 1787–1788,* by Dr. Hove. Bombay, 1855.

SRBG (NS), no. 39[a]. *Reports on the Resources &c. of the Districts of Neriad, Matur, Mondeh, Beejapoor, Dholka, Dhandhooka, and Gogo; the Tuppa of Napar; and the Kusba of Ranpoor; in the Province of Guzerat,* by Lieutenant Colonel A. Walker. Bombay, 1893.

SRBG (NS), no. 114. *Correspondence Relating to the Introduction of the Revenue Survey Assessment in the Kaira Collectorate of the Province of Guzerat.* Bombay, 1869.

SRBG (NS), no. 288. *Papers Relating to the Revision Survey Settlement of the Mehmedabad Taluka of the Kaira Collectorate.* Bombay, 1894.

SRBG (NS), no. 295. *Papers Relating to the Revision Survey Settlement of the Nadiad Taluka of the Kaira Collectorate.* Bombay, 1895.

SRBG (NS), no. 296. *Papers Relating to the Revision Survey Settlement of the Anand Taluka of the Kaira Collectorate.* Bombay, 1895.

SRBG (NS), no. 301. *Papers Relating to the Revision Survey Settlement of the Matar Taluka of the Kaira Collectorate.* Bombay, 1895.

SRBG (NS), no. 305. *Papers Relating to the Revision Survey Settlement of the Thasra Taluka of the Kaira Collectorate.* Bombay, 1895.

SRBG (NS), no. 337. *Papers Relating to the Revision Survey Settlement of the Borsad Taluka of the Kaira Collectorate.* Bombay, 1895.

SRBG (NS), no. 338. *Papers Relating to the Revision Survey Settlement of the Kapadwanj Taluka of the Kaira Collectorate.* Bombay, 1895.

SRBG (OS), no. 10. *Reports on the Portions of the Duskroee Purgunna Situated in the Ahmedabad and Kaira Collectorates*, by Captain J. Cruikshank, Revenue Surveyor, Guzerat. Bombay, 1853.

SRBG (OS), no. 11. *Reports on the Portions of the Dholka Purgunna Situated in the Ahmedabad and Kaira Collectorates; Also on the Mehemoodabad and Nureead Purgunnas, and on the Oomret and Bhaluj Tuppas, in the Kaira Collectorate; and on the Pitlad Purgunna and Nepar Tuppa in the Same Collectorate*, by Captain J. Cruikshank, Revenue Surveyor, Guzerat. Bombay, 1853.

NEWSPAPERS

Bombay Chronicle
Congress Socialist (Bombay)
Indian Social Reformer (Bombay)
Praja Bandhu (Ahmedabad)
Times of India (Bombay)

SECONDARY SOURCES

Ahuja, Ravi. "Labour Unsettled: Mobility and Protest in the Madras Region, 1750–1800." *IESHR* 35, 4 (1998): 381–404.

Alam, Muzaffar. *The Crisis of Empire in Mughal North India: Awadh and the Punjab, 1707–1748*. Delhi, 1986.

Ali, Daud. *Culture and Politics in the Courts of Medieval India*. Cambridge, 2002.

Amin, Shahid. "Gandhi as Mahatma, Gorakhpur District, Eastern UP, 1921–22." In *Subaltern Studies III*, ed. Ranajit Guha, 1–57. Delhi, 1984.

———. *Sugarcane and Sugar in Gorakhpur: An Inquiry into Peasant Production for Capitalist Enterprise in Colonial India*. Delhi, 1984.

———. *Event, Metaphor, Memory: Chauri Chaura, 1922–1992*. Berkeley, 1995.

Anagnost, Ann. "Politics and Magic in Contemporary China." *Modern China* 13, 1 (1987): 40–61.

Anderson, Benedict. *Imagined Communities: Reflections on the Origin and Spread of Nationalism*. Rev. ed. London, 1991.

———. *Under Three Flags: Anarchism and the Anti-Colonial Imaginary*. London, 2005.

Anderson, Clare. "The Politics of Convict Space: Indian Penal Settlements and the Andaman Islands." In *Isolation: Places and Practices of Exclusion*, ed. Carolyn Strange and Alison Bashford, 40–55. London, 2003.

Aravamudan, Srinivas. "Postcolonial Affiliations: *Ulysses* and *All about H. Hatterr*." In *Transcultural Joyce*, ed. Karen Lawrence, 97–128. Cambridge, 1998.

Arnold, David. "Dacoity and Rural Crime in Madras, 1860–1940." *Journal of Peasant Studies* 6, no. 2 (1979): 140–67.

———. "Famine in Peasant Consciousness and Peasant Action: Madras, 1876–78." In *Subaltern Studies III*, ed. Ranajit Guha, 62–115. Delhi, 1984.

———. "Looting, Grain Riots, and Government Policy in South India, 1918." *Past and Present* 84 (1979) 111–45.

————. *Police Power and Colonial Rule: Madras, 1859–1947*. Delhi, 1986.

————. "Touching the Body: Perspectives on the Indian Plague, 1896–1900." In *Subaltern Studies V*, ed. Ranajit Guha, 55–90. Delhi, 1987.

————. *Famine: Social Crisis and Historical Change*. Oxford, 1988.

————. *Colonizing the Body: State Medicine and Epidemic Disease in Nineteenth-Century India*. Berkeley, 1993.

Aston, T. H., and C. H. E. Philpin. *The Brenner Debate: Agrarian Class Structure and Economic Development in Pre-Industrial Europe*. Cambridge, 1990.

Baden-Powell, B. H. *The Land-Systems of British India, Being a Manual of the Land-Tenures and of the Systems of Land-Revenue Administration Prevalent in the Several Provinces*. Vol. 3. Oxford, 1892.

Baker, C. J. "Madras Headmen." In *Economy and Society: Essays in Indian Economic and Social History*, ed. K. N. Chaudhuri and Clive J. Dewey, 26–52. Delhi, 1979.

Basham, A. L. *The Wonder That Was India*. New York, 1954.

Bates, Crispin N. "The Nature of Social Change in Rural Gujarat: The Kheda District, 1818–1918." *MAS* 15, 4 (1981): 771–821.

Bayly, C. A. *Indian Society and the Making of the British Empire*. Vol. 2.1, *The New Cambridge History of India*. Cambridge, 1987.

————. *Rulers, Townsmen, and Bazaars: North Indian Society in the Age of British Expansion*. Cambridge, 1988.

————. *Empire and Information: Intelligence Gathering and Social Communication in India, 1780–1870*. Cambridge, 1996.

————. *Origins of Nationality in South Asia: Patriotism and Ethical Government in the Making of Modern India*. Delhi, 1998.

Bayly, Susan. *Caste, Society, and Politics in India from the Eighteenth Century to the Modern Age*. Vol. 4.3, *The New Cambridge History of India*. Cambridge, 2000.

Benjamin, Walter. *Illuminations: Essays and Reflections*. Ed. Hannah Arendt. New York, 1968.

Bhagavan, Manu. *Sovereign Spheres: Princes, Education, and Empire in Colonial India*. Delhi, 2003.

Bhargava, B. S. *The Criminal Tribes: A Socio-Economic Study of the Principal Criminal Tribes and Castes in Northern India*. Lucknow, 1949.

Bhatia, Bela. "Lush Fields and Parched Throats: The Political Economy of Groundwater in Gujarat." Working paper no. 100, World Institute for Development Economics Research, Helsinki, August 1992.

Bhayani, H. C., and Hasu Yagnik. "Krsna in the Gujarati Folk-Song Tradition." In *Devotion Divine: Bhakti Traditions from the Regions of India*, ed. Diana L. Eck and Francoise Mallison, 39–48. Paris, 1991.

Blyn, George. *Agricultural Trends in India, 1891–1947: Output, Availability, and Productivity*. Philadelphia, 1966.

Booth-Tucker, F. *Criminocurology. A Review of the Work of the Salvation Army among Criminal Tribes in India*. Simla, 1915.

Borradaile, Harry. *Gujarat Caste Rules. Published from the Original Answers of the Castes with the Sanction of Her Imperial Majesty's High Court of Judicature of Bombay*. 2 vols. Bombay, 1884, 1887.

Bottigheimer, Ruth B. "Fairy Tales, Folk Narrative Research, and History." *Social History* 14, 3 (1989): 343–58.

Bourdieu, Pierre. *Outline of a Theory of Practice.* Trans. Richard Nice. Cambridge, 1977.

Breman, Jan. *Patronage and Exploitation: Changing Agrarian Relations in South Gujarat, India.* Berkeley, 1974.

———. *Of Peasants, Migrants, and Paupers: Rural Labour Circulation and Capitalist Production in West India.* Delhi, 1985.

Brenner, Robert. "Agrarian Class Structure and Economic Development in Pre-Industrial Europe." *Past and Present* 70 (1976): 30–75.

———. "The Origins of Capitalist Development: A Critique of Neo-Smithian Marxism." *New Left Review* 104 (1977): 25–92.

———. "Dobb on the Transition from Feudalism to Capitalism." *Cambridge Journal of Economics* 2, 2 (1978): 121–40.

———. "The Social Basis of Economic Development." In *Analytical Marxism,* ed. John Roemer, 23–53. Cambridge, 1986.

Brown, Judith M. *Gandhi's Rise to Power: Indian Politics, 1915–1922.* Cambridge, 1972.

Bryant, Edwin F., trans. *Krishna: The Beautiful Legend of God (Srimad Bhagavata Purana Book X).* London, 2003.

Burghart, Richard. "The Founding of the Ramanandi Sect." *Ethnohistory* 25, 2 (1978): 121–39.

Burns, W., L. B. Kulkarni, and S. R. Godbole. *Grassland Problems in Western India.* Bombay Agricultural Series, Bulletin no. 171. Bombay, 1932.

Callewaert, Winand M. *The Hindi Biography of Dadu Dayal.* Delhi, 1988.

Cashman, Richard. "The Political Recruitment of God Ganapati." *IESHR* 7 (1970): 347–73.

———. *The Myth of the Lokamanya: Tilak and Mass Politics in Maharashtra.* Berkeley, 1975.

Catanach, Ian J. *Rural Credit in Western India: Rural Credit and the Co-operative Movement in the Bombay Presidency, 1875–1930.* Berkeley, 1970.

———. "Plague and the Indian Village, 1896–1914." In *Rural India: Land, Power, and Society under British Rule,* ed. Peter Robb, 216–43. London, 1983.

———. "Plague and Tensions of Empire: India, 1896–1918." In *Imperial Medicine and Indigenous Societies,* ed. David Arnold, 149–71. Delhi, 1989.

Chandavarkar, Rajnarayan. *Imperial Power and Popular Politics.* Cambridge, 1998.

Charlesworth, Neil. *Peasants and Imperial Rule: Agriculture and Agrarian Society in the Bombay Presidency, 1850–1935.* Cambridge, 1985.

Chatterjee, Partha. "Agrarian Relations and Communalism in Bengal, 1926–1935." In *Subaltern Studies I,* ed. Ranajit Guha, 9–38. Delhi, 1982.

———. "More on Modes of Power and the Peasantry." In *Subaltern Studies II,* ed. Ranajit Guha, 311–49. Delhi, 1983.

———. *Nationalist Thought and the Colonial World: A Derivative Discourse?* London, 1986.

———. *The Nation and Its Fragments: Colonial and Postcolonial Histories.* Princeton, 1993.

———. *A Princely Imposter? The Strange and Universal History of the Kumar of Bhawal.* Princeton, 2002.

———. *The Politics of the Governed: Reflections on Popular Politics in Most of the World.* New York, 2004.

Chaturvedi, Vinayak, ed. *Mapping Subaltern Studies and the Postcolonial.* London, 2000.

———. "Of Peasants and Publics in Colonial India: Daduram's Story." *Social History* 30, 3 (2005): 296–320.

———. "Eine kritische Theorie der Subalternität: Überlegungen zur Verwendung des Klassenbegriffs in der indischen Geschichtsschreibung." *Werkstatt-Geschichte,* 41 (2006): 5–23.

———. "The Making of a Peasant King in Colonial Western India: The Case of Ranchod Vira." *Past and Present* 192 (2006): 155–85.

Chibber, Vivek. "Breaching the Nadu: Lordship and Economic Development in Pre-Colonial South India." *JPS* 26, 1 (1998): 1–42.

Choksey, R. D. *Economic Life in the Bombay Gujarat, 1880–1939.* Bombay, 1968.

Cohen, Paul A. *History in Three Keys: The Boxers as Event, Experience, and Myth.* New York, 1997.

Cohn, Bernard S. "Political Systems in Eighteenth Century India: The Benaras Region." *Journal of the American Oriental Society* 82 (1962): 312–20.

———. "The Census, Social Structure, and Objectification in South Asia." In *An Anthropologist among the Historians and Other Essays,* 224–54. Delhi, 1994.

Copland, Ian. *The Princes of India in the Endgame of Empire, 1917–1947.* Cambridge, 1997.

Courtright, Paul B. "The Ganesh Festival in Maharashtra: Some Observations." In *The Experience of Hinduism,* ed. Eleanor Zelliot and Maxine Berntsen, 76–94. Albany, 1988.

Cox, E. C. *Police and Crime in India.* London, 1910.

Crooke, William. *The Popular Religion and Folk-Lore of Northern India.* Delhi, 1968.

Cummings, William. "Rethinking the Imbrication of Orality and Literacy: Historical Discourse in Early Modern Makassar." *JAS* 62, 2 (2003): 531–51.

Curry, J. C. *The Indian Police.* London, 1932.

Darnton, Robert. *The Literary Underground of the Old Regime.* Cambridge, 1982.

———. "An Early Information Society: News and Media in Eighteenth Century Paris." *American Historical Review* 105, 1 (2000): 1–35.

Davis, Mike. *Late Victorian Holocausts: El Niño Famines and the Making of the Third World.* London, 2001.

Dharaiya, R. K. *Gujarat in 1857.* Ahmedabad, 1970.

Dirks, Nicholas B. *The Hollow Crown: The Ethnohistory of an Indian Kingdom.* Cambridge, 1987.

———. "From Little King to Landlord: Colonial Discourse and Colonial Rule." In *Colonialism and Culture,* ed. Nicholas B. Dirks, 175–208. Ann Arbor, 1992.

———. *Castes of Mind: Colonialism and the Making of Modern India.* Princeton, 2001.

Dube, Saurabh. "Idioms of Authority and Engendered Agendas: The Satnami Mahasabha, Chhattisgarh, 1925–1950." *IESHR* 30, 4 (1993): 383–412.

———. *Untouchable Pasts: Religion, Identity, and Power among a Central Indian Community, 1780–1950.* Albany, 1998.

———. *Stitches on Time: Colonial Textures and Postcolonial Tangles.* Durham, 2004.

Eley, Geoff. "Edward Thompson, Social History, and Political Culture: The Making of a Working-Class Public, 1780–1850." In *E. P. Thompson: Critical Perspectives,* ed. Harvey J. Kaye and Keith McClelland, 12–49. Philadelphia, 1990.

———. "Nations, Publics, and Political Cultures: Placing Habermas in the Nineteenth Century." In *Habermas and the Public Sphere,* ed. Craig Calhoun, 288–339. Cambridge, 1992.

Enthoven, R. E. *Tribes and Castes of Bombay.* 3 vol. Bombay, 1922.

Entwistle, Alan W. "The Cult of Krishna-Gopal as a Version of Pastoral." In *Devotion Divine: Bhakti Traditions from the Regions of India,* ed. Diana L. Eck and Francoise Mallison, 73–90. Paris, 1991.

Evans, R. J. "Epidemics and Revolutions: Cholera in Nineteenth Century Europe." *Past and Present* 120 (1988): 123–46.

Farquhar, J. N. *Modern Religious Movements in India.* Delhi, 1967.

Feierman, Steven. *Peasant Intellectuals: Anthropology and History in Tanzania.* Madison, 1990.

Fischer, Michael. "The East India Company's Suppression of the Native Dak." *IESHR* 31, 3 (1994): 319–26.

Forbes, Alexander Kinloch. *Ras Mala; or, Hindoo Annals of the Province of Goozerat, in Western India.* London, 1878.

Forbes, James. *Oriental Memoirs: Selected and Abridged from a Series of Familiar Letters Written during Seventeen Years of Residence in India: Including Observations on Parts of Africa and South America, and a Narrative of Occurrences in Four Indian Voyages.* London, 1813.

Freitag, Sandria B. "Crime in the Social Order of Colonial North India." *MAS* 25, 2 (1991): 227–61.

Frost, Marcia. "Coping with Scarcity: Wild Foods and Common Lands: Kheda District (Gujarat, India), 1824–5." *IESHR* 37, 3 (2000): 295–330.

Fukazawa, H. "Western India." In *The Cambridge Economic History of India.* Vol. 2, ed. Dharma Kumar, 177–206. Cambridge, 1983.

———. "Agrarian Relations and Land Revenue: The Medieval Deccan and Maharashtra." In *The Cambridge Economic History of India.* Vol. 1, ed. Tapan Raychaudhuri and Irfan Habib, 249–60. Cambridge, 1984.

Gandhi, M. K. *An Autobiography: The Story of My Experiments with Truth.* Boston, 1993.

———. *The Collected Works of Mahatma Gandhi.* 100 vols. Ahmedabad, 1958–2000.

Gidwani, Vinay. "Labored Landscapes: Agro-Ecological Change in Central Gujarat, India." In *Agrarian Environments: Resources, Representations, and Rule in India,* ed. Arun Agarwal and K. Sivaramakrishnan, 216–47. Durham, 2000.

———. "New Theory or New Dogma? A Tale of Social Capital and Economic Development from Gujarat, India." *Journal of Asian and African Studies* 37, 2 (2002): 83–112.

———. "The Unbearable Modernity of 'Development'? Canal Irrigation and Development Planning in Western India." *Progress in Planning* 58, 1 (2002): 1–80.

Ginzburg, Carlo. *The Cheese and the Worms: The Cosmos of a Sixteenth-Century Miller.* New York, 1987.

———. *Clues, Myths, and the Historical Method.* Baltimore, 1992.

———. "Witches and Shamans." *New Left Review* 200 (July–August 1993): 75–85.

———. *History, Rhetoric, and Proof: The Menahem Stern Jerusalem Lectures.* Hanover, 1999.

———. *The Judge and the Historian: Marginal Notes on a Late-Twentieth-Century Miscarriage of Justice.* Trans. Anthony Shugaar. London, 1999.

Goody, Jack. *The Interface between the Written and the Oral.* Cambridge, 1987.

———. *The East in the West.* Cambridge, 1996.

Goody, Jack, and Ian Watt. "The Consequences of Literacy." In *Literacy in Traditional Societies,* ed. Jack Goody, 27–68. Cambridge, 1968.

Gopal, Ram. *Lokamanya Tilak: A Biography.* New York, 1965.

Gopal, Surendra. *Commerce and Crafts in Gujarat, 16th and 17th Centuries: A Study in the Impact of European Expansion on Precapitalist Economy.* New Delhi, 1975.

Gordon, Stewart. *Marathas, Marauders, and State Formation in the Eighteenth Century.* Delhi, 1994.

———. *The Marathas, 1600–1818.* Vol. 2.4, *The New Cambridge History of India.* Cambridge, 1998.

Goswami, Manu. *Producing India: From Colonial Economy to National Space.* Chicago, 2004.

Gramsci, Antonio. *Selections from the Prison Notebooks of Antonio Gramsci.* Ed. Quintin Hoare and Geoffrey Nowell Smith. London, 1996.

Guha, Ranajit. "On Some Aspects of the Historiography of Colonial India." In *Subaltern Studies I,* ed. Ranajit Guha, 1–8. Delhi, 1982.

———. *Elementary Aspects of Peasant Insurgency in Colonial India.* Delhi, 1983.

———. "The Prose of Counter-insurgency." In *Subaltern Studies II,* ed. Ranajit Guha, 1–42. Delhi, 1983.

———. *Dominance without Hegemony: History and Power in Colonial India.* Cambridge, 1997.

Guha, Sumit. *The Agrarian Economy of the Bombay Deccan, 1818–1941.* Delhi, 1985.

———, ed. *Growth, Stagnation, or Decline? Agricultural Productivity in British India.* Delhi, 1992.

———. "Theatre State or Box Office State? A Note on the Political Economy of Eighteenth Century India." *IESHR* 31, 4 (1994): 519–24.

———. "Forest Polities and Agrarian Empires: The Khandesh Bhils, c. 1700–1850." *IESHR* 33, 2 (1996): 133–54.

———. *Environment and Ethnicity in India, 1200–1991.* Cambridge, 1999.

Haberman, David L. *Journey through the Twelve Forests: An Encounter with Krishna.* New York, 1994.

Habib, Irfan. *The Agrarian System of Mughal India, 1556–1707.* Bombay, 1963.

———. "Postal Communications in Mughal India." In *Proceedings of the Indian Historical Congress, 46th Session,* 236–52. Delhi, 1986.

Hardiman, David. "The Crisis of the Lesser Patidars: Peasant Agitations in Kheda District, Gujarat, 1917–34." In *Congress and the Raj,* ed. D. A. Low, 47–75. Delhi, 1977.

———. "Baroda: The Structure of a 'Progressive' State." In *People, Princes, and Paramount Power: Society and Politics in the Indian Princely States,* ed. Robin Jeffrey, 107–35. Delhi, 1978.

———. "The Quit India Movement in Gujarat." In *The Indian Nation in 1942,* ed. Gyanendra Pandey, 77–121. Calcutta, 1980.

———. *Peasant Nationalists of Gujarat, Kheda District, 1917–1934.* Delhi, 1981.

———. "The Indian 'Faction': A Political Theory Examined." In *Subaltern Studies I,* ed. Ranajit Guha, 198–232. Delhi, 1982.

———. "From Custom to Crime: The Politics of Drinking in South Gujarat." In *Subaltern Studies IV,* ed. Ranajit Guha, 165–228. Delhi, 1985.

———. "The Bhils and Shahukars of Eastern Gujarat." In *Subaltern Studies V,* ed. Ranajit Guha, 1–54. Delhi, 1987.

———. ed. *Peasant Resistance in India, 1858–1914.* Delhi, 1992.

———. *The Coming of the Devi: Adivasi Assertion in Western India.* Delhi, 1995.

———. *Feeding the Baniya. Peasants and Usurers in Western India.* Delhi, 1996.

Harrison, Mark. "Quarantine, Pilgrimage, and Colonial Trade: India, 1866–1900." *IESHR* 29, 2 (1992): 117–44.

Hatcher, John. "England in the Aftermath of the Black Death." *Past and Present* 144 (1994): 3–35.

Haynes, Douglas E. "Imperial Ritual in a Local Setting: The Ceremonial Order in Surat, 1890–1939." *MAS* 24, 3 (1990): 493–527.

———. *Rhetoric and Ritual in Colonial India: The Shaping of a Public Culture in Surat City, 1852–1928.* Berkeley, 1991.

Haynes, Douglas E., and Tirthankar Roy. "Conceiving Mobility: Weavers' Migrations in Pre-colonial and Colonial India." *IESHR* 36, 1 (1999): 35–67.

Heber, Reginald. *Narrative of a Journey through the Upper Provinces of India, from Calcutta to Bombay, 1824–1825.* Vol. 3. London, 1828.

Heesterman, J. C. *The Inner Conflict of Tradition: Essays in Indian Ritual, Kingship, and Society.* Chicago, 1985.

Hobsbawm, Eric. *Primitive Rebels.* Manchester, 1959.

Holland, A. S. "The Improvement of the Village Police." *Indian Police Association Bulletin* 2 (January 1923).

Inden, Ronald. *Imagining India*. Bloomington, 2000.

Innes, Mathew. "Memory, Orality, and Literacy in an Early Medieval Society." *Past and Present* 158 (1998): 3–36.

Kaiwar, Vasant. "Property Structures, Demography, and the Crisis of the Agrarian Economy of Colonial Bombay Presidency." *JPS* 19, 2 (1992): 255–300.

———. "The Colonial State, Capital, and the Peasantry in Bombay Presidency." *MAS* 28, 1 (1994): 793–832.

Karmarkar, Dattatraya Parashuram. *Bal Gangadhar Tilak: A Study*. Bombay, 1956.

Kasturi, Malavika. *Embattled Identities: Rajput Lineages and the Colonial State in Nineteenth-Century North India*. Delhi, 2002.

Keer, Dhananjay. *Lokamanya Tilak, Father of the Indian Freedom Struggle*. Bombay, 1969.

Kennedy, M. *Notes on Criminal Classes in the Bombay Presidency*. Bombay, 1908.

Klein, Ira. "Imperialism, Ecology, and Disease: Cholera in India, 1850–1950." *IESHR* 31, 4 (1994): 491–518.

Koffsky, P. L. "Postal Systems of India." *Bengal Past and Present* 90 (1971): 47–69.

Kohli, Atul. *Democracy and Discontent: India's Growing Crisis of Governability*. Cambridge, 1991.

Krishan, Shri. "Peasant Mobilization, Political Organization, and Modes of Interaction: The Bombay Countryside, 1934–41." *IESHR* 32, 4 (1995): 429–46.

Kumarappa, J. C. *An Economic Survey of Matar Taluka (Kheda District)*. Reprint. Ahmedabad, 1990.

Lely, F. S. P. *Suggestions for the Better Governing of India, with Special Reference to the Bombay Presidency*. London, 1906.

Lewis, Oscar. *Village Life in Northern India: Studies in a Delhi Village*. New York, 1965.

Lobo, Lancy. *The Thakurs of North Gujarat: A Caste in the Village and Region*. Delhi, 1995.

Mackay, Alexander. *Western India: Reports Addressed to the Chambers of Commerce of Manchester, Liverpool, Blackburn, and Glasgow*. London, 1853.

Maharatna, Arup. *The Demography of Famines: An Indian Historical Perspective*. Delhi, 1996.

Majmudar, M. R. "Dwarka Image of Ranchhodji and the Temple of Dakore." *Journal of the University of Bombay* 15, 4 (1948): 57–91.

Major, Andrew J. "State and Criminal Tribes in Colonial Punjab: Surveillance, Control, and Reclamation of the 'Dangerous Classes.'" *MAS* 33, 1 (1999): 657–88.

Mallison, Francoise. "Development of Early Krishnaism in Gujarat: Vishnu-Ranchod-Krsna." In *Bhakti in Current Research, 1979–1982: Proceedings of the Second International Conference on Early Devotional Literature in New Indo-Aryan Languages*, ed. Monika Thiel-Horstmann, 245–55. Berlin, 1983.

———. "Lorsque Ranachodaraya Quitte Dwarka Pour Dakor, Comment

Dvarakanatha Prit La Succession De Dankanatha." In *Devotion Divine: Bhakti Traditions from the Regions of India*, ed. Diana L. Eck and Francoise Mallison, 196–207. Paris, 1991.

Marriott, McKim. "Feasts of Love." In *Krishna: Myths, Rites, and Attitudes*, ed. Milton B. Singer, 200–12. Honolulu, 1966.

Mayaram, Shail. "Kings versus Bandits: Anti-colonialism in a Bandit Narrative." *Journal of the Royal Asiatic Society* 13, 3 (2003): 315–38.

McAlpin, M. B. *Subject to Famine: Food Crises and Economic Change in Western India, 1860–1920*. Princeton, 1983.

Megged, Amos. "Magic, Popular Medicine, and Gender in Seventeenth-Century Mexico: The Case of Isabel de Montoya." *Social History* 19, 2 (1994): 189–208.

Meghani, Jhaverchand. *Mansaina Diva*. Bhavnagar, 1967.

Melvill, Lieutenant Colonel. "Notes on the Agriculture of the Cherotar District of Gujarat." *JBBRAS* 10 (1845): 276–93.

Metcalf, T. R. *The Aftermath of Revolt: India, 1857–1870*. Delhi, 1990.

———. *Ideologies of the Raj*. Vol. 3.4, *The New Cambridge History of India*. Cambridge, 1995.

Minor, Robert N., ed. *Modern Interpreters of the Bhagavadgita*. Albany, 1986.

Mukherjee, Rudrangshu. *Awadh in Revolt: A Study of Popular Resistance*. Delhi, 1984.

———. "Ashin Das Gupta: Some Memories and Reflections." In *Politics and Trade in the Indian Ocean World: Essays in Honour of Ashin Das Gupta*, ed. Rudrangshu Mukherjee and Lakshmi Subramanian, 6–15. Delhi, 1998.

Nigam, Sanjay. "Disciplining and Policing the 'Criminals by Birth.'" Pt. 1, "The Making of a Colonial Stereotype—the Criminal Tribes and Castes of North India." *IESHR* 27, 2 (1990): 131–64.

———. "Disciplining and Policing the 'Criminals by Birth.'" Pt. 2, "The Development of a Disciplinary System, 1871–1900." *IESHR* 27, 3 (1990): 257–87.

Oberoi, Harjot. *The Construction of Religious Boundaries: Culture, Identity, and Diversity in the Sikh Tradition*. Delhi, 1997.

O'Hanlon, Rosalind. *Caste, Conflict, and Ideology: Mahatma Jotirao Phule and Low Caste Protest in Nineteenth-Century Western India*. Cambridge, 1985.

Omvedt, Gail. *Cultural Revolt in a Colonial Society: The Non-Brahman Movement in Western India, 1873 to 1930*. Bombay, 1976.

Ong, Walter. *Orality and Literacy: The Technologising of the World*. London, 1982.

Orlebar, A. B. "Notes Accompanying a Collection of Geological Specimens from Guzerat." *JBBRAS* 1, 4 (1842): 191–98.

Orr, W. G. *A Sixteenth Century Indian Mystic*. London, 1947.

Pandey, Gyanendra. *The Ascendancy of the Congress in Uttar Pradesh, 1926–34: A Study in Imperfect Mobilization*. Delhi, 1978.

———. "In Defense of the Fragment: Writing about Hindu-Muslim Riots in India Today." *Representations* 37 (1992): 27–55.

Paranjpye, R. P. *Free and Compulsory Education*. Poona, 1916.

Parekh, Bhikhu. *Colonialism, Tradition, and Reform: An Analysis of Gandhi's Political Discourse*. New Delhi, 1989.

Parvate, T. V. *Bal Gangadhar Tilak: A Narrative and Interpretive Review of His Life, Career, and Contemporary Events*. Ahmedabad, 1958.

Patel, Sujata. *The Making of Industrial Relations: The Ahmedabad Textile Industry, 1918–1939*. Delhi, 1987.

Peabody, Norbert. *Hindu Kingship and Polity in Precolonial India*. Cambridge, 2003.

Phoofolo, Pule. "Epidemics and Revolutions: The Rinderpest Epidemic in Late Nineteenth Century Southern Africa." *Past and Present* 138 (1993): 112–43.

Pinch, William R. *Peasants and Monks in British India*. Berkeley, 1996.

Pinney, Christopher. *Camera Indica: The Social Life of Indian Photographs*. London, 1997.

———. *Photos of the Gods: The Printed Image and Political Struggle in India*. Delhi, 2004.

Pocock, D. F. *Kanbi and Patidar: A Study of the Patidar Community of Gujarat*. Oxford, 1972.

———. *Mind, Body, and Wealth: A Study of Belief and Practice in an Indian Village*. Oxford, 1973.

Poddar, Prem, and David Johnson, eds. *A Historical Companion to Postcolonial Thought in English*. New York, 2005.

Prakash, Gyan. *Bonded Histories: Genealogies of Labor Servitude in Colonial India*. Cambridge, 1990.

———. *Another Reason: Science and the Imagination of Modern India*. Princeton, 1999.

Price, Pamela. *Kingship and Political Practice in Colonial India*. Cambridge, 1996.

Rabinow, Paul. *Reflections on Fieldwork in Morocco*. Berkeley, 1977.

Radhakrishna, M. "The Criminal Tribes Act in the Madras Presidency: Implications for the Itinerant Trading Communities." *IESHR* 26, 3 (1989): 269–95.

———. "Surveillance and Settlements under the Criminal Tribes Act in Madras." *IESHR* 29, 2 (1992): 178–98.

Rajasekher, R. "Famines and Peasant Mobility: Changing Agrarian Structure in the Kurnool District of Andhra, 1870–1900." *IESHR* 28, 2 (1991): 73–96.

Ramage, C. *The Great Indian Drought of 1899*. Boulder, 1977.

Rangarajan, Mahesh. "Imperial Agendas and India's Forests: The Early History of Indian Forestry, 1800–1878." *IESHR* 31, 2 (1994): 147–67.

Reddy, M. Atchi. "Work and Leisure: Daily Working Hours of Agricultural Labourers, Nellore District, 1860–1989." *IESHR* 27, 3 (1990): 257–87.

Richards, John. *The Mughal Empire*. Cambridge, 1995.

Robb, Peter, ed. *Rural India: Land, Power, and Society under British Rule*. London, 1983.

Roy, Sarat Chandra. *Oraon Religion and Customs*. Ranchi, 1928.

Roy, Tirthankar. *The Economic History of India, 1857–1947*. Delhi, 2000.

Sahasrabuddhe, Rao Bahadur D. L. *Composition of Important Manures in Western India*. Bombay Agricultural Series, Bulletin no. 174. Bombay, 1933.

Sarkar, Sumit. *Modern India, 1885–1947.* Delhi, 1983.

Scott, James C. *Weapons of the Weak: Everyday Forms of Peasant Resistance.* New Haven, 1985.

———. *Seeing Like a State: How Certain Schemes to Improve the Human Condition Have Failed.* New Haven, 1998.

Shah, A. M., and R. G. Shroff. "The Vahivanca Barots of Gujarat: A Caste of Genealogists and Mythographers." In *Traditional India: Structure and Change,* ed. Milton Singer, 40–70. Philadelphia, 1959.

Shah, Ghanshyam. *Caste Association and Political Process in Gujarat: A Study of Gujarat Kshatriya Sabha.* Bombay, 1975.

———. "Caste and Land Reforms in Gujarat." In *Land Reforms in India.* Vol. 8, *Performance and Challenges in Gujarat and Maharashtra,* ed. Ghanshyam Shah and D. C. Sah, 127–43. New Delhi, 2002.

Shay, Theodore. *The Legacy of the Lokamanya: The Political Philosophy of Bal Gangadhar Tilak.* Bombay, 1956.

Sheel, Alok. "Bubonic Plague in South Bihar: Gaya and Shahabad Districts, 1900–1924." *IESHR* 35, 4 (1998): 421–42.

Shulman, David D. *Tamil Temple Myths: Sacrifice and Divine Marriage in the South Indian Saiva Tradition.* Princeton, 1980.

Siddiqi, Majid. *Agrarian Unrest in North India: The United Provinces, 1918–22.* Delhi, 1978.

Singh, Chetan. "Conformity and Conflict: Tribes and the Agrarian System of Mughal India." *IESHR* 25, 3 (1988): 319–40.

———. "Forests, Pastoralists, and Agrarian Society in Mughal India." In *Nature, Culture, Imperialism: Essays on the Environmental History of South Asia,* ed. D. Arnold and R. Guha, 21–48. Delhi, 1994.

Singh, K. S. "Agrarian Dimensions of Tribal Movements." In *Agrarian Struggles in India after Independence,* ed. A. R. Desai, 145–67. Delhi, 1986.

Singha, Radhika. *A Despotism of Law: Crime and Justice in Early Colonial India.* Delhi, 1998.

Sivaramakrishnan, K. *Modern Forests: Statemaking and Environmental Change in Colonial Eastern India.* Stanford, 1999.

Skaria, Ajay. "Writing, Orality, and Power in the Dangs, Western India, 1800s–1920s." In *Subaltern Studies IX,* ed. Dipesh Chakrabarty and Shahid Amin, 13–58. Delhi, 1996.

———. "Shades of Wildness: Tribe, Caste, and Gender in Western India." *JAS* 56, 3 (1997): 726–45.

———. "Women, Witchcraft, and Gratuitous Violence in Colonial Western India." *Past and Present* 155 (1997): 109–41.

———. "Timber Conservancy, Desiccationism, and Scientific Forestry: The Dangs, 1840s–1920s." In *Nature and the Orient: The Environmental History of South and Southeast Asia,* ed. R. Grove, V. Damodaran, and Satpal Sangwan, 596–635. Delhi, 1998.

———. *Hybrid Histories: Forests, Frontiers, and Wildness in Western India.* Delhi, 1999.

Srinivas, M. N. *Social Change in Modern India.* Bombay, 1972.

Stevenson, Margaret Sinclair. *The Rites of the Twice-Born*. Delhi, 1971.

Stokes, Eric. *The Peasant and the Raj*. Cambridge, 1980.

———. *The Peasant Armed: The Indian Rebellion of 1857*. Ed. C. A. Bayly. Oxford, 1986.

Subrahmanyam, Sanjay. *Penumbral Visions: Making Polities in Early Modern South India*. Delhi, 2001.

Subrahmanyam, Sanjay, and David Shulman. "The Men Who Would Be King? The Politics of Expansion in Early Seventeenth Century Northern Tamilnadu." *MAS* 24, 2 (1990): 225–48.

Subramanian, Lakshmi. *Indigenous Capital and Imperial Expansion: Bombay, Surat, and the West Coast*. Delhi, 1996.

Sundar, Nandini. *Subalterns and Sovereigns: An Anthropological History of Bastar, 1854–1996*. Delhi, 1997.

Tahmankar, D. V. *Lokamanya Tilak: Father of Indian Unrest and Maker of Modern India*. London, 1956.

Thapar, Romila. *Ancient Indian Social History: Some Interpretations*. Delhi, 1990.

———. *Time as a Metaphor of History: Early India*. Delhi, 1996.

———. *Cultural Pasts: Essays in Early Indian History*. Delhi, 2000.

Thiel-Hortsmann, Monika. *Crossing the Ocean of Existence: Braj Bhasa Religious Poetry from Rajasthan*. Wiesbaden, 1983.

Thompson, Edward. *The Making of Indian Princes*. London, 1978.

Thoothi, N. A. *The Vaishnavas of Gujarat*. London, 1935.

Trouillot, Michel-Rolph. *Silencing the Past: Power and the Production of History*. Boston, 1995.

Upadhyaya, K. N. *The Compassionate Mystic*. New Delhi, 1980.

van der Veer, Peter. "Taming the Ascetic: Devotionalism in a Hindu Monastic Order." *Man*, n.s., 22, 4 (1987): 680–95.

———. *Gods on Earth: The Management of Religious Experience and Identity in a North Indian Pilgrimage Centre*. London, 1988.

Voelcker, John Augustus. *Report on the Improvement of Indian Agriculture*. London, n.d. [1893].

Walker, Simon. "Rumor, Sedition, and Popular Protest in the Reign of Henry IV." *Past and Present* 166 (2000): 31–65.

Washbrook, David. "Country Politics: Madras, 1880–1930." *MAS* 7, 3 (1973): 475–532.

———. *The Emergence of Provincial Politics. The Madras Presidency, 1870–1920*. Cambridge, 1976.

———. "Law, State, and Agrarian Society in Colonial India." *MAS* 15, 3 (1981): 649–721.

———. "Progress and Problems: South Asian Economic and Social History, c. 1720–1860." *MAS* 22, 1 (1988): 57–96.

———. "The Commercialisation of Agriculture in Colonial India: Production, Subsistence, and Reproduction in the 'Dry South,' c. 1870–1930." *MAS* 28, 1 (1994): 129–64.

Watts, Sheldon. "British Development Policies and Malaria in India, 1897–c. 1929." *Past and Present* 165 (1999): 141–81.

Wickham, Chris. "Gossip and Resistance among the Medieval Peasantry." *Past and Present* 160 (1998): 3–24.

Wilson, H. H. *A Glossary of Judicial and Revenue Terms and of Useful Words Occurring in Official Documents Relating to the Administration of the Government of British India: From the Arabic, Persian, Hindustani, Sanskrit, Hindi, Bengali, Uriga, Marathi, Guzarathi, Telugu, Karnata, Tamil, Malayalam, and Other Languages.* London, 1855.

Wink, Andre. *Land and Sovereignty in India: Agrarian Society and Politics under the Eighteenth Century Maratha Svarajya.* Cambridge, 1986.

Wolpert, Stanley. *Tilak and Gokhale: Revolution and Reform in the Making of Modern India.* Berkeley, 1961.

Yajnik, Javerilal Umiashankar. "Notices of Hindu Tribes and Castes in Gujarat." *JBBRAS* 10, 28 (1871–72): 93–119.

———. *Notes on Kaira, a District in Fertile Gujarat.* Bombay, n.d.

Yang, Anand. "Peasants on the Move: A Study of Internal Migration in India." *Journal of Interdisciplinary History* 10 (1979): 38–45.

———, ed. *Crime and Criminality in British India.* Tucson, 1985.

———. "A Conversation of Rumors: The Language of Popular *Mentalities* in Late Nineteenth Century Colonial India." *Journal of Social History* 20 (1987): 485–505.

———. "Disciplining 'Natives': Prisons and Prisoners in Nineteenth Century India." *South Asia* 10 (1987): 29–45.

UNPUBLISHED SOURCES

Bajpai, Gita. "Baroda in Transition, 1860–1884." PhD, Maharaja Sayajirao University, Baroda, 1979.

Clark, Alice Whitcomb. "Central Gujarat in the Nineteenth Century: The Integration of an Agrarian Economy." PhD, University of Wisconsin-Madison, 1979.

Den Tuinder, Nico. "Population and Society in Kheda District (India), 1819–1921: A Study of the Economic Context of Demographic Developments." PhD, University of Amsterdam, 1992.

Dhot, Jaspal Kaur. "Economy and Society of Northern Gujarat, with Special Reference to Kheda District, ca. 1750–1850." PhD, Maharaja Sayajirao University, Baroda, 1986.

Frost, Marcia J. "Population Growth and Agrarian Change in British Gujarat, Kaira District, 1802–1858." PhD, University of Pennsylvania, 1995.

Gidwani, Vinay. "Fluid Dynamics: An Essay on Canal Irrigation and Processes of Agrarian Change in Matar Taluka (Gujarat), India." PhD, University of California, Berkeley, 1996.

Hardiman, David. "Peasant Agitations in Kheda District, Gujarat, 1917–34." PhD, Sussex University, 1975.

Kaiwar, Vasant. "Social-Property Relations and the Economic Dynamic: The Case of Peasant Agriculture in Western India, ca. Mid-nineteenth to Mid-twentieth Centuries." PhD, University of California, Los Angeles, 1989.

Kamat, Manjiri. "Labour and Nationalism in Sholapur: Conflict, Confrontation, and Control in a Deccan City, Western India, 1918–1939." PhD, University of Cambridge, 1997.

Patel, H. M. "Adaptation as a Process of Social Change: A Case Study of the Marriage of Baraiya Caste of Village Juni-Ardi." Masters thesis, Maharaja Sayajirao University, Baroda, 1963.

Prakash, Shri. "The Evolution of Agrarian Economy in Gujarat, 1830–1930." PhD, University of Cambridge, 1984.

INDEX

Page numbers in italics refer to illustrations.

accountant *(talati)* legislation and, 40–
43. *See also* Kashibhai Ranchodbhai;
Patidars
Municipal District Pilgrim Tax, 52–53
murders: Chaklasi *badmashes* and, 136;
in Chauri Chaura, 143; village
headmen and, 121. *See also* raids;
underground activities
"mutually conditioned historicity," 18,
229–30

Naranshankar Manishankar, 69, 71, 79,
80–81
Narotamdas Venidas, 103–4
Narsi Bhagat, 203–4, 218–23, 219
Narsiram, 203–6, 205
narwadari system, 34, 35, 36, 105, 134,
154, 244n2. *See also* Charotar tract;
Lewa Kanbis; Patidars
nationalism: concept of, 2–5; imagined
political community and, 3–5; material
and spiritual domains and, 4–5, 229;
peasant politics and, 7, 11–12, 16,
228, 229; in postcolonial era, 158–59.
See also nationalist movement
nationalist movement: Borsad *satyagraha*
and, 146–47; Daduram and, 118, 176–
78; Dharala raids and, 140–41, 151,
156; identity politics and, 13–14, 102,
116–17, 148–50, 151; Kheda *satyagrahas* and, 132–35, 136, 140, 142–
43, 153–55; memories of, 20, 176–
78, 187, 195, 230; Non-cooperation
Movement, 142–43; social relations
with Dharalas and, 148–50, 151–52;
structures of dominance and, 2, 156–
57. *See also* Gandhi, Mohandas K.;
Patidars; raids
newspapers: oral culture and, 92; reports
on raids and, 140–41. See also
*Gujarati Punch; Svadesh Bandhu and
Cambay Gazette*
Non-cooperation Movement, 142–43.
See also nationalist movement
"no-revenue campaigns." See *satyagraha*

Od, village of, 153–54
oral culture: convergence of written word
and, 91–93, 106, 206; Ranchod's ideas
and, 92–93, 96, 98; rumors and, 92–
93, 98; spread of Daduram's ideas and,
109, 172–75, 207; surveillance and,
109–10
oral sources: in Chaklasi, 169–71; escaped
prisoner story and, 199–200; in Hamidpura, 203–6; legacies of Daduram and,
172–83, 196–97, 203–17, 231; lega-

cies of Ranchod and, 169, 170–71,
186–88, 189–92, 193–202; local interest in official documents and, 184–85,
188, 212, 213–14; methodology and,
18–20, 184–85; in Raghupura, 187,
190–92, 193–202

panchayat, 75
Parmar, Garbadbhai Motabhai, 116,
225–26
Parmar, Lallubhai Ramsinhbhai, 225–26
passive resistance, 150
Patel, Chotabhai Marghabhai, 171
Patel, Mr., in Nadiad, 186–87
Patel, Purshottamdas, 171
Patel, Vallabhbhai, 148
Patidar, as term, 245n5
Patidars: abuse of CTA by, 1–2, 125–26,
135, 141, 165, 229; Daduram and,
218–19, 220, 221; factors in rise of,
10–11; forced labor and, 105, 114–
15, 141; government incentives and,
37, 105, 128, 130, 265n5; Kshatriya
identity for Dharalas and, 148–50;
Kshatriyas and, 218–19, 220; nationalism and, 9–12, 227, 231–32; "no-
revenue campaigns" and, 133–35, 136,
153; as oral sources in Chaklasi, 171;
postcolonial policies and, 159, 231–32;
Ranchod's movement and, 187, 195;
solidarity among, 134, 146, 153–54,
156; turbans and, 208. *See also* Lewa
Kanbis; nationalist movement
patron-client bonds. *See* surplus-
extraction relationship
peasant movements: agrarian forms of
politics and, 14–16, 101–2; escaped
prisoner story and, 199–200; modern
legacies of, 18–21, 230 (*see also* oral
sources); strike against colonial land
policies and, 130–31; threat posed by
freedom and, 119. *See also* Daduram's
movement; raids; Ranchod's movement; underground activities
peasant politics: difficulties in writing
about, 182; ethical governance and,
11, 16–18, 111, 228; imagined community and, 7, 11–12, 16, 228, 229;
relationship between Dharalas and
Patidars and, 14–16; roles of Dharalas
and Patidars in, 9–12; strategies of
peasant movements and, 228. *See also*
nationalism; peasant movements
peasant religion: Dakore pilgrimage and,
52–54; nature of, 16–18, 20; spiritual
genealogy and, 179–80, 217. See also
bhagats; bhagat traditions; Daduram's

Text: 10/13 Sabon
Display: Franklin Gothic Demi
Compositor: BookMatters, Berkeley
Indexer: Marcia Carlson
Printer and binder: Maple-Vail Manufacturing Group